New Perspectives on
Black Educational History

New Perspectives on
Black Educational History

edited by
VINCENT P. FRANKLIN
and
JAMES D. ANDERSON

G.K.HALL&CO.
70 LINCOLN STREET, BOSTON, MASS.

Library of Congress Cataloging in Publication Data
Main entry under title:

New Perspectives on Black educational history.

   1. Afro-Americans — Education — History — Addresses,
essays, lectures.   I. Franklin, Vincent P.
II. Anderson, James D., 1944-
LC2801.N48   370'.973   78-2674
ISBN 0-8161-8114-4

This publication is printed on permanent/durable acid-free paper
MANUFACTURED IN THE UNITED STATES OF AMERICA

Dedicated to the Memory of
Carter G. Woodson, Horace Mann Bond and Henry Bullock,
Scholars in Afro-American Educational History.

Contents

Preface

This volume grew out of a session on Black Educational History which took place at the sixty-first annual convention of the Association for the Study of Afro-American Life and History, Chicago, 1976. Aware of the lack of recent published works in the area, we decided to begin to fill this gap in Afro-American historiography through the publication of this book of essays. We basically view the volume as a *reconnaissance,* that is, an attempt by a group of young historians to provide a preliminary survey of current research interests and topics in Afro-American educational history in order to initiate a dialogue with other researchers in this and related fields about the education of black folk in the United States.

Most of the essays are appearing in print for the first time and several were written specifically for this volume. Indeed, for some of the authors this is the first time that they have published essays on these topics, though they have been engaged in research for several years. At the same time, many of the essays are drawn from larger works in progress and thus provide a preview of what we believe will be some of the important issues in Afro-American educational history in the next five or ten years.

The volume, however, should be viewed as a collective effort. Although we were not always able to agree completely on how this movement or that leader or institution should be viewed or interpreted, through the interchange of ideas, methodologies, and information we were able to arrive at a general consensus about the significance of the educational issues examined and the need to present our findings to scholars, students, and the general reading public so that they too can participate in the ongoing search for new knowledge and interpretations. We believe that these case studies in the education of black Americans will assist historians engaged in research on the education of other minority groups in the United States. Although some works have appeared recently which survey the general trends in the education of blacks and other minorities, we believe that detailed accounts of specific educational issues and problems facing minorities, viewed within the larger social, political, and economic context of American society, are the next step in arriving at a more comprehensive interpretation of American educational history in general.

It is our hope that the volume will prove useful for courses in American educational history, Afro-American educational history, and Social Foundations of American Education. We also believe that the book can be utilized in courses on Afro-American history as an accompaniment to general textbooks. But most importantly, we hope that future generations of educators, scholars, and students will benefit from the current generation's new perspectives on black educational history.

January, 1978   *The Editors*

Introductory Essay:
Changing Historical Perspectives on Afro-American Life and Education

Vincent P. Franklin

Historians generally believe that each new generation of scholars writes its own history. This conventional wisdom is accepted not merely because of the availability of new sources and methodologies from one generation to the next, but because the younger researchers often approach the past from a point of view or "perspective" different from that of their predecessors. Whereas during one period economic issues and problems loom larger, in another political concerns and leadership in times of crisis receive the greatest attention from professional historians. These inter-generational differences of perspective are readily apparent in American historiography in the twentieth century. The so-called Progressive historians, most notably Frederick Jackson Turner, Charles Beard, and Vernon Parrington, were those writers who, according to Richard Hofstader, "took their cues from the intellectual ferment of the period from 1890 to 1915, from the demands for reform raised by the Populists and Progressives and from the new burst of political and intellectual activity that came with these demands." These historians tended to believe that political and economic issues and conflicts were essential to historical change and supported the historic movements for political and economic reform as significant to the overall progress of the society. "They attempted to find a usable past related to the broadest needs of a nation fully launched upon its own industrialization, and to make history an active instrument of self-recognition and self-improvement."[1]

The following generation of historians, though trained and influenced by the Progressives, could not easily accept their "guiding principles." Richard Hofstader, one of the leading counter-Progressive or "consensus" historians, explained that "those of us who grew up during the Great Depression and the Second World War could no longer share the simple faith of the Progressive

1

writers in the sufficiency of American liberalism. We found ourselves living in a more complex and terrifying world, and when we set about criticizing the Progressive historians I believe it was with a keener sense of the difficulties of life and of the problem of rendering it in intelligible historical terms."[2] In commenting upon Hofstader's rejection of the Progressive doctrine, Arthur M. Schlesinger, Jr. pointed out that the tendency "to oversimplify and over-dramatize the complex and shifting actuality of our national experience" was objectionable to the leading counter-Progressives. Hofstader and other historians of his generation had concluded that the Progressives "relied too heavily on geographic and economic determinism. They took past conflicts as direct analogues of present conflict. They tended to impute discreditable motives to historical figures on the 'wrong' side."[3]

The counter-Progressive historians downplayed the significance of political action in historical change and looked for the important motive forces of history "inside the mind and psyche of men." Their particular perspectives on history were derived not from politics and economics, but from philosophy, art, literature, and psychology. As Gene Wise in his book, *American Historical Explanations,* puts it, the counter-Progressives focused on "people's pictures of reality as embodied through images, myths, symbols and dramatized in those psychic quests which take men's inner compulsions and project them forward." Whereas the Progressives believed that most people were motivated by economic interests, the counter-Progressives looked to psychic drives for status and success. "Where Progressives tried unmasking ideas to see the real driving things below, counter-Progressives tried unmasking things to see the real driving ideas below."[4]

The counter-Progressive or "consensus" perspective held sway in American historiography through the 1950s and 1960s, but in the latter decade historical studies began to bear the imprint of that new era of "social ferment." The movement for black civil rights which had been gathering momentum before the Second World War burst upon the American scene in the immediate post-war period and grew stronger and stronger so that by the mid-1960s the United States was caught in the grips of a powerful and significant "social revolution." This movement raised the political consciousness of most black Americans and soon began to have an effect upon other historically oppressed groups in the society. Spanish-speaking citizens, Native Americans, women, and even white ethnic groups reexamined their relationships with the dominant political and economic establishment and made new demands on the system on the basis of previous neglect and discrimination as well as perceived contemporary needs. In order to bolster these demands for greater access to the rewards and resources of the society, these groups increasingly turned to "the past" for relevant information, and American social history came into its own. When American historians began to take into account the historical experiences of the various social groups which made up American society, they found that, indeed, the United States had *Many Pasts*. Historians trained in the 1950s and early 1960s could comprehend and appreciate the earlier generation's seeking after "consensus" in the American past, but the counter-Progressive perspective appeared unsupportable in light of the demands of various social groups for historical investigations relevant to their needs and experiences.[5]

Twentieth century Afro-American historiography also reflected changes in perspective from one generation to another. The earliest concerns of historians in this area were related to the need "to tell the Negro's story" within the larger context of American history. Carter G. Woodson, the Father of Negro History, founded the Association for the Study of Negro Life and History in 1915 for "the collection of sociological and historical data on the Negro, the study of peoples of African blood, the publishing of books in this field, and the promotion of harmony between the races by acquainting the one with the other." The *Journal of Negro History* was launched in 1916 in order to stimulate "scientific research" on the Negro and to make "the world see the Negro as a participant rather than a lay figure in history."[6] Imbued with the Progressive spirit of the era, Woodson, W.E.B. DuBois, Monroe Work, and the other scholars active before 1930 emphasized the role of historical research in the social uplift and advancement of blacks in this country. In light of the distortions and inaccuracies about blacks prevalent throughout the society, Woodson placed great faith in the ameliorative or liberating aspects of "historical truth."

> Let truth destroy the dividing prejudices of nationality and teach universal love without distinction of race, merit or rank. With the sublime enthusiasm and heavenly vision of the Great Teacher let us help men to rise above the race hate of this age unto the altruism of a rejuvenated universe.[7]

As editor of the *Journal of Negro History* Woodson published numerous essays which presented the historical truth about the social advantages and deficiencies of Afro-America.[8]

This "racial uplift" motif remained dominant in the historiography on blacks until the 1930s when the Depression led historians to an examination of the "economic" underpinnings of racism and discrimination in American society.[9] Lawrence Reddick in an important essay calling for "A New Interpretation for Negro History" (1937) reemphasized the need for Negro history "To discover and record the role of African peoples in the world.... To awaken and 'educate' a majority population to the significance of this role ... and To inculcate a dynamic pride in the Negro." But he believed that previous historians had not sufficiently analyzed the larger context within which the Afro-American operates. Moreover, current perspectives on American life were being informed by a renewed interest in Marxian economic analysis. Reddick suggested that Negro History too could benefit from more incisive economic interpretations of conditions and problems.

> What has happened to the American Negro since 1865, did not occur in vacuo. In their setting, these developments may be seen as aspects of the rather blatantly aggressive industrialism conditioned by the interplay of population movements, the resistances of public opinion and unchannelized labor protests, plus the rise in Southern life and politics of the yeoman white leadership with its appeals to tradition and antipathy.... In other words, when we see the story of the Negro since Emancipation as the record of the clashes and rationalizations of individual and group impulse against an American social order of an unfolding capitalism, within which operates semi-articulate arrangements and etiquettes of class and caste, we begin to understand the rise of, say, Booker T. Washington, the furor of lynching in the 1890s, and the attitude toward the black worker of the American Federation of Labor.

Reddick believed that the "social philosophy" of previous chroniclers of the race was "sadly lacking in a grasp of dynamic forces," and "turned out to be a rather naive Emersonian gospel of self-reliance, simple optimism and patient regard for destiny." His concluding remarks reemphasized his major points. "If Negro History is to escape the provincial nature of its first phases, it will surely *redefine the area of subject matter in terms of a larger focus; recast its catalog of the determinative influences affecting Negro life; and re-examine the social philosophy implicit throughout the work*" (italics in original).[10]

The 1930s witnessed the publication of several important studies examining the social conditions for Afro-Americans within the developing American political economy. Sterling D. Spero and Abram Harris' *The Black Worker* (1931) set forth "descriptively and analytically the results of a study of the American labor movement in one of its most important aspects, namely, the relation of the dominant section of the working class to the segregated, circumscribed, and restricted Negro minority." Beginning with the relations between black and white workers under the antebellum slave economy, Spero and Harris carry their examination through the rise of trade and industrial unionism among American workers.[11] In 1936 Abram Harris published *The Negro as Capitalist,* an economic study which examined the development of black banking in this country. Harris made clear "the struggle of the Negro to gain economic status and social respectability by erecting within the larger framework of capitalism a small world of Negro business enterprise to develop his own capitalist-employer class and to create employment opportunities for increasing numbers of Negroes in the white collar occupations."[12] The most significant historical analysis of the social and economic conditions for black citizens and workers within the larger American economic framework was W.E.B. DuBois' *Black Reconstruction in America* (1935), which he referred to as "An Essay Toward a History of the Part Which Black Folk Played in the Attempt to Reconstruct Democracy in America, 1860-1880." This classic historical study not only challenged the contemporary interpretations of the Reconstruction era, but was also the first systematic analysis of the input of the black and white working class in the economic development of the South. Previous histories had described the South as primarily a land of masters and slaves. DuBois, however, applied several Marxian concepts and forms of analysis to post-bellum southern society and generated several new insights into that controversial era in American History.[13]

The shifting interpretations and perspectives in Afro-American historiography in general during the first four decades of this century were also reflected in the historical investigations of the education of black folk. Carter G. Woodson's *The Education of the Negro Prior to 1861,* published in 1915, was originally intended to cover the schooling of black Americans from the Civil War to 1915, but upon undertaking the research he found enough sources for a book solely on the colonial and antebellum periods. Woodson documents the formal schooling provided for blacks by religious and philanthropic groups, antislavery societies, public institutions, and by blacks themselves. He examines these educational activities primarily within the immediate social environment of blacks. There is an awareness of the increasing industrialization and urbanization and at times these changes are related to the provisioning of schooling for Afro-Americans. Woodson's strongest point, however, is the vastness of the historical evidence he unearthed. As one reviewer put it, "Every available fact has been garnered and is made accessible to the reader by a painstaking index, while a scholarly bibliography gives the original sources. A valuable set of documents is appended, including many not hitherto laid open to the general public."[14]

Woodson was also profoundly interested in the contemporary educational conditions for Afro-America and in 1933 he published a collection of essays entitled *The Miseducation of the Negro.* The work was basically a critique of the contemporary status of Negro education in America. Woodson believed that black education should serve two purposes: preparation and training for movement into the mainstream of American political and economic life, and the inculcation of "race pride" in the younger generation of black Americans. In this way blacks would be in a position to compete with others for the limited resources of the society and would do so as black men and women proud of their heritage in this country and throughout the world. At that time he believed the greatest drag on Negro education and the general advancement of the race was "the educated class of Negroes." "The only question which concerns us here," Woodson asked rhetorically, "is whether these 'educated' persons are actually equipped to face the ordeal before them or unconsciously contribute to their own undoing by perpetuating the regime of the oppressor." Woodson's overall conclusions were optimistic, however, because of his basic faith in education. "Can you expect teachers to revolutionize the social order for the good of the community? Indeed we must expect this very thing. The educational system of a country is worthless unless it accomplishes this task. Men of scholarship, and consequently of prophetic insight, must show us the right way and lead us into the light which shines brighter and brighter."[15]

The historical investigations of Afro-American education which appeared in the 1930s were generally more restrained in the evaluations of the liberating effects of education. Horace Mann Bond published *The Education of the Negro in the American Social Order* in 1934. This important and comprehensive study presented an analysis of the history and financing of schooling for black Americans to 1930. Bond made very clear the interrelationships between the American social order and the public schooling of blacks historically, and fully documented the "perpetuation of inequality" between blacks and whites through the failure to provide equal or even adequate programs and facilities for blacks in most southern and some northern states. The study took into account the "larger context" of Negro education and was cited by Reddick as one of the "new" interpretations or perspectives on Afro-American history. But Bond did not share Woodson's faith in the "uplifting" or liberating effects of schooling. "Of one thing, at least, we can be sure," Bond warned, "that is the unsoundness of relying upon the school as a cure-all for our ills." He believed there should be a greater awareness of "the limitations and possibilities of the school."

> Better schools cannot of themselves save a population which is condemned by economic pressure to remain in a half-starved, poverty-stricken environment.... Strictly speaking, the school has never built a new social order; it has been the product and interpreter of the existing system, sustaining and being sustained by the social complex. Schools for Negro children can perform the older function of the school; but even more they can adventure beyond the frontier and plan for a new order in those aspects which affect the race. To do this, however, they must function as coordinate elements of a unified system, and not in utter isolation from the world of action and social change.[16]

In *Negro Education in Alabama,* (1939) his prize-winning study of the "social and economic forces" affecting the public schooling of blacks in Alabama from 1865 to 1930, Bond was again concerned with the "larger context" of black education in the state. "Separated by custom and law," wrote Bond, "the two races remained bound together by the inextricable web of the social and economic order of which they are a part." He added that "in a study of this kind ... it is as impossible to speak only of schools for Negro children, as though they were an isolated phenomenon that could be excised from the body social for study at any convenient time, as it would be to trace the natural history of an organ of the human body without reference to the larger whole."[17] By the end of the 1930s historians of Afro-American life and education were in general agreement that the social, political, economic, and educational development of Afro-America must be viewed within the evolving social and economic context of American society in general.

The outbreak of World War II in Europe, the national defense mobilization, and the entrance of the United States into the hostilities brought few challenges to the dominant historiographical perspectives on Afro-America. The obvious need to utilize all available manpower and material to support the Allied cause meant the federal government would be forced to outlaw dis-

crimination against blacks and other minorities by employers receiving government contracts. The low morale and general lack of enthusiasm on the part of
Afro-America for the war effort meant that several concessions had to be
made in order to convince blacks that they had a stake in the war's outcome.
The fascist dictators in Europe appeared less of a threat than the fascist politicians in the United States. As one black college student observed, "The Army
jim crows us. The Navy lets us serve only as messmen. The Red Cross refuses
our blood. Employers and labor unions shut us out. Lynchings continue. We
are disenfranchised, jim crowed, spat upon. What more could Hitler do than
that?"[18] In order to gain a modicum of support among the black masses, the
Negro press launched its campaign for the "Double V" — victory against
fascism at home and abroad.[19]

The thrust of attempts to improve race relations throughout the country
during and immediately following the war was on activities to increase "interracial contacts," which in turn would lead to greater "interracial tolerance and
understanding." Whereas during the 1930s American Marxists and others
placed great emphasis on the role of the capitalist economy in the perpetuation
of racism and discrimination against Afro-Americans, social scientists and
minority group leaders in the 1940s and 1950s stressed "ignorance and intol-
erance" as the major reasons for majority-minority group tensions. Hundreds
of local interracial committees and organizations tried to "educate" the
American majority about minority racial and cultural groups in hopes of
increasing "intergroup understanding."[20] The publication of Gunnar
Myrdal's *An American Dilemma* in 1944 was significant in that it cloaked the
"Negro Problem" in moral terms for white Americans. The failure to extend
freedom and equality to black Americans was considered to be in conflict with
the self-professed "American Creed" which ostensibly supported the ideals of
individual human dignity, the fundamental equality of all men, and of certain
inalienable rights to freedom, justice, and fair opportunity. When Americans
are made aware of the profound conflict between these values and ideals and
the treatment of black Americans, according to Myrdal, they will move to end
the prejudice and discrimination practiced in virtually all areas of American
social life.[21]

Myrdal's overly optimistic assessment of the moral dilemma of white
Americans set the tone for discussions and activities to try and improve the
꞊al social conditions for blacks and other minority groups in the postwar
United States emerged from the war the predominant world power
eeded to impose the "Pax Americana" upon the western industrial-
ions and the prowestern developing countries of the "Third World."
merican government encountered some difficulties, however, in con-
g many of the newly-decolonized "colored peoples" that the United
s supported their entrance into the international community on an equal
ting with other sovereign nations, especially given the way "colored
oples" were treated within its own borders. Moreover, civil rights organiza-

tions, such as the National Association for the Advancement of Colored People (NAACP) and the Communist-dominated National Negro Congress used the United Nations and other international forums to expose the conditions for blacks and other oppressed groups in this country. The continued "bad press" received by the United States following each new lynching and mob action against blacks even spurred some white citizens and organizations to join the ongoing black struggle for equal rights. The advent of white participation in the civil rights movement and the increased media coverage of events in the South meant that the terrorism and barbaric acts which had previously plagued black attempts to secure equal rights could not continue unabated without further exposing the "American system of justice" for what it actually was. By the late 1940s the Executive and Judicial branches of the government gradually began to move to protect the civil rights of black citizens.[22]

Afro-American historiography was not unaffected by these changes in the social conditions of black America. Historians began to look to the past for guidance and information on how the country should best move toward improved race relations. Studies undertaken in this area during the "civil rights era" usually sought either to document the negative impact of isolation and segregation upon black Americans or to demonstrate the efficacy of interracial cooperation or "integration" in bringing about improvements in the social, political, and economic conditions of Afro-America. The important historical studies on black Americans published in the 1940s, 1950s, and 1960s often reflected this "civil rights perspective." In the first edition of *From Slavery to Freedom* (1947) John Hope Franklin approached Afro-American history from the historiographical perspectives developed by earlier generations of scholars as well as the contemporary concern for the improvement of race relations. "I have made a conscious effort to write the history of the Negro in America with due regard for the forces at work which have affected his development," wrote Franklin.

> This has involved a continuous recognition of the main stream of American history and the relationship of the Negro to it....
> I have given considerable attention to the task of tracing the interaction of the Negro and the American environment. It can hardly be denied that the course of American history has been vitally affected by his presence. At the same time it must be admitted that the effect of acculturation on the Negro in the United States has been so marked that today he is as truly American as any member of other ethnic groups that make up the American population. That is not to say that the story of the Negro is one solely of achievement or of success.... The task here has been not to recite his achievements — though naturally some have been so outstanding as to warrant consideration — but to tell the story of the process by which the Negro has sought to cast his lot with the evolving American civilization.

Thus Franklin followed the historiographical guidelines of Woodson, Reddick, Bond, and DuBois, while seeking to demonstrate that blacks were "truly American" and moving toward greater participation or "integration" into the mainstream of American life.[23]

Other important historical works published in the 1950s and 1960s echoed these themes. Rayford Logan's *The Negro in American Life and Thought, The Nadir, 1877-1900,* first published in 1954, sought to shed light on "one of the neglected periods in American history ... when second class citizenship for Negroes was accepted by Presidents, the Supreme Court, organized labor, the General Federation of Women's Clubs — indeed, by the vast majority of Americans, North and South, and by the 'leader' of the race" [Booker T. Washington]. Logan contrasted "The Nadir" with the contemporary circumstances of Afro-Americans.

> Barely visible were "The Roots of Recovery" — the forces that were to gain strength in our times that today the future of the American Negro is as bright as it was gloomy fifty years ago. The contrast should make the faint-hearted in the United States and the honest critics abroad give an eventual affirmative answer to the question that Frederick Douglass posed in 1889, namely, whether "American justice, American liberty, American civilization, American law, and American Christianity could be made to include and protect alike and forever all American citizens in the rights which have been guaranteed to them by the organic and fundamental laws of the land.[24]

Logan's account of "The Nadir," however, was criticized by a contemporary for being *too* negative. In the *Journal of Negro History's* review of the book, George Grimke complained that "in spite of its extensive findings, the work does not yield the total thought on Negroes in America during the era. For example, it omits the humanitarian efforts for Negro uplift in the period which would have restrained liability to charges of bias."

> There were hundreds of Northern men and women who toiled in the South among Negroes, and today monuments stand in institutions to their memories and sacrifices. Moreover, there survive also accounts of millions of dollars which were spent in training Negro leaders who have guided their fellow sufferers out of the slough of despondency, degradation, and ignorance, in which slavery left them. There is practically no mention of white Southerners, many of whom helped behind the scenes and openly. Their efforts silently assuaged much of the ruthless vengeance, which embittered poor white competitors..., would otherwise have wreaked upon the freedmen.

Grimke did believe that the work had some value "as an accompaniment of Woodward's splendid works...;" and that Logan had "inadvertently made a contribution to historical truth."[25]

C. Vann Woodward in *The Strange Career of Jim Crow,* first published in 1955, tried to demonstrate the "relative recency of the Jim Crow laws," placing their origins in the post-Reconstruction era. William Brewer, then editor of the *Journal of Negro History*, believed "this very timely investigation of a difficult and urgent problem by a distinguished historian is probably the most important contribution to the history of the South in 1954. . . . The work will be invaluable to historians and laymen who seek understanding as the South and nation grapple with desegregation in public education and practice Christianity and democracy."[26] In subsequent editions of the book, however, Woodward was forced to qualify his original interpretation, especially in light of the numerous essays and monographs which seem to demonstrate that Jim Crow laws and other segregatory practices were well-defined in most American cities and towns, North and South, before the Civil War.[27]

Other studies which appeared during the integrationist era sought to illuminate various aspects of black life rather than concentrating on interracial activities. Again, Gunnar Myrdal's *An American Dilemma* set the frame of reference for the historical analysis of Afro-American culture and communities. For example, although the Negro community and culture were not primary objects of the study, Myrdal managed to conclude that they were "a pathological form" of American communities and culture.

> In practically all its divergences, American Negro culture is not something independent of general American culture. It is a distorted development or a pathological condition, of the general American culture. . . .
>
> This can be said positively: we assume that it is to the advantage of American Negroes as individuals and as a group to become assimilated into American culture, to acquire the traits held in esteem by the dominant white Americans. . . .
>
> Also not to be taken in a doctrinal sense is the observation that peculiarities in the Negro community may be characterized as social pathology. As a reaction to adverse and degrading living conditions, the Negroes' culture is taking on some characteristics which are not given a high evaluation in the larger American culture. Occasionally the Negro culture traits are appreciated by the whites.[28]

Despite the fact that Myrdal did not wish his observations on the Negro community to be accepted "in a doctrinal sense," historical investigations of urban black communities undertaken in the 1950s and 1960s usually sought to document the "social pathologies" of the "Negro ghetto." Allan Spear's *Black Chicago: The Making of the Ghetto,* Gilbert Osofsky's *Harlem: The Making of a Ghetto,* Meier and Rudwick's *From Plantation to Ghetto,* Kenneth Kusmer's recent study of blacks in Cleveland, *A Ghetto Takes Shape,* and similar works discussed many of the so-called "social pathologies" which developed as a result of the isolation and segregation of blacks in urban America.[29]

Unfortunately, these studies of the "rise of the black ghetto" have shed little light on the evolution and development of urban black communities. Historians and sociologists who examined the social conditions for blacks in the ghettos merely compared them with conditions for blacks in other cities and white immigrants. The political, social, and economic comparisons were the essence of the significant information contained in these works. Politically, we learned that the white immigrant groups advanced by attaching themselves to the dominant political machines in the various cities, while black political activity seemed to stagnate during the first three decades of this century, with blacks in Chicago registering the only solid political advances. Socially, we learned that as the number of blacks increased in any urban area, race relations began to deteriorate and violence sometimes erupted, and blacks became more and more segregated. Economically, we learned that the white immigrants made significant occupational gains through control of the trade and industrial labor union movements and employment in urban industry. Blacks occupied what appeared to be a permanent position at the bottom of the urban occupational ladder. The remainder of these "black ghetto studies" was usually a somewhat detailed examination of the social pathologies of the ghetto. The instability of the black family in the urban setting, the social class antagonisms, the inability of urban blacks to make and retain political advances were some of the "Negro Problems" investigated. The black ghetto studies provided very little information on the internal functioning of black communities in urban America.[30] Several essays in this collection, however, provide an "inside view" of how blacks in several American cities educated themselves.

Historical research on the education of black Americans produced in the 1950s and 1960s also reflected the dominant integrationist perspective. Willard Range's *The Rise and Progress of Negro Colleges in Georgia, 1865-1949,* published in 1951, was considered "vindication of the dreams, hopes, and visions of the men and women who sacrificed themselves not only in Georgia, but throughout the Southland in behalf of educational opportunity for colored young men and women."[31] Elizabeth Peck's *Berea's First Century, 1855-1955* (1955) discussed the futile attempts of the liberal founders of the college to provide "interracial education" in Kentucky in the face of wide-spread opposition to the practice. In a 1955 review, historian Charles Walker Thomas expressed his belief that the book "should be required for those who must wrestle with the problems of integration. When they are seen in historical perspective, as Mrs. Peck presents, they will prove to be neither novel nor insoluble."[32]

Separate and Unequal by Louis B. Harlan appeared in 1958. It examined the impact of northern philanthropy and southern racial beliefs on the development of the public educational systems of North Carolina, Virginia, South Carolina, and Georgia. Harlan analyzed the relationship between the economies of the various states and their public school systems, following the pattern established by Horace Mann Bond in *Negro Education in Alabama* (1939). Harlan recognized the limitations of the "separate" public schools, but believed that "the improvement of white education in the South has been one of the means by which Negroes of the region *may* expect eventually to secure their heritage of human rights." However, Harlan also stated that "education by itself, without other forms of action, including intelligent protest, would never solve the major racial problems; on the contrary public schools might inculcate orthodox racism, and sometimes have." Harlan found very little evidence that public schooling and increases in income had any great impact upon the overall racial beliefs and practices of southern whites.[33]

The most important historical investigation of the education of Afro-Americans to appear in the 1960s was Henry Bullock's *A History of Negro Education in the South from 1619 to the Present* (1967). The prizewinning study surveys the elementary, secondary, and higher education of southern blacks primarily from the Civil War to 1965. The integrationist or "civil rights" perspective was explicit. "This book is concerned with the historical development of educational opportunities for Negroes in the South, and with the manner in which these evolving opportunities facilitated the desegregation movement now occurring in the United States." The contemporary leadership of the civil rights movement had been educated in the segregated schools of the South and Bullock believed that this was one of the "unintended" positive outcomes of southern Negro education. This "historical accident" helps account for the current "changes in American race relations we are now experiencing...." Bullock believed that the changes were "the result of a 'sneak attack' directed by the larger purpose of human society against the biases of individuals and through the force of a segregated educational system that was never created for such end."

> Basic, therefore, is the central idea that our current educational and social revolution was never intended, but has developed instead out of liberating responses elicited by the nation's efforts to maintain the status quo; that Negro education in the South repeatedly served as the main leverage for this movement; and, despite purposeful efforts to the contrary, has been pushing the movement toward the complete emancipation of the Negro American as a person.[34]

Bullock also expressed his belief that with the development of Negro education in the South, "new and higher levels of interracial accommodation ... came into existence...."[35]

The 1970s have witnessed the beginning of another shift in the dominant historiographical perspectives on Afro-American life and education. The civil rights-integrationist concern with race relations has given way to renewed interest in the development and evolution of Afro-American culture and communities. Many previous historians failed to describe or even acknowledge the existence of a truly Afro-American culture under slavery. Kenneth Stampp in the *Peculiar Institution* (1956) stated that "the Negro slave existed in a kind of cultural void."

> He lived in a twilight zone between two ways of life, neither of which now afforded him much opportunity to develop the attributes which dis-

tinguish man from beast. [Frederick Law] Olmsted noted that slaves normally acquired, by example or compulsion, some of the external forms of white civilization; but this was poor compensation for "the systematic withdrawal from them of all the usual influences which tend to nourish the moral nature and develop the intellectual faculties, in savages as well as in civilized free men." Indeed, the development of a true Afro-American culture had to await the end of slavery.

What, then, filled the leisure hours of the slaves? Not surprisingly, these culturally rootless people devoted much of their free time to the sheer pleasure of being idle.[36]

John W. Blassingame in his study of *The Slave Community* (1972), however, identified several distinct Afro-American cultural developments.

> Antebellum black slaves created several unique cultural forms which lightened their burden of oppression, promoted group solidarity, provided ways for verbalizing aggression, sustaining hope, building self-esteem, and often represented areas of life largely free from the control of whites. However oppressive or dehumanizing the plantation was, the struggle for survival was not severe enough to crush all of the slaves' creative instincts. Among the elements of slave culture were: an emotional religion, folk songs and tales, dances, and superstitions. Much of the slave's culture — language, customs, beliefs, and ceremonies — set him apart from his master.... The more his cultural forms differed from those of his master and the more they were immune from the control of whites, the more the slave gained in personal autonomy and positive self-concepts.[37]

Blassingame discussed how the slave culture facilitated the development of group solidarity and identification.

> The most important aspect of this group identification was that the slaves were not solely dependent on the white man's cultural frames of reference for their ideals and values. As long as the plantation black had cultural norms and ideals, ways of verbalizing aggression, and roles in his life largely free from his master's control, he could preserve some personal autonomy, and resist infantilization, total identification with planters, and internalization of unflattering stereotypes calling for abject servility.[38]

According to previous historians the black family did not fare well under slavery. Matriarchal and disorganized by the ravages of the interstate slave trade, the slave family was considered one of the weakest components of the slave culture. Sociologists E. Franklin Frazier and Daniel P. Moynihan and historians U. B. Phillips and Kenneth Stampp believed that the slave family was not of great assistance in the freedmen's transit from slavery to freedom.[39] However, Herbert Gutman in his recent study, *The Black Family in Slavery and Freedom* (1976) documented the intricate kinship networks of black extended families under slavery which survived the disruption of Emancipation, Civil War, Reconstruction, and Redemption. The Afro-

American cultural pattern of naming offspring for near and distant relations was identified by Gutman through the examination of plantation records from throughout the South. Gutman was able to trace the names of slaves freed in 1865 to relatives who lived on the same plantations two or three generations earlier.[40] Moreover, other aspects of the slave culture have recently become the subject of historical investigation. Slave folktales, spirituals and other musical forms, religious practices, and other Afro-American cultural forms having their origins in slavery have been the subject of renewed discussion and analysis by historians during the 1970s.[41]

The new perspectives on black educational history presented in this volume focus primarily upon the education of Afro-American communities, leaders, and professionals. The descriptions and accounts of the development of "black ghettos" rarely contained information on "education," other than public schooling. The major topic of concern was usually the problem of increasing segregation in the public schools of various cities and the concurrent deterioration in the quality of public instruction and facilities available to blacks following the "transformation of the schools." There was usually no discussion of how the black ghetto or "community" was educated and educated itself. The first two essays in this volume examine schools of "higher learning" which were provided for and by blacks in late nineteenth century Philadelphia and Augusta, Georgia. The authors not only discuss the history and development of the schools, but also describe the interactions between the faculty and students at the schools and the local black communities.

Linda Perkins examines the Institute for Colored Youth, a Quaker sponsored secondary school for blacks in Philadelphia. The Quaker practice of racial segregation in their own schools meant that any formal education provided for blacks for philanthropic, religious, or other reasons would have to be carried out by "qualified Negro educators" employed by the Friends. Ms. Perkins discusses the degree of black control and input in the running of the Institute between 1852 through 1903. Her findings challenge the prevailing historiography in the area which denies the significance of black input in the functioning of Quaker-endowed schools for blacks.

The earliest schools for blacks in Augusta, Georgia were founded by local blacks and later the Freedmen's Bureau. With the opening of public schools in the city for whites, the pre-existing black schools were eventually incorporated into the local public school system. In the late 1870s the Richmond County School Board decided to support the establishment of high schools for whites, but only reluctantly agreed to help finance black secondary schooling in the city. June Patton documents the struggle of black Augustans to maintain the Ware High School for blacks and their attempts to gain public support for the school. Ms. Patton's essay provides the background information on one of the most important decisions by the Supreme Court on public secondary schooling for blacks in the United States.

The most famous secondary school in the South for Afro-Americans during the nineteenth century was Hampton Institute, with General Samuel T. Armstrong as Principal. A great deal has been written about the school and its principal, but most of it was based on sources provided by the General and his friends. James Anderson presents a detailed analysis of the "industrial education" program provided at Hampton between 1867 and 1900. Utilizing a wide array of letters, newspaper articles, speeches and eyewitness accounts of the activities at the school, Anderson is able to document *both* the educational philosophy and practices of General Armstrong. This is the first scholarly account of the actual schooling provided at Hampton Institute which trained a large percentage of the leadership class of Afro-America.

Whereas Hampton was the leading industrial secondary school for blacks in the late nineteenth and early twentieth century, Fisk University in Nashville was the most important collegiate institution. The schooling provided at Fisk was designed primarily to train the "educated class of Negroes" for their positions as leaders of the race. However, several northern white philanthropists who were interested in blacks remaining the reserve industrial labor force for the South objected to the "militant racial egalitarianism" spouted by the students and graduates of the college. Thus in order to insure that Fisk produced the type of Negro leader who would not challenge the social status assigned blacks in the South, several "industrial philanthropists" decided to take over the Fisk Board of Trustees and arrange the appointment of teachers and administrators at the school sympathetic to their cause. James Anderson documents the machinations of the industrialists and describes how the Fisk student body was able to thwart the "philanthropic" intervention.

The next two essays examine the education of two northern black communities during the early decades of the twentieth century. Vincent Franklin describes the educational activities of black social organizations in Philadelphia between 1900 and 1930 and reports that the types of educational programs sponsored were related to the specific social, political, and economic needs of the black community. He believes that the examination of community-wide educational activities provides new insights into the overall social environment of urban black communities. In the same vein, Lillian Williams details the founding and educational programs of the Michigan Avenue YMCA for blacks in Buffalo between 1922 and 1940. The funds for opening a separate black YMCA were donated by local white philanthropists and members of the black community. However, the entire YMCA educational program was under the control of the black members of the various committees which ran the institution. Ms. Williams describes how the YMCA was used to improve the social, economic, and educational conditions of blacks in Buffalo. These two essays are the first to document the role of "community education programs" in the social development of urban black communities.

Howard University Law School trained more black lawyers than any other school in the United States during the 1920s and 1930s. One of the major reasons for this accomplishment was the high quality and academic standards of the school's faculty. Genna Rae McNeil recounts the transformation of Howard Law School between 1920 and 1935 from an unaccredited, marginal institution for the legal training of blacks, to one of the leading schools of law, black or white, providing training in civil rights law and other legal areas of significant interest to black Americans. Ms. McNeil describes these important changes at Howard within the overall context of American legal education during the period, while documenting the professional and collective commitments of the black administrators and professors at the school. Darlene Hine examines the changes at Meharry Medical College between 1921 and 1938 and provides many important insights into the problems facing blacks desiring medical training during that period. Lack of professional recognition, incompetent instructors, inadequate facilities, and prejudiced white administrators were only some of the drawbacks with which students had to contend. Ms. Hine's essay, based on previously unavailable sources, presents the preliminary findings on what will very likely be an entirely new perspective on the history and evolution of black medical and professional education in the United States.

The discussions of the conditions at predominantly black colleges and professional schools accentuates the need to clarify the relationship between traditional American social goals and values historically, and the provisioning of segregated schooling for the black minority in the United States. In the final essay, Vincent Franklin surveys the formal schooling of black Americans from the early nineteenth century to the present and offers some explanations as to why certain types of schooling were provided for blacks at various points in time. Franklin's essay attempts to place into historical perspective the contemporary opposition to the desegregation of American public education.

Afro-Americans historically have been educated by a wide variety of institutions and agencies for a number of different and sometimes conflicting purposes. With this book of essays we have begun to fill the gap in our knowledge of the education of Afro-Americans and have tried to provide some new information and perspectives on this important area of American educational history.

NOTES

1. Richard Hofstader, *The Progressive Historians: Turner, Beard, and Parrington* (New York, 1968), pp. xii, xvii.

2. Ibid., p. xv. Some of the famous "counter-Progressive" historians are Louis Hartz, John Williams Ward, Daniel Boorstin, and Clinton Rossiter.

3. Arthur M. Schlesinger, Jr., "Richard Hofstader," in *Pastmasters: Some Essays on American Historians,* Marcus Cunliffe and Robin W. Winks, editors (New York, 1969), p. 284, passim; *see also* Arthur Mann, "The Progressive Tradition," in *The Reconstruction of American History,* John Higham, editor (New York, 1962), pp. 157–179.

4. Gene Wise, *American Historical Explanations: A Strategy for Grounded Theory* (Homewood, Illinois, 1973), pp. 84, 107, passim; *see also* Bernard Sternsher, *Consensus, Conflict, and American Historians* (Bloomington, Indiana, 1975), pp. 1–27.

5. For an excellent introduction to and samples of American social history *see* Herbert Gutman and Gregory S. Kealey, editors, *Many Pasts: Readings in American Social History, Volume I, 1600–1876,* and *Volume II 1865–The Present* (Englewood Cliffs, N.J., 1973). The introductory essay discusses the rise of American social history.

6. Carter G. Woodson, "Ten Years of Collecting and Publishing the Records of the Negro," *The Journal of Negro History (JNH),* 10 (October 1925):598.

7. Idem, quoted in Earl E. Thorpe, "The Philosophy of Black History," in *The Central Theme of Black History* (Durham, N.C., 1969), p. 35; *see also,* Thorpe, *Black Historians: A Critique* (New York, 1971), passim.

8. A perusal of the volumes of the *JNH* edited by Woodson (1-37) reveals that he was concerned with the history and uplift of Africans in Latin America, and the Caribbean as well as in the United States and Canada.

9. For another statement of the "uplift" perspective on Negro History, *see* Charles Wesley, "The Reconstruction of History," *JNH,* 20 (October 1935): 411–427.

10. Lawrence D. Reddick, "A New Interpretation For Negro History," *JNH,* 22 (January 1937): 19, 26–28.

11. Sterling D. Spero and Abram L. Harris, *The Black Worker: The Negro and the Labor Movement* (1931, reprinted New York, 1969), p. xv.

12. Abram L. Harris, *The Negro As Capitalist: A Study of Banking and Business Among American Negroes* (1936, reprinted College Park, Maryland, 1968), p. ix.

13. W.E.B. DuBois, *Black Reconstruction in America* (New York, 1935). The 1976 edition of the book (Kraus-Thompson) contains a new and informative introduction by Herbert Aptheker.

14. J. F. Gould review of *The Education of the Negro Prior to 1861* in *Survey Magazine* quoted in Earl E. Thorpe, "The Father of Negro History," in *The Central Theme of Black History,* p. 60.

15. Woodson, *The Miseducation of the Negro* (Washington, D.C., 1933), pp. xi-xii, 1, 145.

16. Horace Mann Bond, *The Education of the Negro in the American Social Order* (1934, reprinted New York, 1966), pp. 12, 13.

17. Idem, *Negro Education in Alabama: A Study in Cotton and Steel* (1939, reprinted New York, 1969), p. 287.

18. Quoted in Harvard Sitkoff, "Racial Militancy and Interracial Violence in the Second World War," *The Journal of American History,* 58 (December 1971): 665.

19. Ibid., *see also,* Lee Finkle, "The Conservative Aims of Militant Rhetoric: Black Protest During World War II," *The Journal of American History,* 60 (December 1973): 692–713.

20. Ibid. *A Monthly Summary of Events and Trends in Race Relations* was published by Fisk University and provided on-going information on activities to improve race relations throughout the country from 1943 through 1948.

21. Gunnar Myrdal with the assistance of R. Sterner and A. Rose, *An American Dilemma: The Negro Problem and Modern Democracy* (New York, 1944), pp. xlv-lix, 1–25, passim.

22. The postwar conditions for black America are discussed in John Hope Franklin, *From Slavery to Freedom: A History of Negro Americans,* 3rd edition (New York, 1967), pp. 608–622.

23. Ibid., first edition (New York, 1947), pp. vii, viii; *see also,* Franklin, "The New Negro History," *JNH,* 42 (April 1957): 89–97.

24. Rayford Logan, *The Negro in American Life and Thought, The Nadir, 1877–1900* (New York, 1954), preface. This work was enlarged and reissued under the title, *The Betrayal of the Negro: From Rutherford B. Hayes to Woodrow Wilson* (New York, 1965).

25. George Grimke review of Logan, *The Negro in American Life and Thought,* in *JNH,* 40 (July 1955): 283–284.

26. William Brewer review of Woodward, *The Strange Career of Jim Crow,* in *JNH,* 40 (October 1955): 380–381.

27. Woodward issued new editions of *The Strange Career of Jim Crow* in 1957, 1965, and 1974. For discussions and critiques of the Woodward thesis, *see The Origins of Segregation,* Joel Williamson, editor (Boston, Mass., 1968).

28. Myrdal, *An American Dilemma,* pp. 928–930.

29. Allan Spear, *Black Chicago: The Making of A Ghetto, 1890-1920* (Chicago, 1967); Gilbert Osofsky, *Harlem: The Making of A Ghetto, Negro New York, 1890-1930* (New York, 1966); August Meier and Elliot Rudwick, *From Plantation to Ghetto: An Interpretive History of Negro Americans* (New York, 1966); and Kenneth Kusmer, *A Ghetto Takes Shape: Black Cleveland, 1870-1930* (Urbana, Ill., 1976).

30. The black ghetto studies are discussed in detail in Vincent P. Franklin, "Ghetto On Their Minds: Afro-American Historiography and the City," *Afro-Americans in New York Life and History,* 1 (January 1976): 111–119.

31. William Brewer review of Willard Range, *The Rise and Progress of Negro Colleges in Georgia, 1865-1949* (Athens, Ga., 1951), in *JNH,* 40 (April 1955): 199.

32. Charles Walker Thomas review of E. Peck, *Berea: First Century, 1855-1955* (Lexington, Ky., 1955) in *JNH,* 40 (October 1955): 377.

33. Louis B. Harlan, *Separate and Unequal: Public School Campaigns and Racism in the Southern Seaboard States, 1901-1915* (1958, reprinted New York, 1968), pp. xiii-xviii.

34. Henry Bullock, *A History of Negro Education in the South From 1619 to the Present* (New York, 1967), pp. xiii, xv, xvi.

35. Ibid., xvi.

36. Kenneth Stampp, *The Peculiar Institution: Slavery in the Antebellum South* (New York, 1956), p. 364.

37. John W. Blassingame, *The Slave Community: Plantation Life in the Antebellum South* (New York, 1972), p. 76.

38. Ibid., p. i. *See also,* Vincent P. Franklin, "Slavery, Personality, and Black Culture: Some Theoretical Issues," *Phylon,* 35 (March 1974): 54–63.

39. For excerpts from these books on the "disorganization of the black family," *see, Black Matriarchy: Myth or Reality,* edited by John Bracey, et al. (Belmont, Calif., 1971); *see also,* Stampp, *The Peculiar Institution,* pp. 240–271.

40. Herbert Gutman, *The Black Family in Slavery and Freedom, 1790-1925* (New York, 1976), passim.

41. *See,* for example, Leslie Owens, *This Species of Property: Slave Life and Culture in the Old South* (New York, 1976); Lawrence Levine, *Black Culture and Black Consciousness: Afro-American Folk Thought From Slavery to Freedom* (New York, 1977); James D. Anderson, "Aunt Jemima in Dialectics: Genovese on Slave Culture," *JNH,* 61 (January, 1976): 99–114.

Quaker Beneficence and Black Control: The Institute for Colored Youth 1852–1903

Linda Marie Perkins

Members of the Society of Friends, also known as Quakers, were widely known for their anti-slavery efforts and contributions to the education of blacks throughout the eighteenth and nineteenth centuries.[1] However, several educational historians have recently attributed Quaker philanthropy toward blacks to certain "guilt feelings" on their part generated from Quaker participation in the institution of slavery. Thus, contributions to black education were merely considered to be payment of the "just debt" the Quakers owed to the black race. These historians have also pointed out that these benefices were often given paternalistically, condescendingly, and in some instances for the purpose of self-aggrandizement.[2] While charges of Quaker bigotry and their desire to oversee the most minute details of their black institutions have been documented,[3] the traditional view that blacks had little or no input in directing and controlling Quaker sponsored institutions needs further examination. In this essay we will examine the history of the Institute for Colored Youth (ICY), the most important Quaker financed educational institution for blacks of the nineteenth century. In particular, we will describe the role of the black faculty and administrators in the determination of the educational objectives and practices at the Institute, and discuss the contributions of the school to the social, economic, and intellectual advancement of blacks in the Philadelphia area and throughout the nation during the period 1852 to 1903.

In 1832, by the bequest of a Philadelphia Quaker goldsmith, Richard Humphreys, $10,000 was left for "the benevolent design of instructing the descendants of the African Race in school learning, in the various branches of the mechnik [*sic*] arts and trades and in Agriculture: in order to prepare and fit and qualify them to act as teachers in such of those branches of useful business as in the judgement of the said society they may appear best qualified for ...

19

under [the] care, management, and control of such Persons only as are or may be member of the Yearly Meeting of the Religious Society of Friends commonly called Quakers."⁴ Humphreys left the above sum in the trust of thirteen fellow Quakers specifically designated in his will.

Four months after Humphreys' death in June, 1832, nine of the thirteen trustees met to discuss implementation of the bequest; however, it was not until five years later (1837) that the group met again to further discuss the establishment of a school for black students. At this time, the group established the "Association" whose purpose was to carry out the wishes of Humphreys' will. The organization was comprised of the original trustees named in the Humphreys will and twenty-one other Quakers. (The Association was later renamed the Corporation in 1842). By early 1840, a 136-acre farm had been purchased seven miles from Philadelphia by the Association, and on October 5, 1840, five boys from the Shelter for Colored Orphans in Philadelphia were enrolled at the "farm school" as students with a white superintendent, matron and instructor. It was the plan of the Association to enroll ten to fifteen boys from the Shelter for Colored Orphans under their exclusive control until the boys reached twenty-one years of age. The boys were to be instructed in the "ordinary branches of education ... in gardening or other work around the farm or house under the direction of a superintendent and subject to the control of the Managers."⁵

The farm school was actually a manual labor school with stringent rules and regulations which required the students to follow a strict schedule of activities from 6:00 A.M. until 8:00 P.M. Due to financial problems, in September, 1843, the Managers ordered the day school closed and all of the students' time was to be devoted to farm labor. This change prompted the first of a series of student runaways and in 1844, a fire of "suspicious circumstances" was started in some combustible material outside one of the buildings. In March, 1845, the rules of the school were made even more stringent, and the students were required to follow a 5:00 A.M. to 9:00 P.M. schedule.⁶ Again, the students' response to the revised schedule seem to be the setting of the barn on fire the following May; and by April, 1846, all but one of the fourteen students had run away from the school. Since the boys were not receiving monetary or educational compensation for their work at the farm school, they very likely saw little point in remaining. Thus, the school closed in April, 1846. The Quaker Managers had been completely unsuccessful in their farm school effort due to their preoccupation with the financial concerns of the school. In addition, the inability of the white staff to influence favorably the behavior of the students also contributed to the demise of the farm school.⁷

It was not until 1848 that the Board of Managers met again to discuss plans for another school. After considering several possibilities, they decided to apprentice students to black mechanics in Philadelphia. During this period, the influx of European immigrants had intensified racial hostilities in Philadelphia, resulting in numerous race riots in the 1830's and 1840's. These conditions very likely influenced the decision of the Managers to apprentice the students to black tradesmen exclusively. However, the fact that Quakers could also save money by paying the black tradesmen less than they would have had to pay skilled white workers may have also attributed to the choice. In any case, the decision to employ black artisans was to have a profound effect on the shaping of the Quaker-sponsored schooling for blacks in the city. The black mechanics agreed to apprentice the students at fifty dollars per student, and more importantly, proposed to the Quakers the idea of providing a literary education to the students whereby they would have an opportunity for schooling in the "higher branches." Apparently, the men had planned the proposal prior to their meeting with the Quakers, because in addition to their suggestion, they offered a plan for the implementation of the new school. The tradesmen proposed apprenticing the students by day and the opening of an evening school for the teaching of the "literary subjects" with "well trained persons" as teachers. Although several white organizations aided in the education of blacks in Philadelphia, blacks primarily provided their own schooling. Prior to 1860 there were fifty-six private black schools in the city with only twelve of them being conducted by whites. Publicly-sponsored elementary education had been available to blacks in Philadelphia since 1822, but there was no opportunity for them to receive a high school education.[8] With the recent establishment of the Central High School for whites in Philadelphia, it is likely that this resulted in the black tradesmen suggesting to the Quakers that a high school for blacks be opened.

The Quakers responded favorably to the proposal and gave the gentlemen full authority to select the teacher and pupils, and to oversee generally the entire effort. The men immediately formed the "Board of Education Auxiliary to the Guardianship of the Estate of Richard Humphries [*sic*] bequesting a legacy for the instruction of colored Boys in trades, literature and Agriculture." Officers were selected for the organization and a circular was issued in the black community announcing the plans for the school and soliciting applications from boys who possessed "good moral character" and "knowledge of the elementary branches." In October, 1849, the men were able to have a black man, Ishmael Locke, hired as teacher for the evening school which opened in a room on Barclay Street near Sixth in South Philadelphia. Within a month of the school's opening, thirty pupils were enrolled, and by the end of the 1850 school term, forty-three boys had attended the school. In contrast to the earlier farm school failure, the apprenticeship program and the evening school proved to have been a successful venture providing the students with skills for gainful employment as well as advanced academic training.

In an attempt to have the educational opportunities expanded to larger numbers, the black tradesmen appealed to the Quakers to open a day school and to increase the amount paid for the students' apprenticeships. Increased fees would encourage white mechanics to apprentice black youth, and the black tradesmen pointed out to the Managers, "the present compensation is no inducement to white mechanics to have the obloquy and contempt that will attend their efforts to give trades to colored boys."[9]

The fee was not increased, but plans were made to establish a day school to accommodate thirty boys. Ishmael Locke resigned as teacher in September, 1850, to accept a better paying position in Rhode Island and another black man, John Rock, was hired. Rock remained only until March, 1851, when the evening school was closed to prepare for the day school. Approximately sixty students had been apprenticed since the school's opening in 1849 and had been instructed in the subjects of reading, writing, defining, written and mental arithmetic, grammar, geography, philosophy, physiology, anatomy, hygiene, elocution, logic, composition, and phrenology.[10]

In 1852 a building was erected in the heart of the black community and named the Institute for Colored Youth (ICY). Charles A. Reason, a distinguished black educator from New York was chosen as principal; and Grace A. Mapps, also of New York, was named head of the Female Department. The opening of the day school signaled a complete break with the agricultural emphasis suggested in Humphrey's will. Reason immediately began to establish the Institute as a strong academic institution. A library was opened and a lecture series of primarily scientific topics commenced during his first year at ICY. Both the library and lectures were made available to the entire black community. Capitalizing on the cooperation of the Quaker board, Sarah M. Douglass, a black teacher who conducted classes in her Philadelphia home, wrote the Managers concerning the possibility of including her school within the Institute. The Managers agreed, and in May, 1853, a Preparatory Department offering the elementary courses was opened within the Institute, headed by Sarah Douglass. Thus with the financial backing of the Quakers and the organized activities of the black tradesmen, Charles Reason and Sarah Douglass, the Institute for Colored Youth had been tailored to meet the educational needs of the mid-nineteenth century Philadelphia black community.

Under the leadership of Principal Charles Reason, ICY was provided with a strong academic base. Having been a teacher of mathematics at New York Central College prior to coming to the Institute, Reason made sure that this subject was stressed at the school. In addition, he introduced bookkeeping into the curriculum and had a visiting teacher give a course in elocution and lectures on natural philosophy. The Institute enjoyed an enviable reputation in Philadelphia and drew considerable acclaim under Reason's leadership. So impressive was the scholarship of the students at the annual public examinations and commencements that even the Governor of Pennsylvania, James Pollock, attended the exercises in 1855. Despite Reason's outstanding record at ICY, in November, 1856, he resigned as principal and returned to New York due to "important matters relating to his personal interest."[11]

Reason was replaced with still another outstanding black scholar, Ebenezer Bassett, a graduate of the Connecticut State Normal School and a former student at Yale College. In addition, Robert Campbell, a native of the British

West Indies, reputed to be well versed in the sciences, was also employed as a teacher. Maintaining its academic reputation under the principalship of Bassett, the classes of the Institute were systematized and trigonometry, higher algebra, Latin, and Greek were added to the curriculum. The public exhibitions and commencements continued to generate widespread interest among the public. One white observer from Lancaster, Pennsylvania, considered a "veteran in the cause of education", was so astonished by the students' performance on the annual examination of 1857 that he wrote of the experience in the official organ of the Department of Public Instruction, the *Pennsylvania School Journal*. In the Annual Report of 1857, the Managers reported that the Institute had begun "to attract the attention of intelligent persons in various parts of the country and [had] been more frequently visited by strangers than heretofore." Many of the visitors were reported to have been southern whites. In addition to the students' performance, the teachers of the Institute served as an especial source of pride to the black community. One ICY parent remarked to Bassett during the 1857 school term, "You cannot think how proud I am of that Institute, and how grateful I am to the managers for its library, its schools, its lectures, and its colored teachers. Oh, it is a great thing for our people." This enthusiasm and support of the community continued, and by 1862, two thousand persons attended the closing exercises of the school with the event being expanded over a two-day period.[12]

The Civil War years witnessed an expansion in the functioning of the Institute for the black community. Despite the passivist tendencies of the Quakers in politics, Bassett, who was active politically, replaced many of the scientific lectures with those of a more political nature. Such men as Frederick Douglass, Alexander Crummell, Henry Highland Garnet, and Robert Campbell were brought in as lecturers. Although the Managers voiced no opposition to the change in focus of the lectures, they did suggest to Bassett that Douglass confine his remarks to the "peaceable principles of the Friends." The lectures were well attended by the black community and Bassett informed the Managers that speakers such as Garnet and Douglass were "a continued and unanswerable argument in behalf of the ability, energy and worth of the colored race; and their presence in the community cannot but be beneficial to their own people, as well as to others." The lectures continued throughout the Civil War years and in 1863 when Pennsylvania Governor Andrew Curtin called for volunteers for the Union Army, the Institute opened its doors as the recruitment headquarters for the black community.[13] Clearly, ICY was a political as well as educational center for black Philadelphians.

During this decade, the first black teaching appointments to the city's public school system were made. In 1862, John Quincy Allen was appointed as a teacher and in 1864, Jacob C. White, Jr., was appointed principal of the small Roberts Vaux School in the City. Both men were graduates and former teachers at the Institute for Colored Youth. These appointments demonstrated the need for a strong normal program at the Institute to prepare its students for the city's teachers' examination. Bassett, in a lengthy letter to the Managers in May, 1863, told of the need for well-trained black teachers in the city of Philadelphia. He proudly stated that John Allen competed with thirty whites for the position he received in the school system; and Cordelia Jennings, a 1860 ICY graduate who maintained a private pay school at her home, took advantage of a law which allowed any school with thirty or more students to apply for public school status. After doing so, Miss Jennings was also in charge of the "public" school. Bassett stressed to the Managers the importance of black teachers to black students, and stated that many black parents sacrificed a great deal to send their children to private pay schools with black teachers rather than to free public schools with white teachers. After a normal program was instituted at ICY, Bassett told the Managers that "we may see all the public colored schools of our city taught by colored teachers, competent, and loving their work, [with] Allen and Cordelia being [the] pioneers."[14]

The Managers enthusiastically endorsed Bassett's suggestion and in their Annual Report of 1863 appealed to the Corporation for financial support in the endeavor. By September, 1864, Bassett had initiated the negotiations which eventually brought Fanny Jackson (later Fanny Jackson Coppin) to the faculty of the Institute. Miss Jackson was a student in the Collegiate Department of Oberlin College. At Oberlin, she was an outstanding student, and distinguished herself by becoming the first black person to teach in the Preparatory Department of the College. Also, she established an evening school for the freedmen who poured into the city during the Civil War. Fanny Jackson graduated from Oberlin in August, 1865 and arrangements had been made by the Managers for her to begin teaching at the Institute in September of that year.[15]

Although the Managers were supportive of the proposed new building and additional staff, a circular issued by them in the spring, 1863, revealed their initial apprehension concerning the ability of blacks to pursue "advanced" studies. The circular stated that the present ICY had been an "experiment to test the capability of colored youth to attain the knowledge of the higher educational branches, those that required close study, deep thinking and thorough instruction."[16] However, a better understanding of the ICY Board of Managers best explains their apprehensions about black intellect. The Board of Managers of the Institute was comprised of members of the Orthodox Society of Friends who attended the Arch Street Meeting in Philadelphia. They were generally considered the most conservative Quakers in the city. As was the case with many other white benevolent groups, these Quakers strictly adhered to the practice of segregation in their relations with blacks. Sarah M. Douglass, a black Quaker and ICY teacher, discontinued her membership with the Arch Street Meeting in the 1830's because of the segregated seating policy at the services. Of the Quakers, Miss Douglass stated, "I have heard it frequently remarked and have observed it myself, that in proportion as we become intellectual and respectable, so in proportion does their [the Quakers'] disgust and prejudice increase." But, she noted there were "a noble few who have cleansed their garments from the foul stain of prejudice.'' One such Quaker was Alfred Cope, an ICY Manager since 1842, whose financial support and influence made most of the proposals of the black staff of ICY possible. The black faculty early recognized Cope's importance on the Board and they usually addressed their suggestions and proposals for the school's improvement to him. Cope's contributions to the Institute were numerous during the period of 1842 to 1875. In 1859, for example, he established a fund for the purpose of awarding cash prizes to outstanding graduates at commencement, and was instrumental in the establishment of the building fund for the Institute by providing $10,000 toward the effort. It was Alfred Cope who corresponded with the officials of Oberlin College to secure Fanny Jackson as a teacher at the Institute; he even sent her eighty dollars upon hearing of her financial hardship at the College. Prior to his death in 1875, Cope established a "Scientific Fund" for the Institute to develop a scientific and technical department which could offer courses in medicine, polytechnics, applied sciences, and industrial arts. He corresponded with Edward Bouchet in 1874, then a senior Physics major at Yale College, and encouraged Bouchet to remain at Yale for further studies in order that he could be in a position to head the proposed science department upon completion of his studies. Cope financed the young scientist's remaining education at Yale, and in 1876, Bouchet became the first black person in the nation to receive a Ph.D. degree.[17]

Prior to Fanny Jackson's arrival at the Institute in 1865, Bassett presented a proposal to the Managers in June of that year to revise the curriculum and administrative structure of the Institute. His plan provided for a head principal responsible to the Managers for all departments, and a female principal with full authority over the Girls' High School. Students entering the Preparatory Departments were to be at least eleven years of age and have knowledge of the elementary subjects. In addition, no student would be allowed into the Preparatory Department who did not intend to matriculate in the high school department for at least one year. The revised curriculum also introduced additional "classical" courses of study. Hence, Bassett arranged that Fanny Jackson's position and the revised curriculum become institutionalized into the formal bylaws of the Institute.[18]

When Fanny Jackson arrived at the Institute in September, 1865, she was welcomed to the city by members of the black community. The *Christian Recorder* in August, 1865, had applauded her appointment, stating that she was qualified academically, morally, as well as religiously. Miss Jackson's impact upon the Institute was felt immediately. After her first week at the Institute, the Managers reported after visiting her classes that they believed she was a "very valuable acquisition" to the faculty. They were impressed by the ability of Miss Jackson and her assistant, Mary Jane Patterson, also an Oberlin graduate, to give "thoroughness and perfect understanding" to every portion of the student recitations. The ladies' experience in public speaking and elocution at Oberlin were reflected in their teaching. Already, the Managers noted a "greater animation of manner and a louder and clearer mode of speaking among the girls."[19]

The Institute moved into its new quarters at 9th and Bainbridge Streets in March, 1866. The three-story building included a library, reading room, laboratory, apparatus room, in addition to classrooms for the Preparatory and high school departments. With its new building and competent corps of teachers, the Institute equalled and surpassed many high schools of the nation.[20]

In March, 1869, President Ulysses S. Grant appointed ICY principal Ebenezer Bassett as United States Minister to Haiti. Fanny Jackson was immediately appointed as acting Principal and subsequently Principal of the Institute. Although there had been several males associated with the Institute for a greater number of years, Alfred Cope, in a letter to Octavius V. Catto, an ICY teacher, pointed out that Fanny Jackson was more qualified than Catto or even Bassett, to serve as principal. Cope informed Catto,

> Thou [Catto] had not kept thyself somewhat fresh in all those branches which are allotted to the station of Principal ... I think thou wilt see on reflection, that if the school had occupied its present advanced position at the time when Ebenezer D. Bassett became Principal, we could not have placed him at the head of the Institute.[21]

Throughout the first year of her principalship, Jackson worked diligently to establish a normal department within the Institute. She took a leave from the school to visit normal schools in the Philadelphia area, as well as Millersville, Pennsylvania and Trenton, New Jersey. The first class to complete their entire studies in the high school under Fanny Jackson graduated in December, 1869, and was the largest graduating class in the history of the Institute — a total of eighteen students. In an attempt to improve the quality of education at the Institute, Miss Jackson encouraged greater interaction between the school and the parents of the students. For example, she sent monthly conduct reports to parents informing them of the academic performance, behavior, and attendance of their children. In addition, she met with the parents each month to discuss their children's academic progress. By 1871, she formally introduced the normal program into the school. Moreover, these efforts did not go unnoticed by the Managers or the black community. The Managers reported to the Corporation in 1873, "Our esteemed principal, Fanny M. Jackson, has throughout the year applied herself with unremitting zeal and energy to the interests of the pupils." In 1875, they took note of her influence upon the faculty by pointing out that "the teachers perform their duties in the various departments with commendable faithfulness and assiduity and we feel it is largely due to the energy and thorough devotion to the work of our principal, Fanny M. Jackson that the lively interests of those connected with the school is so fully maintained, and the administration is so efficient." Similarly, the

Christian Recorder praised Fanny Jackson's character and influence on the black community and described her remarks to the graduating class of 1875 as "apples of gold in pitchers of silver." Ten years later, her influence and value to the Philadelphia black community had not diminished and the *Recorder* again remarked, "For the education of the colored youth of this city, there is no institution, perhaps, which has done and is doing more in that direction than the Institute for Colored Youth, under the principalship of Mrs. F.M.J. Coppin, the good accomplished by this school is plainly evidenced by the large number of graduates annually, who may be found usefully employed in various professional and business enterprises."[22]

The Institute maintained such an outstanding academic reputation within the black community that even during the Depression of the 1870s enrollment remained above two hundred, with many students on the waiting list. While the number of graduates of the Institute totaled fifty-seven prior to Jackson's principalship, only six years later in 1875 the number had nearly doubled to 109. While many high schools of the nation were barely worthy of the name in 1875, ICY's strong curriculum of classics, higher mathematics and sciences easily rivaled the course of studies of many colleges such as Oberlin. The black Philadelphia community was well aware of the Institute's merit and in 1875 the *Recorder* informed its readers that "the course of study persued [*sic*] in the institute [ICY] is quite full; equal to that of the average college." In June, 1876, Edward A. Bouchet, received a Ph.D. in Physics from the Sheffield Scientific School of Yale College and joined the ICY faculty the following September. Bouchet's presence on the faculty was reflected in the many ICY students who subsequently pursued scientific vocations. By the early 1890's the Institute was attracting an international student body.[23]

Manager Alfred Cope died in December, 1875. His financial backing and progressive attitude towards the Institute would be an irreplaceable loss to the faculty as well as the black community. Without Cope, Jackson's strategies for insuring acceptance of her proposals for the Institute by the more conservative members of the Board would have to be somewhat different. The issues of tuition and the Preparatory department were the first important tests of Fanny Jackson's influence with the Board of Managers without Cope. In 1866, tuition fees were imposed for attendance at ICY, but from the beginning, Miss Jackson viewed this as a hardship for the parents of the students and generally refused to dismiss those students who were delinquent in their tuition payments. When this refusal to collect the payments was discovered by the Managers, the issue became explosive. A special committee delegated to investigate the problem reported to the Board of Managers:

> The names of delinquents have rarely if ever been reported to the Board whilst on the other hand the Principal claims that she has never had authority to discharge such delinquents. Whilst she has well said in her communication to the committee that "a law is mere dictum without

power to execute it," yet it could hardly be expected that the Board would give her authority to discharge delinquents without having their names before it as was originally designed. The pupils and their parents have gradually come to believe that the payment of those fees is optional, and their ability to pay has been diminished by the hard times the number who have taken the options not to pay, has increased. The well known opposition of our Principal to the collection of fees has no doubt had its influence in still further diminishing the number who pay as well as the view which the committee fear has been promulgated among the parents that they are to be abolished.... Whilst the committee think that if the original plan had been adhered to from the first and dismissal from the school made the penalty for non-payment of the fees, the difficulty in collecting them which we now experience would not have assumed its present proportions, yet we believe that in view of affairs now existing, it will be almost impossible to restore the system. We therefore feel disposed to recommend the abolition of the tuition dues.[24]

In this instance, Jackson was acutely aware of the difficulties facing black students at the Institute during the 1870's and acted in what she considered to be the most appropriate manner. The failure to collect tuition greatly disturbed the Board of Managers, but the non-payment of fees in no way threatened the quality of the schooling being provided at the school, and finally the Managers came to support the position of the Principal and agreed to abolish tuition fees.

In an attempt to save money after the loss of the tuition revenues, the Managers in 1877 voted to close the Boys' Preparatory Department. They viewed the Preparatory Department as a temporary adjunct to the Institute which was considered a school of "higher learning." However, when Principal Jackson was notified of the changes, the committee that handled curriculum matters reported to the Managers that Jackson "was decidedly of the judgement that the best interests of the School would be promoted by the adoption of a plan somewhat different from that agreed upon by the Board and the *Committee did not think it best to dissent therefrom* — the schools were therefore open upon this basis." (Emphasis added.) As an alternative, Fanny Jackson merged the Boys' Preparatory Department with the Girls' Preparatory Department to save money for the Institute. She assigned students of the normal class to teach in the consolidated department, thus eliminating the hiring of a new teacher and also providing some teaching experience for the students.[25]

With the establishment of many schools for blacks in the South during the period of Reconstruction, Fanny Jackson saw a need to prepare teachers for that area of the country. She suggested to the Managers that the Institute establish a dormitory for students who were from outside the Philadelphia area. She impressed upon the Managers the importance of having southern students at ICY and emphasized that such students would be able to return to the South and contribute to the education of the black race. Normally very direct in her approach with the Managers, Fanny Jackson told them, "If the Managers of this school intend this Institute to be merely local in its usefulness, the argument is closed," but warned, "if what I have said is without weight, I must be told so decidedly or I shall bring it up again." When the Managers refused to follow her suggestion, Jackson secured a house next door to the Institute and paid the rent for the students. After her marriage in 1881 to Levi Coppin, a minister of the African Methodist Episcopal Church, many students lived in their home. Reverend Coppin reported that between the small boarding house and their home, approximately fifteen students were provided housing each year.[26]

Although there were other areas that were transformed and improved during the early years of her principalship, Jackson's most outstanding contribution to the school and the Philadelphia black community was the establishment of an Industrial Department in 1889. During the Centennial Exposition of 1876 in Philadelphia, an exhibit by Victor Della Vos of the Moscow Imperial Technical School in Russia generated nation-wide attention and was by far the most noteworthy feature of the International Exhibition. Vos demonstrated his newly-developed approaches to the teaching of the mechanical arts, in which he organized each trade into a series of graded exercises using drawings, models, and tools. Since one of the main themes of the Centennial was the relationship between education and national progress, the Vos method sparked immediate interest among American educators. Recognizing the concern of many educators about the lack of technical education in the United States, Fanny Jackson observed, "if this deficiency was apparent as it related to the white youth of the country, it was far more so as it related to the colored."[27]

In what she termed an "Industrial Crusade," Fanny Jackson set out on a two-fold mission: (1) to impress upon blacks the need for cooperation in business, and (2) to emphasize the importance of technical and industrial training to the community. Discrimination in employment opportunities had become one of the gravest problems facing blacks in Philadelphia. With Quaker and other benevolent assistance no longer assured, it became imperative that blacks develop methods for aiding themselves. In March, 1877, Miss Jackson spoke before a well attended audience of the Bethel Literary Association of the Mother Bethel AME Church in Philadelphia on the topic of "Co-operative Associations." In her lecture, she stressed the practicality and economic advantages in joint-stock corporations and co-operative associations. Since the failure of the Freedman's Bank in 1874, many blacks were apprehensive of further cooperative ventures. But, Fanny Jackson asked the audience if "numbers of white banks have not failed since the failure of this [Freedman's] bank involving the loss of hundreds of millions of dollars but had this for a moment deterred the establishment of new banks and as freely as though no banks had broken, and did not even colored men put their money in white banks with as much confidence as ever?" She ended by cautioning her audience that blacks were often "behind the times" and did not make the most of opportunities that were sometimes presented.[28] This was one of the many consciousness raising lectures for self-reliance and self-help for which Fanny Jackson was to become noted. Several weeks after the above lecture, the *Christian Recorder* endorsed her proposal and urged the black community to follow her advice.

> Day by day, we are becoming more and more circumscribed. Old employments are taken from us nor do new ones open to us. The Irish and the Germans are snatching the aprons from our men; John China-man is stealing the irons from our women.[29]

To reach a national audience, Miss Jackson introduced in 1878 a column entitled "Women's Department" into the weekly *Christian Recorder* under the pen name of Catherine Casey. Through this column she reported achievements of women in education and employment, as well as the benefits of cooperation among black Americans. Her column also urged women to remain financially independent of men and often gave career tips. Informing her readers that there was little need for more dressmakers or beauticians, Jackson told them to open floral or millinery shops, stating the women should pursue "fairer fields and pastures new!" She also told them to consider nursing as a profession because, "This is one profession for women that is not overcrowded, and where women can earn good wages. The chief qualifications are good health, good temper, general intelligence and a fair common-school education."[30]

At the Institute, cooperative efforts were introduced by Fanny Jackson and were an important aspect of the students' education. Each week, the students gave voluntarily one cent to several different charitable societies within the school. Thus, at the year's end, the treasuries amounted to $75 to $100. With these funds contributions were made to various charities. In addition to being an example of the power of cooperative efforts, the exercises in cooperation provided a practical mode of teaching the pupils bookkeeping, how to purchase money orders, and how to write checks.[31]

By the summer of 1878, Fanny Jackson was able to have the black community also test the merits of cooperative efforts. At this time, the *Christian Recorder* began experiencing extreme financial problems and was in danger of being discontinued. Although the paper was a publication of the AME Church and Fanny Jackson was a member of another denomination, she viewed the *Recorder's* problem as one that should concern all black people irrespective of religious affiliation. In an attempt to aid the newspaper, she planned a "World's Fair" modeled on the Centennial Exhibition of 1876. In addition to helping the newspaper, Jackson saw this as an opportunity for black women to display their artistic and creative talents. On this point, she commented, "With some very honorable exceptions, we are positively indifferent to much of the talent displayed by colored men and women."[32]

Pointing out that the Centennial Exhibition had been a success due to co-operation between people and nations, she stressed that the Fair on behalf of the *Recorder* could do likewise. The event was scheduled for the winter of 1879, thus, she had a year to gather art work, inventions, and other original items from black artisans and craftsmen. Throughout 1879, Fanny Jackson spoke on the topic of self-help and continued the message in her column. She also worked to secure better job opportunities for blacks by appealing to large mercantile houses, public libraries, and similar institutions to hire black workers.[33]

In publicizing the Fair, Miss Jackson made clear to the readers of her column the significance of the *Christian Recorder* to both the local and national black communities. She issued a circular prior to the Fair in the fall of 1879 that clarified the issues at hand:

> The Publication Department of the *Christian Recorder* is weighed down by a comparatively small debt, which cripples its usefulness and thus threatens its existence. This paper finds its way into many a dark hamlet in the South where no one ever heard of the Philadelphia *Bulletin* or the New York *Tribune*. A persistent vitality has kept this paper alive thru a good deal of thick and thin since 1852. In helping pay this debt we shall also help to keep open an honorable vocation to colored men, who, if they will be printers, must "shinny on their own side."[34]

The "World's Fair" was held at the Masonic Temple in Philadelphia for a week's duration during the month of December, 1879. The event was an overwhelming success displaying articles made by blacks from twenty-four states. More importantly, the Exposition cleared the debt of the newspaper. The attendance had been massive at the Fair, and the *People's Advocate,* a black newspaper of Washington, D.C., reported, "Nothing like this Bazaar has been held in Philadelphia within the memory of the present generation."[35]

With the success of the Fair as an example of the power of cooperative projects, Fanny Jackson urged blacks to apply this principle to other areas and businesses. She told her audiences that although blacks may not have great wealth individually, collectively their few dollars could add up to millions, as the Freedmen's Bank clearly illustrated. She believed this was particularly necessary among blacks in the South who were victims of the crop-lien system.[36]

The second important area of concern in Jackson's "Industrial Crusade" was the need for industrial training for black youth. In 1879 she addressed the issue before the Board of Public Education in Philadelphia which held a meeting to consider the status of industrial education in the public schools of the city. She told the Board that presently the only place a black person could learn a trade was in the House of Refuge or State Penitentiary and even there they learned only how "to make brooms and cane chairs." In her autobiography written in 1913, she recalled the importance of the meeting. She stated, "It was to me a serious occasion. I so expressed myself. As I saw building after building going up in the city, and not a single colored hand employed in the constructions, it made the occasion a very serious one to me."[37] After the conference, the wife of one of the school directors donated fifty dollars towards

Fanny Jackson's effort. Although the sum was small, Miss Jackson believed, "We [blacks] only needed a feather's weight of encouragement to take up the burden." With this small sum as a beginning, she went on to carry her message to the black communities of Newport, Rhode Island, New York City, and Washington, D.C., emphasizing those occupations from which blacks were barred because of discrimination and lack of training.[38]

By the end of 1881, the Scientific Fund which was donated to the Institute by the late Manager Alfred Cope in 1874 was due to receive $15,000 in maturities. Since the fund was to be used for technical education, Fanny Jackson approached the Managers with a plan of implementation in June, 1881. The black community anticipated a positive response from the Managers, and the *Christian Recorder* reported, "Miss Fanny M. Jackson is working earnestly in the cause of industrial education, her object being to start a polytechnic school in the Fall." She had organized the students and faculty of the Institute, along with members of the community, to raise funds for the proposed technical school. The *Public Ledger,* a local white newspaper, endorsed her efforts and encouraged the citizens of Philadelphia to respond favorably. The newspaper repeated Jackson's argument that persons unskilled or unable to find employment would soon fill the city's jail. ICY was complimented on its history of quality education and outstanding graduates, but the paper noted that all the students of the school were being trained to become teachers, and stated, "There is no reason why they should all choose such a field."[39]

Despite the massive campaign for a technical program at the Institute, in December 1881, the Managers announced that they saw no practical way to include such an addition to the school. Also, the Managers informed the Institute's donors that the school had sufficient funds to maintain itself and contributions to the school were no longer necessary.[40] Both announcements were shattering to Fanny Jackson. The Managers' decision was made during the week of her wedding in Washington, D.C., and she probably did not receive the news until after the New Year (1882). However, the information altered both her personal plans as well as those she had for the Institute. It was her intent to resign from ICY after the technical program was started, and her decision to marry in December was very likely based upon the assumption that the industrial program was to start after the bond maturities were received. She had met her husband-to-be, Levi Coppin, during the Fair she sponsored for the *Christian Recorder* in 1879. Coppin, a native of Maryland, had been pastor of the local Mother Bethel AME Church, but in June, 1881, was transferred to a church in Baltimore. The following September, convinced that the Scientific Fund would be used to open the technical school, Fanny Jackson announced to the Managers her plans of marriage. This series of events eventually led the black community to believe that technical school was now to be shelved but in February, 1882, the *Christian Recorder* issued a strong statement from Fanny J. Coppin: "Mrs. Fannie Coppin [*sic*] nee Jackson, says the project of an industrial school never has been nor ever will be abandoned."[41]

Thus, committed to starting a technical school, she remained at ICY while her husband returned to his church in Baltimore.

More determined than ever, Fanny Coppin took her campaign back to the black community. The project became a near obsession and John Durham, an ICY graduate, recalled:

> Rain, snow, heat, cold had no terrors for her [Fanny J. Coppin]. No so-called literary society or church festival was too humble to command her attendance. No matter what theme they prescribed for her, she talked "Industrial School." Her school work extended late into the afternoon but her evenings were devoted to "Industrial School." We feared that she would become "Industrial School" mad.[42]

Initially, the response of the black community to the industrial school was something less than enthusiastic. This can best be attributed to the confusion as to what was being advocated. The terms manual, industrial, polytechnical, and trade education were being used interchangeably in black newspapers, and oftentimes, the issues were presented and debated in such a manner that industrial education appeared to be the antithesis of classical education. Fanny Coppin viewed classical education as foremost in black education but saw industrial education as a temporary and immediate solution to the employment problem of blacks in the growing industrial nation. It was not her intent to replace one type of education with another, but rather to make available to blacks training in areas other than teacher education.[43] She informed the Managers in 1884 that many students withdrew from the Institute when they discovered that only teacher training was offered. By the Spring of 1884, the Managers had been convinced of the necessity of the addition to the Institute and agreed to offer courses in the "mechanic arts." The Annual Report of 1884 announced the plan for the anticipated department and appealed to donors for financial support to the project. A group of Managers visited the New York Trade Schools, the City College of New York, and Spring Garden Institute of Philadelphia to gather information for operating the new department. After the visits, the Managers decided to model the new department after the New York Trade School, an institution which offered trade courses three nights a week to men between the ages of sixteen and twenty-one. This decision was based on the Managers' belief that the New York Trade School was "best adapted to the situation of the colored people." The fact that the New York Trade School program was the most inexpensive to imitate was very likely another important reason for the choice. Cautious of their new undertaking, the Managers informed Coppin that the only trades to be offered in the new department would be those that could be taught quickly, economically, and with the least financial risk. The courses to be offered initially were carpentry and bricklaying for the men, and dressmaking for the women. Far short of the industrial program Fanny Coppin had envisioned for the Institute, she was grateful for even this small beginning.[44]

It was not until the Spring of 1888 that the Managers were able to raise sufficient funds to launch the new department. Of the $40,000 received, $2,600 had been contributed by the black community. Although the sum was small, Coppin pointed out that the sum could have been twenty times as much but she refused to accept more than one dollar per person, stating she was unwilling to "press poor people beyond what I thought they could give."[45]

On January 4, 1889, the Industrial Department of the Institute opened with only a class in carpentry for men, but by the end of the school year, bricklaying, shoemaking, dressmaking, millinery, and cooking were also offered. Although there had not been any public announcements, notices, or solicitation of applications, the response of the black community was great, with eighty-seven students enrolled and 325 on a waiting list only two months after the department opened. Joseph Hill, an ICY graduate, had been appointed Secretary of the new Department and reported to the Managers that he had been flooded with applications which demonstrated the eagerness of the black community to take advantage of the new educational opportunities. Hill visited the New York Trade School and Pratt Institute of New York in March, 1889, and upon returning told the Managers he "saw much that could be introduced in the Institute." He suggested adding house-painting, printing, and plumbing to the curriculum, and submitted a list of 412 persons desiring instruction in tailoring, engineering, upholstering, blacksmithing, short-hand, and millinery. The list demonstrated the black community's belief that the Institute was sensitive and responsive to their educational needs. Yet, the Managers responded to their request by stating that even though the new department helped "the colored people to raise themselves in the scale of dignity and self-respect," an expansion of classes would necessitate the hiring of additional teachers and require a much larger sum than they presently had. In reporting the progress of the Institute to their donors, the Managers stated there had been pressure to add courses in the Industrial Department, but they decided to avoid "entering inconsiderately upon any experiments which might be unsuccessful."[46] However, the potential contributors were informed that if they wished to contribute further to the new department, the contribution would be used. As with the Academic Department, the Managers viewed the Industrial Department as another "experiment" to test the capabilities of blacks. In addition to the general skepticism Quakers held concerning black intellect, lack of funds prevented them from granting many of the requests of the faculty and the black community. After the death of Alfred Cope in 1875, it was rare that Fanny Coppin requested anything from the Managers without first justifying the cost.

Despite the Managers' lukewarm attitude towards the new department, Fanny Coppin continued her efforts to raise funds for the school. In 1888, as president of the Women's Home and Foreign Missionary Society of the AME Church, she was sent as a delegate to the Centenary of Missions Conference held in London. There she carried the message of the need for technical education for blacks in America. *Anti-Caste,* an English newspaper, reported:

> [Fanny Coppin] graphically pictured how in such cities as Philadelphia, with its 30,000 colored inhabitants, the colored youth are confronted by an insurmountable barrier, being boycotted on account of their color from all the staple trades and handicrafts of the nation — such as smithing, carpentry, house, ship, and carriage building, engineering, factory work of all kinds, shop serving, etc. and in fact from nearly all of those occupations which are ordinarily open to young people of similar age and culture... From this terrible restriction flow two evils (1) the few channels of honest labor open to them — principally those of a menial or servile character — are pitifully overcrowded; (2) the mechanical and commercial talents and skill of this whole people lies dormant and undeveloped, or is faultily represented.... Mrs. Coppin is greatly interested in the founding of a technical school for young people in Philadelphia.[47]

Coppin raised three hundred dollars while abroad for the Industrial Department. The department also received $2,000 from an anonymous donor in 1891, and $37,752 from two Quaker charities in 1892.[48] The pressure from the ICY faculty and the black community for the Managers to add more courses to the curriculum could not be ignored. By 1890, plastering, printing, and tailoring had been added to the curriculum, and by 1893, typing and stenography were also included. Thus, ten trades were offered the black community of Philadelphia.[49] Even though it had taken Fanny Coppin over a decade to have the Industrial Department included into the Institute, with the help of the black community, she succeeded in having the school expand its usefulness to a larger portion of the city's black population.

As the nineteenth century came to a close, the Quakers in Philadelphia had become practically indistinguishable from their non-Quaker contemporaries. The older Managers who wore the broad-brimmed hats, plain coats without lapels, and dark colors when Fanny Coppin first arrived at ICY were few in number by 1895. The Board of Managers was no longer comprised solely of the conservative Arch Street Friends, but included the more affluent and "worldly" Friends from other Meetings in the city and area. Men such as lawyer George Vaux, Jr., insurance executive Charles Roberts, banking and real estate businessman Edward M. Wistar, Harvard-trained Haverford College professor Francis B. Gummere, the Friends' Select Headmaster J. Henry Bartlett and the Friends' Select Professor David H. Forsythe, were the most influential members of the ICY Board.[50]

By the mid-'90's, however, the Managers and Coppin's views on the direction of ICY drew farther and farther apart. As historian Philip Benjamin observed: "The educational philosophy to which the Quakers subscribed in the nineties was that of Booker T. Washington, ... [and] as they became part of the educational empire of Booker T. Washington, Friends remained insensitive to black cultural needs, urged Negroes to remain on Southern farms, and settled and markedly reduced aspirations for the objects of their philanthropy." Therefore, as Quakers assimilated into mainstream America, discarding their plain dress and "quietist beliefs," their attitude concerning the race question came to resemble that of the larger society.[51]

Booker T. Washington was in direct communication with the Quaker Managers through the "Friends' Association of Philadelphia and its Vicinity for the Relief of Colored Freedmen" (FFA). The FFA was formed in 1863 by a group of philanthropic Friends from the Philadelphia Meeting to aid blacks in the South. Most of the ICY Managers were members of the FFA. One of the schools supported by FFA was the Christianburg Institute of Virginia. Christianburg Institute was a normal school located forty miles from Roanoke. Although the school was not founded by the Quakers, in 1873 the FFA began a policy of making an annual contribution to the school. In 1893, Fanny Coppin was sent to Christianburg Institute to observe the school and make recommendations for improving the school's program. An academic department with industrial courses similar to ICY resulted for the school. However, when Booker T. Washington visited the Christianburg Institute at the request of the FFA in 1896, he was very critical of the school. He reported to the Quakers that "There is still [at Christianburg] too much tendency towards the superficial or top heavy work. The industrial is not given an equal chance with the literary work." Washington also pointed out that at the school, "there were almost no signs of thorough sweeping, dusting, scrubbing, keeping up repairs, etc. These are the lesson that our people need." Submitting a plan for Tuskegee to take over the school, Washington stated that he observed that at Christianburg, "The teachers now there, except the principal, seem to be persons that could be moulded into new channels" and suggested a Tuskegee Institute graduate, Charles Marshall, as principal. Assuring the Quakers that he intended to create a "Tuskegee at Christianburg," Washington cautioned the Quakers, "Unless necessary, I prefer that my name not be used in connection with this report." The FFA voted unanimously to accept Washington's plan, and the Christianburg Institute was henceforth staffed exclusively with students of Hampton and Tuskegee Institutes. By 1898, land had been purchased to start an agricultural program, and in 1901 the name of the school was officially changed to "Christianburg Normal and Industrial School."[52]

These events paralleled the closing of the Institute for Colored Youth in Philadelphia. After Washington's 1896 report of Christianburg Institute to the FFA, the ICY Managers warned Fanny Coppin that:

> The [ICY] teachers should guard against the tendency to devote too much time and attention to those studies which lie entirely beyond the future careers of the scholars, and which are hardly valuable even as a means of mental training.[53]

After Christianburg Institute became predominately manual training and agricultural in 1898, the ICY Managers issued a statement informing the public that ICY would emphasize the elementary courses and "manual training." Throughout the late '90's, Washington made repeated visits to Philadelphia urging manual training for blacks, and denouncing black political aspirations. He drew considerable support from the white press, and in February 1899 the Philadelphia *Evening Bulletin* reviewed a Washington speech and directly attacked schools such as ICY:

> The Tuskegee Institute is not, unlike many educational enterprises that philanthropy has set up for the negro, a mere nursery of "genteel" or "respectable" colored men who think that nature has endowed them to be statesmen or scholars or something of that kind.... There has been much which the observing have had occasion to notice in Philadelphia of the pitiable or the ludicrous ambition of young colored men to become "professional" men, when in many cases it must have been evident to anyone who might have dispassionately advised them that they were only entering a crowded market, and that there could hardly be a success for them even if nature had made them more clever.[54]

By September, 1900, the ICY curriculum was transformed to reflect the "new" industrial emphasis of the school. History and the Latin classics such as Cicero and Horace were eliminated, and many of the studies of science and mathematics were consolidated. In September, 1901, the Managers reported that they anticipated the resignation of Fanny J. Coppin. This course of events was not coincidental. As was the case with the Christianburg Institute, the Institute for Colored Youth had been captured by the "Tuskegee Machine." A special Committee to Re-organize the Institute was formed immediately after Coppin's anticipated resignation was announced, and a delegation of Managers went to Tuskegee to confer with Washington on the hiring of the next principal.[55] By February, 1902, the special committee reported to the Board of Managers that Hugh M. Browne, principal of the Colored High School and Training School in Baltimore and former Hampton teacher, had been endorsed by Washington and Dr. Hollis Frissell of Hampton Institute. The report revealed what hiring Browne, a Washington disciple, would mean.

> It is due to the Board to know that the administration of such a man [Hugh M. Browne] must mean radical changes in the Institute.... Radical changes in the future will not of course discredit the work of the past great advances have been made recently towards the solution of the problem of Negro education and doubtless Francis J. Coppin would be the first to wish for the future of our work the highest standard of efficiency and most approved means of real progress to this end.[56]

Browne accepted the principalship in March, 1902, and by June, the first of many "radical changes" was instituted when he ordered the Academic Department closed for the following year. Unlike the faculty of Christianburg Institute, that Washington observed in 1896 were "persons that could be moulded into new channels," the faculty of ICY held high the principles of academic excellence. Thus, their dismissal would be necessary to carry out the plan of "re-organization." In the fall of 1903, the Institute for Colored Youth moved to a farm in Cheyney, Pennsylvania, twenty-five miles outside of Philadelphia. The new school, which was ironically reminiscent of the original farm school the Managers first opened for blacks in 1840, was to be modeled after Hampton and Tuskegee Institutes.[57] Removed from the black community was the institution that for fifty years provided not only education for the youth of the area, but also lectures, a library and reading room, and trade education for the adult community as well.

In assessing relationships between blacks and the Philadelphia Quakers, Philip Benjamin asserted that, "Friends generally won applause from the black community for their philanthropic and educational efforts." However, blacks did not endorse all the practices of the Quakers. In 1875, the *Christian Recorder* asked, "Why do our Quaker friends keep up the color-line by not sending their children to the school [ICY]?" Similarly, in 1890, John Durham, an ICY graduate, stated that "had she [Fanny Coppin] not had to struggle against the characteristic conservatism of the Society of Friends, she would have been one of the most famous of America's school reform instructors." Most blacks in Philadelphia supported the statement of black abolitionist Samuel Riggold Ward, in 1855, that "they [Quakers] will aid in giving us a partial education — but never in a Quaker school, beside their own children. Whatever they do for us savors of pity, and is done at arm's length." This was even more the case in 1902 than in the year the words were originally spoken. However, the greatest opposition from the black community came with the closing of the Institute and the dismissal of the Academic faculty in 1902. Many of the Institute's graduates and friends never accepted the new ICY at Cheyney as their alma mater and refused to send their children to the school. At Booker T. Washington's speaking engagements in Philadelphia, few blacks attended, and the *Christian Recorder* expressed dissatisfaction with the Washington educational philosophy.[58] The ICY had been considered an important part of the black community, and once the school was removed from its presence, most Philadelphia blacks divorced themselves from the new ICY.

Established at the request of members of the Philadelphia black community in 1849, throughout the fifty-year existence of the Institute for Colored Youth, the three principals, Charles Reason, Ebenezer Bassett, and Fanny Jackson Coppin, shaped the school's programs to meet the needs of the black population. Reason strengthened the curriculum by including more advanced mathematical and scientific courses, and introduced a public lecture series at the Institute. Bassett sponsored lectures on political issues and had the school serve as a recruitment center for the Union Army. He shaped the school's classical curriculum, was instrumental in advocating the normal department, worked for the establishment of a new building, revised the administrative structure, and insured that these changes were institutionalized in the by-laws of the school. In addition, Bassett was directly responsible for the hiring of Fanny Jackson Coppin, Mary Jane Patterson, and Edward Bouchet, all outstanding black scholars. The black community of Philadelphia was well served by the Institute through the leadership of Reason and Bassett. The school had such great significance to black Philadelphia that when the Institute was moved to larger quarters on 9th and Bainbridge Streets in 1866, members of the black community bought the old ICY building at 6th and Lombard, and renamed it "Liberty Hall."[59]

Fanny Jackson Coppin's thirty-seven years of service (1865-1902) to ICY and the black community made her one of the best known, most respected, and influential blacks in Philadelphia in the latter nineteenth century. She not only displayed exceptional leadership in the administrative functions of the Institute, but also exhibited outstanding community leadership during a difficult period for blacks in the city. Foreign immigration and economic depressions decreased employment opportunities for the city's blacks in the 1870s. By 1895, approximately 15,000 more blacks had migrated to Philadelphia, most of them destitute and unskilled.[60] It was to this group that Fanny Coppin devoted much of her efforts. She sought employment for the race in the developing industries of the city, and lectured constantly in the black community on cooperative businesses. She labored for a decade to establish the Industrial Department in the Institute.

Many students of the Institute were aided financially by Coppin, and, through her encouragement, many eventually went into the professions. John Durham, an 1876 ICY graduate who later became a civil engineer and United States Consul to San Domingo and Minister to Haiti recalled that Fanny Coppin had encouraged him to become an engineer. Recollecting the lectures she had given him on the importance of blacks entering the professions, Durham pointed out, "She [Fanny Coppin] pictured to me the great work to be done by specialists in the learned professions, great cures to be made by great colored doctors, cases to be won by colored lawyers, books to be made by colored writers..." He remembered that the lectures were not unique to him but that Coppin had done the same for "scores, hundreds of other pupils now successfully working in various parts of the country."[61]

The greatest believer in her students, Fanny Coppin rarely made a report to the Managers without mention of the success of one of the Institute's students. The records of the graduates of ICY listed among them teachers, doctors, nurses, pharmacists, lawyers, engineers, architects, governmental officials, and private businessmen and women.[62] And it was a rare student at ICY who was not influenced either directly or indirectly by Fanny Coppin. She concerned herself not only with their educational development but also their living, health, and employment conditions.

These concerns were also exhibited for the black community. Her column in the *Christian Recorder* attempted to develop race pride and offer career information to her readers. Avoiding social class biases, Coppin addressed the column to women of all income and educational backgrounds. One Philadelphia observer noted that "even with her [Coppin's] rare learning, she never made even the humblest appear uncomfortable."[63] Despite the responsibilities of the principalship of the Institute, she was at the forefront of most activities for the improvement of the black community. Of her influence in the community, Levi Coppin observed:

> Miss Jackson [Coppin] was not only the recognized scholar among school teachers, but gained a reputation of being a platform speaker with few equals even among the other race varieties. These facts, backed up by an irreproachable character, gave her undisputed leadership in all matters of race advancement. She was the one person whom the whole city would follow.[64]

By the close of the nineteenth century, the Institute for Colored Youth was referred to by most black Philadelphians as simply, "Mrs. Coppin's School." At a testimonial given in her honor after her retirement in 1902, Fanny Coppin told the audience that throughout her years in Philadelphia she had two schools, the Institute and the community. It was this belief that sustained the bond between the Institute and the community throughout the school's history.[65]

As the Institute closed its doors in 1903, the Philadelphia black community recalled with great pride the accomplishments of the students and faculty of the school. Quaker beneficence had made the physical existence of the Institute possible, but the black leaders of the Institute and in the community molded and shaped its direction and developed the school into one of the most outstanding black educational institutions of the nineteenth century.

NOTES

1. For a discussion of Quaker contributions to anti-slavery activities and black educational endeavors, see Ira V. Brown, *The Negro in Pennsylvania History*, No. 11 (University Park, Pennsylvania: The Pennsylvania Historical Association, 1970), passim; Sydney V. James, *A People Among Peoples: Quaker Benevolence in Eighteenth Century America* (Cambridge, Massachusetts: Harvard University Press, 1963), Ch. XII: Thomas Woody, *Early Quaker Education in Pennsylvania* (New York: Teachers College, Columbia University, 1920), Ch. XI.

2. Harry C. Silcox, "A Comparative Study in School Desegregation: The Boston and Philadelphia Experience, 1800-1881," (Ed.D. dissertation, Temple University, 1972), p. 71; Phillip S. Benjamin, *The Philadelphia Quakers in the Industrial Age, 1865-1920* (Philadelphia: Temple University Press, 1976), p. 28.

3. See article by Quaker Henry Joel Cadbury, "Negro Membership in the Society of Friends," *Journal of Negro History* 21 (1936): 151-213; Benjamin, *The Philadelphia Quakers,* Ch. 6, pp. 126-147; Leon F. Litwack, *North of Slavery* (Chicago: The University of Chicago Press, 1971), pp. 204-208; Benjamin Quarles, *Black Abolitionist* (London: Oxford University Press, 1969), pp. 72-74.

4. Quoted in Charline F. H. Conyers, "A History of the Cheyney State Teachers College, 1837-1951," (Ed.D. dissertations, New York University, 1960), p. 50.

5. Ibid., pp. 62-64, 69.

6. Ibid., pp. 71-72. The students were required to adhere to the following schedule in 1845: 5:00 A.M., rise and do chores; 6:00 A.M., breakfast; 7:00 A.M., start manual labor; 12:30 P.M., dinner; 2:00-6:00 P.M., manual labor; 6:30 P.M., supper and necessary duties; 9:00 P.M., bedtime.

7. Ibid., pp. 89-90, 93. In the five and a half years of the farm school's existence, it had three different superintendents and matrons and four different teachers.

8. Ibid., pp. 98-100; W.E.B. DuBois, *The Philadelphia Negro* (New York: Schocken Books, 1967), pp. 27-32; Silcox, "A Comparative Study," p. 66.

9. Quoted in Conyers, "A History of Cheyney," pp. 102-105.

10. Ibid., pp. 103, 107.

11. Ibid., p. 114; ICY Annual Report of 1856; Fanny Jackson Coppin, *Reminiscences of School Life and Hints on Teaching* (Philadelphia: AME Book Concern, 1913), p. 139; Harry C. Silcox, "Philadelphia Negro Educator: Jacob C. White, Jr., 1837–1902," *Pennsylvania Magazine of History and Biography*, 97 (January, 1973): 80; Campbell resigned from ICY in 1859 to go to Africa through the sponsorship of the American Colonization Society.

12. Coppin, *Reminiscences*, pp. 140, 155–156; Annual Report of 1856; *Pennsylvania School Journal* V(12), 1857: 387–388; quoted in ICY Managers Minutes of May 18, 1857, Richard Humphrey Foundation, Series two, Administrative Papers — Managers Minutes, 1855-1866, Box 1, Friends Historical Library, Swarthmore College (hereafter referred to as *Managers Minutes*).

13. ICY Annual Report of 1863; Harry C. Silcox, "Nineteenth Century Black Militant: Octavius V. Catto (1839–1871)," *Pennsylvania History* 44 (January, 1977).

14. *Managers Minutes*, May 4, 1863; Annual Report of 1863.

15. Ibid; *Lorain County News* (Ohio), February 4, 1863; February 10, 1864; February 15, 1865.

16. Circular in *Managers Minutes*, May 4, 1863.

17. *See* letter from Robert Campbell to Alfred Cope, November 17, 1856, Richard Humphreys Foundation Papers, Miscellaneous Papers, 1837–1922, Series two, Box 5, Friends Historical Library, Swarthmore College; Alfred Cope to Octavius V. Catto, April 23, 1869, O. V. Catto Papers, Leon Gardiner Collection, Box 3GA, folder 5, Historical Society of Pennsylvania; Coppin, *Reminiscences*, p. 13; Sarah Douglass to William Bassett, December, 1837, in Gilbert H. Barners and Dwight L. Dumond, *Letters of Theodore Dwight Weld, Angelina Grimke Weld, and Sarah Grimke, 1822–1844*, 2 vols. (New York, 1934), 1: 830–831; Conyers, "A History of Cheyney," p. 127; Alfred Cope to Board of Managers in *Managers Minutes*, February 10, 1865; *Managers Minutes*, November 18, 1873, February 17, 1874, March 18, 1874, April 28, 1874; Annual Report of 1876; also see *The Cheyney Record*, September, 1940.

18. *Managers Minutes*, June 13 and September 12, 1865.

19. *Christian Recorder*, August 26, 1865; *Managers Minutes*, September 21, 1865.

20. *Managers Minutes*, October 31, 1866.

21. Alfred Cope to Octavius V. Catto, April 23, 1869.

22. *Managers Minutes*, October 11, 1871, October 15, 1872; *Christian Recorder*, June 24, 1875, October 8, 1885; Annual Reports from 1869–1875.

23. *See* "Pencil Pusher Points" in *Philadelphia Tribune*, March 30, 1912; undated letter from Fanny J. Coppin to Manager Howard Comfort in Monthly Reports; also see Annual Report of 1892. *Christian Recorder*, October 28, 1875; Coppin, *Reminiscences*, pp. 139–191.

24. Annual Report of 1866; Minutes of the Committee for Discipline and Instruction of ICY, February 15, 1875, March 16, 1875, August 19, 1876, Series two, Box 5,

Richard Humphrey Foundation — Administrative Papers,Committee on Discipline and Instruction Minutes, 1871–1884, Friends Historical Library, Swarthmore College; Report of the Committee on Tuition and Fees in *Managers Minutes,* March 20, 1877.

25. Annual Reports, 1877, 1879; Minutes of the Committee on Discipline and Instruction, March 25, 1875, May 16, 1877, September 18, 1877; Report on Tuition and Fees.

26. Monthly Report of ICY Boys' High School Department, May 19, 1884, Richard Humphrey Foundation — Administrative Papers, Series two, Box 6 (hereafter referred to as Monthly Report), Friends Historical Library, Swarthmore College; Levi J. Coppin, *Unwritten History* (New York: Negro Universities Press, 1919; reprint ed., 1968), p. 361.

27. Lawrence Cremin, *Transformation of the School* (New York: Alfred A. Knopf, 1969), pp. 24–25; Fanny Coppin, *Reminiscences,* p. 23.

28. Fanny Coppin, *Reminiscences,* p. 28; *Christian Recorder,* March 15, 1877.

29. *Christian Recorder,* April 12, 1877.

30. Ibid., June 27 and September 29, 1878.

31. Fanny Coppin, *Reminiscences,* pp. 34, 60.

32. *Christian Recorder,* July 18, 1878.

33. Ibid., *see also* July 25, 1878.

34. Fanny Coppin, *Reminiscences,* pp. 29–31.

35. *People's Advocate,* December 13, 1879.

36. Fanny Coppin, *Reminiscences,* pp. 34, 60; for a discussion of the crop-lien system *see* Nell Irvin Painter's *Exodusters* (New York: Alfred A. Knopf, 1977), pp. 58–63.

37. Fanny Coppin, *Reminiscences,* p. 28.

38. Ibid.; Levi J. Coppin, *Unwritten History,* p. 359.

39. Minutes of Committee on Discipline and Instruction, May 13, 1881; *Christian Recorder,* June 2 and June 9, 1881; *Public Ledger and Transcript,* June 28, 1881.

40. Minutes of Committee on Discipline and Instruction, December 20, 1881.

41. Ibid., September 2, 1881; Levi J. Coppin, *Unwritten History,* pp. 353–362; *Christian Recorder,* February 23, 1882.

42. *New York Age,* November 8, 1890.

43. *See New York Age,* January 5 and March 1, 1884; Since many of ICY students were either partially or totally self-supporting, Fanny Jackson viewed industrial training as an expedient means of the students earning decent wages until their education was complete. *See* Monthly Report, February 17, 1897.

44. Annual Report of 1884; Committee on Industrial Education Report in *Managers Minutes,* January 20, 1885.

45. Annual Report of 1886; Fanny Coppin, *Reminiscences,* p. 29.

46. Annual Report of 1890.

47. Article from *Anti-Caste* reprinted in the *Christian Recorder,* October 4, 1888.

48. Ibid.; $2,671 was given by the Bee Hive School and approximately $35,000 by the Emlen Institute for the Benefit of Children of African and Indian Descent. (*See Managers Minutes,* May 4, 1892, and Annual Report of 1892.)

49. Annual Reports of 1890 and 1893.

50. Gummere suggested that the courses of the Institute be "toned down" in 1894. (*See Managers Minutes,* May 15, 1894); and Bartlett, Warner, Vaux, and Forsythe comprised the Committee to Re-Organize the Institute. (*See Managers Minutes,* February 18, 1902.)

51. Benjamin, *The Philadelphia Quakers,* pp. 142, 147.

52. Frank O. Wargny, "Education of the Freedman by Philadelphia and Baltimore Quakers During the Civil War and Reconstruction Period," (M.A. Essay, The Johns

Hopkins University, 1947), p. 28; *Managers Minutes,* February 4, 1893; Friends Freedmen Association Executive Committee Minutes, April 3 and April 20, 1896; June 11, 1901.

53. *Managers Minutes,* September 21, 1897.

54. *Evening Bulletin,* February 15, 1889, clipping in scrapbook entitled ''Booker T. Washington'' at Cheyney State College Archives; Annual Report of 1898.

55. *Managers Minutes,* September 18, 1901; Annual Report of 1901.

56. Report of the Committee to Re-Organize the Institute in *Managers Minutes,* February 18, 1902.

57. The students had a prescribed schedule as with the original farm school. (*See* Conyer, ''A History of Cheyney,'' p. 205.)

58. Benjamin, *The Philadelphia Quakers,* p. 145; *Christian Recorder,* June 24, 1875, July 2, 1902; *New York Age,* November 8, 1890, quoted in Quarles, *Black Abolitionists,* p. 72; the *Christian Recorder* quoted in the *Standard-Echo,* December 21, 1895, clipping in a scrapbook entitled ''Booker T. Washington,'' Cheyney State College Archives; Conyer, ''A History of Cheyney,'' p. 198; Mrs. Sarah R. Isaac, interview with Linda Perkins, August 18, 1976, Philadelphia, Pennsylvania.

59. *See* deed to shares of Liberty Hall bought from Elisha Weaver by O. C. Catto, May 12, 1870. O. V. Catto Papers.

60. DuBois, *The Philadelphia Negro,* p. 47.

61. *New York Age,* November 8, 1890.

62. Information on ICY graduates can be found in Fanny Coppin, *Reminiscences,* pp. 139–191; *see also* DuBois, *Philadelphia Negro,* p. 353.

63. ''Pencil Pusher Points,'' in *Philadelphia Tribune,* February 1, 1913.

64. Levi Coppin, *Unwritten History,* p. 353.

65. *Christian Recorder,* October 22, 1902.

The Black Community of Augusta and the Struggle for Ware High School 1880–1899

June O. Patton

After examining the development of formal schooling in the antebellum South, W.E.B. DuBois concluded that there were two major obstacles to the advancement of public schooling during that period and in the early post-Civil War era. The first impediment was the large number of white property owners who questioned the wisdom of providing public schools at the taxpayers' expense. The second was the southern white working class which failed to see the value of public schooling and thus made few demands for its provision.[1]

At the same time, however, many black southerners, slave and free, demonstrated a strong desire for schooling dating from the pre-Civil War period. The legal restrictions and other prohibitions upon educating slaves and free blacks serves as an indirect testimony to the reality of this desire. This contention is further supported by the evidence of a number of clandestine schools for blacks discovered during and immediately after the hostilities between the states.[2] Moreover, evidence that this enthusiasm for education continued after the war is abundant in the reports of northerners who visited the South during those years. These soldiers, teachers, and missionaries described the myriad classes and little school houses opened by blacks in order to prepare themselves for their new life.[3]

In Augusta, Georgia, for example, which had a small free black population, numbering only 386 in 1860, blacks supported at least two schools in the decade before the Civil War.[4] In the years immediately following the war, the Augusta black community became even more active in providing schooling, and were able in 1880 to bring about the opening of the first publicly-supported high school for blacks in the state. Blacks in Augusta worked diligently for the opening and maintenance of Ware High School from the end of the Reconstruction era to the last years of the nineteenth century, and were to

45

take their campaign for equal secondary education all the way to the Supreme Court, only to be crushed by the Court's ruling in the case of *Cumming v. Richmond County Board of Education* (1899). In previous investigations of the history and development of black education in the South, very little emphasis has been placed upon the role of blacks in initiating and supporting the maintenance of public secondary schools. This essay attempts to shed some much needed light on both the role of a southern black community in the provision of public secondary education during the last quarter of the nineteenth century and the nature of white opposition to black public schooling during the period.

By the early 1800s the city of Augusta was one of the emerging urban centers of the Piedmont region of the South.[5] Situated on the Savannah River, Augusta was not only a railroad hub but also one of the leading manufacturing and commercial centers in Georgia from the 1820s through 1860.[6] As a result, black freedmen and slaves were employed in a wide variety of occupations including jobs in commercial and industrial areas. They were retained at shipping docks, railroad yards, mills, factories, and trading houses.[7] The majority of free blacks were employed in an assortment of service trades as barbers, tailors, piano tuners, blacksmiths, etc. Others were skilled and unskilled hired laborers, and a few owned grocery stores and other small business concerns.[8] While there were a number of artisans and craftsmen among the slaves, it is probable that most were domestic servants.[9] Some slaves, however, were employed by the railroads, the federal arsenal, various industries, and at times the city for public works projects.[10]

The Civil War did not completely disrupt the growth of Augusta because no actual fighting took place there. During the last two years of the conflict, the city's population was greatly expanded by a wave of fleeing white refugees and a large influx of blacks. At the end of the war, many of these individuals departed, but Augusta's population still continued to grow. In 1860, for example, the total population in the city was 12,943; by 1870 it had risen to 15,389. The population persistently increased in the post Reconstruction era, so that by 1880 there were over 21,000 persons in the city. The vast majority of Augusta's work force through 1880 was engaged in manufacturing and commercial activities. In 1870 blacks were over one third of the total population, and in 1880 there were 10,120 blacks, making up almost forty-five percent of the total.[11] Blacks were employed in an even wider variety of areas after the war, becoming butchers, bookkeepers, and cotton buyers. The advent of a black professional class made up of teachers, doctors, dentists, businessmen, and public officials added a new "upper strata" to the social class structure of the black community. Also, whereas in the 1870s most black skilled and semi-skilled workers were employed by whites, by the 1880s many blacks were self-employed.[12]

The leadership class in the Augusta black community also grew rapidly during the post-Civil War era and rose to prominence in the educational campaigns of the 1870s and 1880s. As in most southern cities, the early leadership was provided by blacks who had been free before the general Emancipation, and who were active in church and civic organizations. Gradually, the leadership ranks were swollen by the young and newly educated freedmen. One of the most distinguished leaders from the older generation was William Jefferson White. Born of free parents, White had before the war become a prosperous cabinetmaker in Augusta.[13] In 1853, he began to organize clandestine schools for free blacks and slaves around the city.[14] In 1855 White became a member of the Springfield Baptist Church in which he established a Sunday school in 1859. He served as the school's superintendent for nine years and in 1866, while holding that position, was ordained as a Baptist minister. Two years after becoming a preacher, White founded and became pastor of Harmony Baptist Church in Augusta. By the early 1870s, Rev. W. J. White had become one of the most powerful black religious leaders in the state holding a number of church offices, including the presidency of the Colored Georgia Baptist Sunday School Convention.[15]

White's spiritual commitments in no way diminished his activities in the field of education. Immediately following the war he joined with other black leaders in an effort to stimulate black Augustans to start schools and he was instrumental in the organization of the Summer Literary Society and Lending Library of that city.[16] When the Freedmen's Bureau began operations in Georgia, White became a bureau agent and traveled throughout the state establishing schools for the newly-freed slaves.[17] Prior to the establishment of his church, White aided Richard C. Coulter in the organization of the theological seminary that was to become the Augusta Baptist Institute; this school was opened in 1867 in the Springfield Church with 38 pupils.[18] In that same year, the Freedmen's Bureau ended its work in Augusta and placed the black schools in Rev. White's charge.[19] Recognized as an outstanding educator throughout the state, he was elected to the Board of Trustees of Atlanta University in 1871, and Spelman College in 1888.[20] Rev. White was also active in Republican politics in the state and held both elective and appointive offices, and his influence as a leader was greatly enhanced through his newspaper, *The Georgia Baptist,* which DuBois described as "probably the most universally read Negro paper in the South" in the 1880s and 1890s.[21]

By the end of the 1870s a younger and more educated group of blacks began to share in the leadership of Augusta's black community. Outstanding among them were Lucy Craft Laney and Charles T. Walker. Laney, born in Macon, Georgia in April 1854, was the seventh of David and Louisa Laney's ten children. Her father, a carpenter by trade and an ordained Presbyterian minister, was a man of initiative. While a slave in South Carolina, he saved enough money to purchase his freedom, and moved to Macon where he was employed by a number of slaveowners to teach his carpentry skills to their slaves. Lucy's mother at the time of her marriage to David was the property of the prominent Campbell family of Macon. To assure the freedom of his children, David

Laney purchased his wife's freedom, though she continued to work for the Campbell family as the maid of one of her ex-master's daughters. It was the young Miss Campbell who provided the daughter Lucy with some early education. After studying for a time at Lewis High School in Macon, fifteen year old Lucy Laney, aided by her mother's mistress, entered Atlanta University and was graduated in 1873.[22]

After teaching in the public schools of Macon and Milledgeville, Georgia for a few years, Laney was persuaded by Rev. W. J. White to assume charge of the Fourth Ward Grammar School in Augusta.[23] Laney soon came to be considered one of the best teachers in the Augusta system. In 1880 she accepted a position in Savannah, but was induced by black parents to return to Augusta in 1883 to open a private school.[24] In 1887, Laney appealed to the General Assembly of the Presbyterian Church for financial aid for her school and with the help of one "Mrs. Haines," eventually received assistance. As a show of gratitude, the school was renamed "Haines Normal and Industrial Institute."[25] Miss Laney remained an outspoken advocate of education and was one of the leaders in the campaign for adequate public schools for blacks in the city.

Like Lucy Laney, Charles T. Walker came from a large family, being the youngest of eleven children. He was born in slavery sixteen miles southwest of Augusta near Hephzibah, Georgia, in 1859. He received his early education in various schools conducted by the Freedmen's Bureau.[26] In 1874, "with only $6.00 in his pockets," Walker entered the Augusta Baptist Institute to study to become a minister. A short time thereafter, his educational expenses were assumed by three men from Dayton, Ohio who continued their support for five years. In 1885, he organized the Tabernacle Baptist Church and became its Pastor.[27] Walker's ability as a preacher eventually earned him a wide reputation and he attracted large crowds wherever he spoke.[28] With the exception of Bishop Henry McNeal Turner, Walker was the most widely known black preacher in the state of Georgia in the 1880s and 1890s.[29] Having been a teacher in Georgia during his youth, Walker was sensitive to the educational needs of his people. Walker is credited with the introduction of the resolution to the American Baptist Home Mission Society Board which in 1893 led to the founding of Walker Baptist Institute in Augusta.[30] As a local political leader, he was active in the black struggle for schools and used the influence of his position to that end. Rev. White, Lucy Laney, Charles Walker and several others were members of the multigenerational leadership class of black Augusta in the 1870s and 1880s which organized and led the struggle for the Ware High School.

In the second issue of the *Colored American* (December 21, 1865), the first black newspaper in Georgia, editor John T. Shuften urged black parents in Augusta to "toil a little harder and a little longer so as to allow your sons and daughters the inestimable privilege of learning. . . . Remember they will have to take your place in the great drama of life, which is vastly more responsible

now, than when you were like them ... they will have to take care of themselves ... and nothing ... can aid them to do this better than a good education."[31] Blacks in Augusta had established at least seven schools in various
black churches and other parts of the community by 1865.[32] There was, however, a need for more schools, and the Freedmen's Bureau sponsored several in
1865. By November 1866, the Bureau had established at least eleven schools,
most of which were also partially supported by the black community.[33]

The Freedmen's Bureau ended its operation in Augusta in 1867, and the
schools were turned over to the black community.[34] It was not until 1870 and
1872 that school laws were passed in Georgia which allowed for "separate but
equal" schools "as far as practicable" for black children. Between 1867 and
1872 the Augusta black community supported its own schools, but with the
establishment of the Board of Education of Richmond County (Augusta) in
January, 1873, Rev. W. J. White, then Chairman of the Board of Trustees of
the black schools in the city, offered the school buildings owned by blacks to
the School Board for the opening of black public schools.[35] Rev. White informed the School Board that the Trustees were prepared to relinquish their
three schools to the Richmond County School Board "perpetually", provided
the buildings were used only for schools and under the condition that the
schools be repaired and maintained. They also asked that a fence be placed
around the schools, and shade trees planted in the yards, and that the schools
be insured for $2,000 and that the policy be placed in the name of Chairman of
the Board of Trustees.[36] The School Board agreed to these terms and the black
schools in the first, second, and fourth wards of the city became a part of the
public school system of Augusta.[37]

The Board of Education of Richmond County, which controlled the public
schools in Augusta, reported that for the city proper in 1873 there were 452
black and 434 white pupils enrolled in the public schools.[38] Initially, the black
public schools were considered superior to the schools available to white. In
May 1873 *The Augusta Constitutionalist,* a local white paper, reported that
"the school rooms of whites, except in two districts, are destitute of every con-
venience and comfort, both for the teachers and students." But because the
black schools had been well-maintained by the members of the black community, the newspaper reported that "the houses are large, well ventilated and
comfortable, provided with benches, desks, black boards, maps, etc. ... they
also have convenient playground." However, the writer did express faith in the
future of the public schools. "The system is in its infancy and as time pro-
gresses ample provision will be made for education of all children in the
county. All that is necessary now is patience."[39]

Whatever progress was made in the operation and facilities in the
Augusta public schools during the first decade was usually confined to the
white schools. In some wards adequate public schools were not provided for
black children, in others where schools were provided, they remained un-
graded throughout most of the decade, while the white schools were graded

one through three (primary), four and five (intermediate), and six and seven (grammar).[40] The salaries for black teachers were, of course, lower than those of whites.[41]

In April 1874 the School Board decided that it could not afford to provide a high school for white boys, but that it would pay up to $30.00 per year for the matriculation of any (white) public school student who wished to enroll in a private secondary school in the city.[42] Then in 1876 the Neely High School for white girls was opened by the Richmond County Board and assistance was given to the Hephzibah High School in the village of Hephzibah to assure secondary education for white children in that community. Two years later the name of the Neely School was changed to Tubman High, after Mrs. Emily H. Tubman presented the Board with the new building for the school.[43] Therefore, in October 1878, several blacks in Augusta began to submit petitions to the Board for the opening of a high school for blacks. The petitions pointed out that the state law which mandated that separate schools for blacks and whites be opened also "provides that the same school facilities shall be provided for both classes. We therefore request as a matter of right under the law, that you provide a school commencing with the next school term to which these children of ours and others of like advancement may be sent. . . ."[44] But the School Board informed the black community in 1878, 1879, and 1880 that they could not afford to open a high school for blacks.[45]

In July 1880, black parents, teachers, and interested citizens held a meeting and produced still another petition for the School Board, but this time they not only provided the names of black pupils who were ready to attend high school, but they also made it clear that they were willing "to pay ten dollars for the scholastic year" for each black pupil. After blacks expressed their willingness to pay for secondary schooling and there were sufficient students, the School Board finally agreed to support the opening of a high school for blacks.[46]

Richard Robert Wright, an Atlanta University graduate and formerly principal of Howard Elementary School in Cuthbert, Georgia, was hired in October 1880 by the Richmond County School Board as principal of the new "Colored High School," later known as E. A. Ware High School. Opened in one of the existing black school buildings in the city of Augusta in November of 1880, Wright was initially the only teacher and the "high school" consisted solely of the eighth grade in which thirty-six pupils were enrolled.[47] The first session went fairly well, but in the second year of operation, a severe outbreak of measles in the fourth ward where the school was located resulted in a sharp drop in attendance.[48] In 1883 and the succeeding five years, the school was inundated by the rising Savannah River. In 1887 flood waters in the class rooms reached as high as eight feet, and left six inches of mud when they subsided. Much of the furniture in the building was damaged, the floors turned-up, and the school yards were completely ruined.[49] Efforts to clean and open the school were hampered by an epidemic of typhoid fever which later swept the area.[50]

The following year (1888) on the anniversary of the famous 1886 earthquake, Augusta experienced the worst flood in its history.[51] These events forced the closing of the school for various periods of time and generally disrupted its activities. The expenses incurred as a consequence of these calamities only added another dimension to the general financial insecurity of the Ware High School during the period 1880 to 1887. While the Board of Education in Richmond County was committed to the letter of the School law on the question of separate schools, it was indifferent to the statute's requirements that the facilities be "the same." Moreover, the economic discrimination against the Ware High School took many forms and occurred on various levels. For example, from the school's founding in 1880 through most of 1894 only one teacher was provided. Richard R. Wright was hired at $75.00 per month, a salary which was half of that paid the principal of the city's white high school and five dollars less than that received by his white assistant. Fourteen years later in 1894 when the black school finally received an assistant teacher, the salary was fixed at $35.00 per month.[52] While the white public high schools consisted of three grades, 8th, 9th and 10th, the Ware School opened with only the 8th grade, and the 9th was later added; but it was never able to offer all three high school grades because of the School Board's refusal to hire additional teachers.[53]

This financial neglect by the Board of Public Education was even more conspicuous in the area of maintenance and improvements. In 1879 the fourth ward school was an old wood-framed building located at 1109 Reynolds Street. It had been one of the three buildings turned over to Rev. White by the Freedmen's Bureau in 1867, and by White to the Richmond County School Board in 1872.[54] The school consisted of Lucy C. Laney's grammar department, an intermediate class, and a primary class. In 1880, Lucy C. Laney was replaced by R. R. Wright and the "grammar department" became the "high school." The intermediate and primary classes continued to share the building with the "new" high school.[55] This arrangement continued until Wright resigned and the school was closed. When Henry L. Walker became principal in 1891 the school was reopened in another old building at the corner of Tenggs and Walton Streets.[56]

The minutes and reports of the Richmond County Board of Education from 1880 to 1897 contain numerous references to appropriations for both the maintenance and the improvement of the white high schools. For example, during the summer of 1883 the School Board provided $552.00 for repairs at the Tubman High School. This was followed two years later with a grant of $385.00 for the purchase of fifty new desks. In 1891 this same school was appropriated $5,000.00 to buy a lot adjacent to the school so that an addition could be made to the building, and in 1894 the Tubman High School was provided $9,012.17 for improvements.[57] While numerous suggestions were made that inquiries as to needs of the "Negro High School" be elicited, and many committees were created to evaluate the status of the "public" institution, the school records indicate that no improvements were made at the expense of the "public."

The major consequence of the school's financial problems was its inability to provide a "proper" secondary education for the city's black population. Between 1880 and 1893 the school's enrollment averaged only thirty-one mainly because of R. R. Wright's steadfast opposition to admitting more students than there were seats and for whom he felt he could provide a "proper" secondary education.[58] This position was supported by most members of the black community, and Wright's successor, Henry L. Walker, was able to maintain the same position until 1894.[59]

Throughout the period 1880–1897, blacks held meetings, formed committees, and filed petitions with the School Board asking for another teacher, a longer school year, additional space, and better maintenance of their school.[60] Blacks also took it upon themselves to furnish and support private secondary schools for blacks in Augusta. In 1883, Haines Institute and Paine College were opened, and in 1894 another private school was opened when Walker Baptist Institute was moved from Waynesboro, Georgia to Augusta.

Another indication of the School Board's failure to provide adequate secondary education for blacks was the high enrollments in these private schools. Lucy C. Laney's Haines Institute, for example, opened with 75 students and by the end of the second year had a student body of 234.[61] These schools charged tuition comparable to and cheaper than that of the public high school and yet as late as 1886 R. R. Wright reported that more students applied to the public high school than could be accommodated.[62] The black community tried to pressure the Board into providing support for the public high school, but achieved no significant successes.

It is ironic that the major response of the black community to the School Board's refusal to establish sufficient secondary education for black children was used as an excuse for ending financial support to the black public high school altogether. From its organization the attitudes of white citizens toward the institution were mixed. The sentiments generally ranged from silent indifference to resounding opposition. Some questioned the wisdom of providing "higher" schooling for blacks, and almost all resented being taxed to provide it. A major force in keeping the school open, however, was the school commissioner, W. H. Fleming, who in 1878 and 1880 pleaded with the Board to comply with the wishes of the black petitioners to open a high school.[63]

Benjamin B. Neely, school commissioner from 1880 to 1882, was also basically supportive of the school, and in 1882 he attempted to persuade the Board to hire an additional teacher for the school. However, it was Commissioner Lawton B. Evans who had the most significant impact on the history and evolution of Ware High School. Elected in 1882, Evans held the office of School Commissioner of Richmond County for 52 years, and the changes in Evans' ideas and beliefs about black education (and ultimately his attitude toward the black public high school) mirrored the shift in white opinion which was occurring throughout the South during the period.[64] In the early years Evans appeared favorably disposed toward the school's continued existence. When the entire high school department came under attack during a protest against school taxes in 1883, Evans informed the Board that it was his intent to provide the advantages of "full and free education" for every child in the county, white and black.[65] Throughout the 1880s Commissioner Evans wrote and spoke in glowing terms of the work being accomplished by the high school in providing public school teachers for Richmond County and the adjoining counties. Evans had only the highest praise for Principal Wright and his students, and he often lectured the School Board on the reasons why blacks needed intelligent and capable leadership in the schools. In sum, Evans viewed the high school as a positive good for the community at large and believed Wright was doing an excellent job.[66]

In the late 1890s, however, Commissioner Evans' ideas about black public education began to change. When the "high school" for blacks was organized it was supposed to provide the same program as the high school for whites. In 1895, Evans began to question this policy. In his report to the Board, Evans stated that black children were "born to work ... to work with their hands ... they find their best service and happiest employment in manual labor." Later in the same year, he recommended that cooking and sewing be introduced into the Ware High School.[67] Coinciding with ascent of Booker T. Washington, Evans came to believe that blacks were receiving the "wrong kind of education" and that this instruction made them "anxious to pursue some profession and obtain financial, social, and political equality with the white race."[68] The Commissioner now saw as the major job of the public schools the instruction of black children in those "industrial pursuits" for which they were destined. Evans believed that only "exceptional" black children should be educated to be teachers and leaders, and his views were shared by a growing number of School Board members. Eventually, overt opposition to the black high school increased.[69]

In 1891 after R. R. Wright resigned the principalship of the Ware High School to become President of the first publicly supported black college in the state, the Richmond County Board voted not to reopen the black public high school. The black community protested and several blacks signed petitions against this action. Then the Board decided to open the school under the conditions that, (1) at least thirty students enrolled, and (2) $2.00 be paid by each pupil at the time of entrance and the balance of $8.00 by November 1. If a student refused to pay his tuition fees in advance he would not be admitted, and the Board let it be known that if enrollment fell below thirty, the school would be closed. On October 5, 1891 Henry L. Walker, a teacher in the Second Ward Grammar School, was promoted to principal of the Ware High School and the institution was opened October 12, with thirty-six pupils.[70]

The end of R. R. Wright's tenure as principal marked the beginning of a new period of constant struggle between the black community and the Richmond County Board of Education over the Ware High School. The School Board debated whether or not the school should be reopened at the beginning of each new school year.[71] The school's opponents charged that it was not necessary to provide a public high school for blacks since Paine College, Haines and Walker Institutes provided secondary education.[72] They also pointed out that there were hundreds of black children in the city presently deprived of a "primary" education, and that the funds spent on the high school could best be used for public elementary schools.[73] The School Board members pointed out that some black students had not paid all their tuition and that the total enrollment of the school was too low to justify continued public support.[74]

Most members of the black community, however, believed that the school was needed and that under the law they were entitled to it. As for enrollment, they pointed out the school had only one teacher who could handle only so many students without an assistant. With regard to tuition payments, Henry Walker pointed out in a letter to the School Board in 1896 that in his years as principal of the school all financial responsibilities had been fully met and that on many occasions blacks had paid more than the required fees.[75]

To head off charges of low enrollment a drive was begun by members of the black community to increase the enrollment at the high school in 1893, and by January of 1894 there were over one hundred students registered and more than $400.00 had been paid in tuition.[76] In that year Principal Walker again requested an assistant teacher, and this time the Board agreed.[77] While registration dropped off somewhat in 1895, the average enrollment from 1894 to 1897 was seventy-one students.[78] Then in June, 1897 the School Board decided that three secondary schools for blacks was sufficient, and voted to close the Ware High School.[79] Armed with yet another petition, Rev. W. J. White appeared before the Board on July 15, 1897 and made one last plea for the school. This petition was refused by the members of the School Board and they voted overwhelmingly to close the school.[80]

After exhausting other avenues for redress, black citizens then turned to the courts. In September of 1897, Albert S. Bladgeth, J. W. Cumming, Jerry M. Griffin, Mr. Harper, and Mr. Ladevenge filed a suit in the Superior Court of Richmond County asking for an injunction compelling the School Board to reopen the black high school and enjoining the tax collector from receiving the portion of the taxes levied for high schools until such time that the school for blacks was re-established.[81] When the School Board was directed by the Court to show cause for closing the black school, its members became so enraged that they voted to remove the word "temporarily" from their order closing the Ware High School.[82] On December 22, 1897, the Superior Court of Richmond County ruled that the Board could not use any monies raised for the support of high schools until it provided an equal facility for blacks.[83] The School Board members appealed to the Supreme Court of Georgia which on March 23, 1898 reversed the lower court's decision and pointed out that while blacks believed their constitutional rights had been violated, they had not stated exactly what provisions were in question. The Court argued that it saw no civil rights violations.[84] Black Augustans then went to the Supreme Court of the United States, and on October 30, 1899 their lawyers argued that black citizens paid taxes which were used for public secondary education, but none was provided for their children. Black citizens believed that the School Board's action was a denial of the equal protection clause of the United States Constitution, and the Court was asked to restrict the use of the public funds for "high schools" until one was provided for blacks. The Board of Education, however, denied that it had established "a system of high schools," but admitted giving assistance to private high schools in the county. They insisted that the Ware High School should be closed and the money be spent on elementary education. They noted that blacks had three private secondary schools in the city which could satisfy the black demand for secondary education.

On December 18, 1899 the Supreme Court's landmark decision, *Cumming v. Richmond County Board of Education,* was rendered. Justice John Harlan, author of the opinion, stated that granting the injunction requested by the plaintiffs would either compel the Board of Education to close the white high schools or "impair their efficiency." Neither of these actions, however, would advance the cause of public secondary education for black children in Richmond County. Thus the principle of "equality" could not justify denying such educational opportunities to white children. The Supreme Court also concluded that the School Board did not have to establish a high school for blacks.[85]

> It was said at the argument that the vice in the common school system of Georgia was the requirement that the white and colored children of the state be educated in separate schools. But we need not consider that question in this case. No such issue was made in the pleadings.... While all admit that the benefits and burdens of public taxation must be shared by citizens without discrimination against any class on account of their race, the education of people in schools maintained by state taxation is a matter belonging to the respective states, and any interference on the part of Federal authority with the management of such schools cannot be justified except in the case of a clear and unmistakable disregard of rights secured by the supreme law of the land. We have here no such case to be determined.

With this decision, the first phase of the struggle of Augusta's black community for a publicly supported high school ended. After the Supreme Court's verdict it became all but impossible to gain public support for black secondary education and the city of Augusta was not to provide another publicly supported high school for blacks until 1937.[86]

It is important to note that this decision represented the first time the Supreme Court of the United States ruled upon the question of race and education. More significantly, this verdict established the legal precedent used to exclude black children from public high schools, when these institutions were becoming an integral part of the American common school system. The Southern white opposition and indifference toward public education in the antebellum period, DuBois observed, was replaced in the late nineteenth century by increasing enthusiasm for this northern institution. Consequently, in Augusta's dual public school system blacks found themselves in competition with whites for the limited educational funds which were to be spent on public schooling. The vogue in American public education in the late 1890s was to prepare children for the positions they would occupy in American society, and many white decision makers in Augusta gradually came to believe that blacks were born to labor with their hands. The exceptional few who needed a high school education could be accommodated by the various private schools in the area. By the end of the nineteenth century the Richmond County Board of Education and the United States Supreme Court had decided that it was not a public responsibility to provide secondary education for blacks at public expense.

NOTES

1. W. E. Burgbardt DuBois, *Black Reconstruction,* (New York, 1935), p. 641.

2. Ibid., pp. 637–669; *see also,* Carter G. Woodson, *The Education of the Negro Prior to 1861* (New York, 1915), passim; National Archives Microfilm Publications, Records of the Educational Division of the Bureau of Refugees and Freedmen, and Abandoned Lands 1865–1871, monthly and other school reports (Washington, D.C.), passim (hereafter cited as Freedmen's Bureau Archives).

3. Ibid., *see also American Missionary,* December 1861 to July 1871, passim and Henry L. Swint, *The Northern Teacher in the South, 1862–1870* (Nashville, Tenn., 1941), passim.

4. The number of free blacks in Augusta in 1860 is taken from *The Population of the United States in 1860, Compiled from the Original Returns of the Eighth Census* (Washington, D.C., 1864), p. 74. Mention of schools for blacks in Augusta before the war are cited by Florence Fleming Corley, *Confederate City* (Columbia, S.C. 1960), p. 103; Willard Range, *The Rise and Progress of Negro Colleges in Georgia 1865–1949* (Athens, Georgia, 1951), p. 8; Ridgely Torrence, *The Story of John Hope* (New York, 1948), p. 8.

5. Robert S. Starobin, *Industrial Slavery in the Old South* (New York, 1975), p. 8.

6. Corley, *Confederate City,* p. 6; *see also* Charles Jones and Salem Dutcher, *Memorial History of Augusta, Georgia,* (1890, reprinted Spartanburg: The Reprint Company, 1966), Chapters 27, 30 and 31. Also, E. Merton Coulter, *Georgia, a Short History* (Chapel Hill, N.C., 1947), pp. 257–258, 297–282.

7. Corley, *Confederate City,* pp. 49–50, 89. *See also* Starobin, *Industrial Slavery,* passim and Dutcher, *Memorial History,* passim.

8. The 1850 census for the city of Augusta is printed in the *Constitutionalist,* January 3, 1851, cited by Corley, *Confederate City,* p. 15.

9. Richard C. Wade, *Slavery in the Cities* (New York, 1964), p. 30. Census schedules for 1840, 1850 and 1860 do not indicate the occupations of slaves consequently there is no precise statistical data.

10. Starobin, *Industrial Slavery, passim; see also,* Corley, Confederate City, pp. 49–50; 89, and Dutcher, *Memorial History,* passim.

11. Population of Augusta for 1860, 1870, and 1880 taken from *10th Census 1880, Social Statistics of Cities,* Part 2, p. 163. Black population for 1870 cited in C.W. Norwood, *Georgia State Gazeteer and Business Directory for 1879–1880,* (Atlanta, Georgia, 1879), p. 351.

12. Chronicle and Constitutionalist, *Augusta City Directory,* (Augusta, Ga., 1872, 1879, 1880, 1882, 1883, 1886); also R. L. Polk and Company, *Augusta City Directory* (Augusta, Ga., 1886, 1888, 1889).

13. Torrence, *John Hope.,* p. 54; *see also* Range, *Negro Colleges in Georgia,* p. 8.

14. Ibid.

15. William J. Simmons, *Men of Mark* (1887, reprinted Chicago, 1970), p. 791.

16. Torrence, *John Hope,* p. 55.

17. Range, *Negro Colleges in Georgia,* p. 8; *see also* Swint, *Northern Teacher,* p. 97–98.

18. Torrence, *John Hope,* p. 55; *see also* Range, *Negro Colleges in Georgia,* pp. 24–25.

19. Freedmen's Bureau Archives, Georgia, November 1865–December 1870, Report of School Superintendent Eberhart, October 1867; *see also The Augusta Chronicle,* Anniversary edition, 1960 cited in Frank Vernon Jones, "Education of Negro in Richmond County Georgia," (unpublished Master's paper, Atlanta University, 1962), pp. 38–39.

20. Clarence A. Bacote, *The Story of Atlanta University,* (Atlanta, Ga., 1969), p. 97; *See also* Range, *Negro Colleges in Georgia,* p. 108.

21. Quoted in Torrence, *John Hope,* p. 55.

22. Benjamin Brawley, *Negro Builders and Heroes* (Chapel Hill, N.C., 1937), pp. 279–282; *see also* Torrence, *John Hope,* p. 4.

23. Torrence, *John Hope,* p. 55; *see also* Brawley, *Negro Builders and Heroes,* p. 280.

24. Ibid.

25. Brawley, *Negro Builders and Heroes,* pp. 280–281; *see also* Jones, "Education of Negro," p. 46.

26. Cornelius Troup, *Distinguished Negro Georgians* (Dallas, Texas, 1962), p. 186; *see also* W. N. Hartshorn, *An Era of Progress and Provise 1865–1910* (Boston, Mass., 1910), p. 495.

27. S. X. Floyd, *A Sketch of Rev. C. T. Walker, D.D.,* (Augusta, 1892), p. 2, cited in Range, *Negro Colleges,* p. 122.

28. Troup, *Negro Georgians,* p. 186; *see also* August Meier, *Negro Thought in America 1880–1915,* (Ann Arbor, Mich., 1966), pp. 221–222.

29. Clarence A. Bacote, "Negro Proscriptions, Protests, and Proposed Solutions in Georgia, 1880–1908," in *The Negro in the South Since 1865,* Charles E. Wynes, editor (University, Ala., 1965), p. 177.

30. Troup, *Negro Georgians,* p. 186.

31. *Colored American* (Augusta, Georgia), December 21, 1865, p. 1.

32. *Colored American,* December 30, 1865, p. 3; *see also* Freedmen's Bureau Archives, G. L. Eberhart's report, November 30, 1865.

33. Freedmen's Bureau Archives, Georgia, G. L. Eberhart's report, November 1866.

34. Ibid., October, 1867; *see also* Jones, "Education of Negro," pp. 38–39.

35. The Ordinary of Richmond County reported in 1870 that there were eight or nine colored schools in the county with an eight to nine hundred pupils in attendance cited in Jones, *Negro Education,* p. 38; *see also* Dutchers, *Memorial History,* pp. 323–324.

36. Richmond County Board of Education Minutes and Proceedings (hereafter cited as Board Minutes), January 11, 1873, p. 17 and April 12, 1873, p. 59.

37. Ibid., *see also* Board minutes, April 9, 1892, pp. 67-68; it should be noted that there were no blacks on the Richmond County Board of Education.

38. Cited in *Augusta Constitutionalist,* March 23, 1873, p. 3.

39. *Augusta Constitutionalist,* May 11, 1873, p. 3.

40. All of the schools for blacks in the city were not graded until 1879. *See Augusta Constitutionalist,* October 2, 1879, p. 3. *See also Seventh Annual Report of Public Schools of Richmond County* (hereafter cited as Annual Report). Almost from conception the school system of Augusta did not provide enough schools to accommodate all the black children who applied. *See* Board Minutes, 1873-1879.

41. For example, in 1880 there were two white grammar schools, one teacher was paid $75.00 per month and the other $65.00. Lucy Laney was the only black grammer school teacher in this city and her salary was $45.00. In all five primary schools for whites, the teachers were paid $40.00, while all three of the black teachers received only $35.00. The greatest discrimination however, occurred on the intermediate level, the average salary of teachers in the five white schools was $59.00 as opposed to $17.00 for the four black schools.

42. Board Minutes, April 11, 1874; *see also Chronical and Sentinal,* April 12, 1874, p. 3.

43. J. C. Bancroft Davis, reporter, *United States Reports,* Vol. 175. Cases adjudged in the Supreme Court, October, Term, 1899, The Banks Law Publishing Co. (New York, N.Y., 1900), p. 531.

44. This petition was only one of many blacks were to submit in behalf of the high school. Original copies of these petitions are folded in the pages of the Board Minutes for Oct., 1878, p. 36; July 10, 1880, p. 133, and p. 137.

45. Board Minutes, November 9, 1878 and July 12, 1879, p. 76.

46. The meeting held by blacks is cited in Board Minutes, July 10, 1880. The original petition from black citizens is folded in the pages. The recommendation of the high school committee that the school be established is in Board Minutes for July 10, 1880, p. 137.

47. Board Minutes, October 9, 1880, election of R. R. Wright, that school was established in 4th ward school, see Augusta City directory 1880; for number of teachers, grade levels and number of pupils see *9th Annual Report of the Superintendent of Richmond County Schools* (hereafter cited as Annual Report), December 31, 1881, pp. 10-16.

48. Board Minutes, April 9, 1881, p. 153.

49. *Richmond County Board of Education Quarterly Report* (hereafter cited Quarterly Report), August-September, 1887, p. 2; *see also* Board Minutes, November 12, 1887, p. 2.

50. Dutcher, *Memorial History,* p. 270.

51. Ibid., pp. 189 and 190.

52. *See* footnote 41.

53. Board Minutes, October 9, 1880, pp. 133-135; *see also* Board Minutes, October 13, 1894, p. 200; 9th Annual Report, 1881, p. 16.

54. Torrence, *John Hope,* p. 60; Board Minutes, June 15, 1897, p. 370; and Jones, "Negro Education," pp. 38-39.

55. *Augusta City Directory,* 1879 and 1880; Board Minutes, pp. 239-241.

56. Board Minutes, June 12, 1897, pp. 370-372.

57. Board Minutes, passim; *see also* Board Minutes, July 14, 1883, p. 231; October 13, 1883, pp. 237 and 244; November 14, 1885, p. 315; July 11, 1891, p. 12 and June 9, 1894, p. 191.

58. This average is based upon reports provided to the school board by the principal of the school. The attendance figures given in the superintendent's published reports

are inflated. R. R. Wright report on Ware High School (hereafter cited as Wright Report), June 30, 1886, is folded in pages of Board Minutes, June 30, 1886, p. 349; *see also* 9th Annual Report, 1881, p. 16 and Board Minutes, July 9, 1881, p. 163; April 8, 1882, p. 189.

59. Petition from H. L. Walker to Board of Education November 9, 1891. Located between pp. 144 and 145 of Board Minutes, November 9, 1893; *see also* petition from members of black community presented by Judson W. Lyons to Board June 10, 1893 in Board Minutes, June 10, 1893, p. 132.

60. Board Minutes, 1880–1897, passim.

61. Jones, "Negro Education," p. 45.

62. Wright Report, June 30, 1886, *see also National Reporter System, South Eastern Reporters,* vol. 29 (St. Paul, Minn., 1898), p. 489 and *United States Reports,* vol. 175, Cases adjudged in the Supreme Court, October term, 1899, p. 533.

63. Board Minutes, July 10, 1880, p. 126 and October 12, 1878.

64. 9th Annual Report, 1881, p. 16; Jones, "Negro Education," pp. 42–43.

65. Board Minutes, July 21, 1883, p. 244.

66. Ibid., 1880–1890, passim, particularly see July 14, 1883, p. 226; July 12, 1884, p. 278; July 10, 1886, p. 337.

67. Commissioner of Education's Report, 1895, in Board Minutes, November 9, 1895, p. 309. Evans recommendation for class in cooking and sewing in Board Minutes, January 12, 1895, p. 229.

68. Ibid., Commissioner of Education Report.

69. Ibid.

70. Board Minutes, July 11, 1891, p. 17; October 10, 1891, p. 20–26.

71. Board Minutes, 1891–1897, passim.

72. Ibid., June 10, 1893, pp. 121–122; July 18, 1893, p. 126 and July 12, 1897, pp. 370–372.

73. Ibid. It should be noted that there were private white schools that provided secondary education for whites, e.g., Richmond Academy.

74. Ibid., April 9, 1892, p. 58 and July 12, 1897, pp. 370–372.

75. Petition from members of black community presented by Judson W. Lyons to Board on June 10, 1893, p. 132; Walker's report to the Board is found in Board Minutes, February 8, p. 288.

76. Board Minutes, October 14, 1893, p. 137; July 18, 1893, p. 126 and September 13, 1894, pp. 197–198.

77. Ibid., September 13, 1894, pp. 197–198; *see also* October 13, 1894, p. 200.

78. This average is based upon the data in the Board Minutes as opposed to the published Superintendent's report. The Board figures were taken from reports made by the principals of the various schools, but the superintendent's report was used by the state to determine Richmond County's share of the state school fund. Consequently the Superintendent's figures tend to be inflated.

79. Board Minutes, June 12, 1897, pp. 370–372.

80. Ibid., July 15, 1897, pp. 379–380.

81. Ibid., October 9, 1897, p. 386; *see also* Board Minutes, October 9, 1897, p. 386–394; *Cumming v. Richmond County Board of Education,* 175 United States Supreme Court 528 (1899).

82. Board Minutes, October 9, 1897, p. 388.

83. Ibid., n.d. p. 394. *See also Cumming v. Richmond County Board of Education.* 175 United States Supreme Court 528 (1899).

84. Ibid.; *see also National Reporter System, South Eastern Reporters,* vol. 29, pp. 488–491.

85. Ibid.

86. Jones, "Negro Education," p. 78.

The Hampton Model of Normal School Industrial Education, 1868–1900

James D. Anderson

Between 1880 and 1900, the leading businessmen-philanthropists and Southern school reformers came to recognize "Negro industrial training" as the appropriate form of education to assist in bringing racial order, political stability, and material prosperity to the American South. In their opinion the model most suitable for the socialization of the newly emancipated black people, and hence the amelioration of Southern racial and political conflict, was being developed by Samuel Chapman Armstrong at Hampton Normal and Agricultural Institute in Hampton, Virginia. While it has been reported elsewhere that Negro industrial and agricultural education was generated primarily by the national industrial education movement, emphasizing self-help and economic and moral uplift, such arguments do not adequately explain the development and function of the Hampton model.[1] The essence of the Hampton model of black industrial education lay not only in its aims to develop habits of industry, build character, and instill a feeling for the dignity of labor, but in its primary mission to train a cadre of conservative black teachers who were expected to help adjust the Afro-American minority to a subordinate social role in the Southern political economy.

The traditional emphasis on Hampton as an agricultural and industrial school has obscured the truth that it was founded and maintained primarily to train black teachers for the American South. The Institute did not even offer trade certificates until 1895. Still, in 1900, only 45 of Hampton's 656 black students were enrolled in the Trade School, and only four students were in agriculture. From its inception until well into the twentieth century, the Institute was almost wholly devoted to teacher training. Indeed, the "intention to remain through the whole course and become a teacher," was a condition for

I wish to thank Mr. Fritz Malval and his staff for assisting my research in the Hampton Institute Archives.

61

admission at Hampton in the early years. Not surprisingly, between 1872 and 1890, 604 of Hampton's 723 graduates became teachers. It should be kept in mind, however, that this trend was consistent with Armstrong's view of Hampton's primary mission. He always saw the Institute as a unique industrial normal school designed especially to produce "an army of black educators" who were expected to model particular social values and transmit them to the Afro-American South.[2]

Thus, Hampton should be analyzed more in the context of post-Civil War black Normal School training than as part of the era's general trend toward technical, trade, and agricultural education. In contrast to Hampton's concern with teacher training, the late nineteenth century industrial education movement stressed three basic types of training. First, and of the highest status, were the schools of applied science and technology, whose purpose it was to train the engineer, architect, chemist, and the like, for professional work in the emerging technology-based economy. A second and widely different class of industrial schools were the trade schools. They were organized to train the actual workers in industry and to educate them for their prospective individual occupations in life. In contrast to technical schools which trained the overseers and superintendents of labor, the trade school sought to educate the individual operatives. The third class of schools were comprised of those where manual instruction was introduced, mainly as a supplement to the traditional academic curriculum, in order to promote habits of industry, thrift, and morality. Several years before Hampton was established, institutions such as Mt. Holyoke Seminary for Women, Wellesley College, and Oberlin College had required students to do some manual labor to acquire fixed habits of industry and to provide financial support for the colleges. This concept of manual training instruction was urged for inclusion in the common school curriculum to teach the young the value of hard work and other virtues.[3]

Hampton's manual labor routine was designed partly to teach students steady work habits, practical knowledge, and good Christian morals. But, as shall be demonstrated, Armstrong viewed industrial education primarily as an ideological force that would provide the type of instruction suitable for adjusting blacks to a subordinate social role in the emergent New South. Significantly, he identified Hampton with the conservative wing of Southern reconstructionists who supported new forms of external control over blacks, including disfranchisement, segregation, and civil inequality. Armstrong's philosophy of "Black Reconstruction," widely publicized as the "Hampton Idea," essentially called for the effective removal of black voters and politicians from Southern political life, the relegation of black workers to the lowest forms of labor in the Southern economy, and the establishment of a general Southern racial hierarchy. He expected that the work of adjusting blacks to this kind of social arrangement would be carried out by indigenous black educators, particularly teachers and principals, aided by Hampton-styled industrial normal schools, state departments of education, local school boards, and Northern white philanthropists. Hence, Hampton developed an extensive manual labor routine because the schools' faculty believed that a particular combination of hard work, political socialization, and social discipline would mold the appropriate kind of conservative black teachers. In 1888, Atticus G. Haygood, the General Agent of the John F. Slater Fund, touched upon Hampton's central mission when he stated that the school's faculty viewed industrial training as the best intellectual and moral discipline for "those who are to be teachers and guides of their people." Haygood went to the heart of the matter. Hampton's teacher-training program and its attendant political values focused mainly on the relationship of black "teachers and guides" to the larger issues of Southern political and economic reconstruction.[4]

The Political Bias of the Hampton Idea

Hampton's ideological and pedagogical framework was derived mainly from the racial, political and economic views of Armstrong, the Principal from 1868 until his death in 1893, and from Hollis Burke Frissell, the Vice Principal and Chaplain from 1880 to 1893 who succeeded Armstrong and served as principal until 1917. Armstrong, with the help of the American Missionary Association, founded Hampton Institute in April of 1868. Four years after the Institute was established he initiated and edited the *Southern Workman*, an illustrated monthly, to present his views on the freedmen's place in the developing New South. The paper was created ostensibly as Hampton's official news organ; but, from the outset, Armstrong aimed to create a forum much more far-reaching than a typical school newspaper. As he wrote to his friend and Hampton trustee, Robert C. Ogden, "We mean to push it by mail, up and forwards — think of this — the paper may become, and I mean it will be a power." The *Southern Workman* became a "power," especially among Northern philanthropists and Southern white moderates who favored graded school and normal school education for blacks and who were basically opposed to black higher education, equal job opportunities, civil equality, and equal political rights. Although Armstrong attempted to promote the *Southern Workman* as a nonpolitical "instructive monthly," the paper, which expressed vividly his ideas of black reconstruction, sided with conservative political groups who wanted to disfranchise the freedmen and create a legal and customary racial hierarchy. Two years after the founding of the *Southern Workman*, a black newspaper concluded that Armstrong's monthly had "become so conservative that it leans the other way."[5]

To Armstrong, the removal of black people from any effective role in Southern politics was the first step toward "proper" Reconstruction. He wrote almost exclusively of the immorality and irresponsibility of black voters; he excoriated black politicians and labeled the freedmen's enfranchisement as dangerous to the South and the nation. In his view, the "Colored people" could "afford to let politics severely alone." He described black politics in South Carolina as resulting in a "shameless legislature" that had "ruined the credit of a great state." Armstrong instructed black leaders to stay out of politics because they were "not capable of self-government" and he blamed the black voters for creating situations which "no white race on this earth ought to endure of will endure." "The votes of Negroes have enabled some of the worst men who ever figured in American politics to hold high places of honor and trust," argued Armstrong. "Such votes marshalled by cunning knavery are dangerous to the country in proportion to their numbers." Thus he advised blacks to leave politics and urged "every colored leader" to refuse public office for generations to come.[6]

Armstrong waged a campaign against black political rights that should have embarrassed a self-proclaimed "friend of the Negro race," and occasionally it apparently did. He stated, in 1876, that he did not intend to "denounce as such every colored man who takes part in politics." In 1882 he even admitted that a few "colored politicians" could be "trusted." But these isolated statements tended to appear when Armstrong perceived that black political power was disintegrating. He was convinced that the 1877 withdrawal of Union soldiers from the South represented the end of black influence in Southern politics. Therefore, he angrily noted in 1879 that "the colored vote was reappearing as a political force." When this vote influenced the 1879 elections in Virginia, few "Rebels" were more reactionary than Samuel Armstrong:

> The Colored vote has suddenly the balance of power and gives victory to the readjusters. There is a split in Conservative ranks. Ex-Confederate leaders are arrayed against each other. The heroes of the war are replacing one-legged soldiers who fought under them with colored men who might have fought against them.

In Armstrong's view, this "calamity" threatened "Virginia's honor or standing in the markets of the world." The black race, he warned, "will act up to its light, but its best light is dim and therefore unsafe." The masses were "weak and blind" and "their so-called leaders" were, in general, "ignorant, immoral preachers or selfish politicians."[7]

Armstrong insisted that the freedmen should refrain from participating in Southern political life because they were culturally and morally deficient and therefore unfit to vote and hold office in "civilized" society. He fell heir to a particular cultural theory of racial subordination while growing up as the son of a missionary in the Hawaiian Islands. His father, Richard, entered Hawaii as a missionary in 1831 and by 1840 he was Minister of Public Instruction and he eventually became president of the Board of Education. Samuel Armstrong learned that his father's missionary career was "noble work for the savage race." This missionary inheritance was reinforced and consolidated in the milieu of the postwar South. The Southern "darkies," like the Polynesian "savages," were "so possessed with strange notions" that they had to be "most carefully watched over." The "darkies" were "emotional in their nature," improvident by habit, and "not capable of self-government." The Hampton principal easily shifted his missionary views from the Polynesians to the black Southerners. Indeed, he observed that "there was worked out in the Hawaiian Islands the problem of emancipation, and civilization of the dark-skinned Polynesian people in many respects like the Negro race." In both instances, Armstrong maintained that it was the duty of the superior white race to rule over the weaker dark-skinned races until they were appropriately civilized. The civilization of the dark-skinned races, in Armstrong's estimate, would take several generations of moral and religious development.[8]

In his political and educational thought, Armstrong attributed the "barbarism" of dark-skinned people largely to historical and environmental conditions. He occasionally invoked heredity arguments in his attempt to rationalize the dominance of whites over blacks. But the heredity concept, on the one hand, set unchangeable patterns which did not readily support the moral and educational reform commitments of missionary movements. On the other hand, mental or academic achievement was more measurable and came much sooner than moral development, thus supporting more rapid social change than Armstrong was willing to withstand. In arguing for the indefinite exclusion of all blacks, educated and noneducated, from active participation in Southern politics, Armstrong invoked moral development as the chief criteria for self-government. For him, exclusive white rule was legitimate because the race had developed exceptionally "in moral strength, in guiding instincts, in power to 'sense things' in the genius for this or that." The Negro, on the other hand, could not "see the point of life clearly, he lacks foresight, judgment and hard sense." The critical problem with the black race, according to Armstrong, was "not one of brains, but of right instincts, of morals and hard work." The freedmen's chief misfortunes were "low ideas of honor, and morality, want of foresight and energy, and vanity." In short, Armstrong contended that the white race was mentally and morally strong, and the black race was mentally capable but morally feeble. He attributed the moral capacity of the races to historically determined conditions:

> The [American] white race has had three centuries of experience in organizing the forces about him, political, social and physical. The Negro has had three centuries of experience in general demoralization and behind that, paganism.

This historical legacy of paganism and demoralization, Armstrong argued, robbed the black race of the moral wisdom and foresight necessary for responsible political activity.[9]

Armstrong used concepts such as "guiding instincts," and "moral strength," with slight regard for definition or accurate meaning. But despite the theoretical poverty of his social philosophy, it was highly convenient doctrine to support his Reconstruction policy of white rule and black disfranchisement. In 1877, when three black men were elected from the Hampton district to serve in the Virginia State Legislature, Armstrong commented: "This district will be represented in both houses by men of intelligence, but of no moral standing." In his view, "political ambition had proved unhealthy for the brightest minds of the [black] race." Thus, until a moral foundation was broadly laid, counseled Armstrong, "no sensible colored man could wish to see his race take a leading part in government." In the long run, however, the black race could "develop those guiding instincts and institutions that the Anglo-Saxon has reached through ages of hard experience." Moral intuition was largely automatic, instinctive, and historically determined and yet it was changeable. But this was possible "only by a series of experimental tests, which must of necessity include successive generations." Since the Anglo-Saxon race was morally strong, precisely because of its unique historical experiences, it seemed natural to Armstrong that the whites would supply and evaluate the "experimental tests" which led to "civilized" life.[10]

In posing morality, rather than intelligence, as the criteria for admission to the body politic, Armstrong rejected the idea of traditional higher academic training as either a civilizing force or an appropriate preparation for political activity. In his cultural theory of racial subordination, mental aptness was not considered an important measure of moral development; on the contrary, it was viewed more as characteristic of savageness. As Armstrong put it,

> Most savage races are not mentally sluggish. The African Zulu tests the wit and resources of an educated missionary. The Polynesian cannibal is a natural orator and takes to law and theology with readiness. The Aborigines of Australia are quickwitted.

Similarly, Armstrong observed that black children were mentally "capable of acquiring knowledge to any degree, and to a certain age, at least, with about the same facility as white children." "Most savage people," Armstrong warned, "are not like 'dumb driven cattle'; yet their life is little better than that of brutes because the moral nature is dormant." Thus, as long as the Negro's moral nature remained in abeyance, Armstrong believed that it was the whites' duty to suspend black political activity. The Hampton Idea was at once a conservative, gradualist, and paternalistic reform ideology.[11]

The Economic Basis of the Hampton Idea

When Armstrong maintained, as he frequently did, that the black race was "low but not degraded," he usually meant that it was the habit of labor, acquired under slavery, that saved the race from "moral ruin." "The Negro has one source of strength," he argued, "the habit of industry acquired in the time of slavery." This source of strength was important to Armstrong's platform of Southern economic reconstruction. "Southerners must make the best of Negro labor"; he said, "they cannot afford to do otherwise; with them it is that or none." In Armstrong's view, Northern capital and cheap black labor were critical to Southern economic reconstruction and reunion with the Northeast. "The Eastern states have the capital and experience," he announced in 1875, "while the South has the cheap labor; to bring the two together is to cement a real peace between the sections." This union, he believed, was hindered mainly by the political and racial turmoil in the South which discouraged capital investments from the Northeast. To Armstrong, the debate over black political participation "kindled the passions of war" and blocked the "swift return of Southern prosperity through immigration and capital from the North." He viewed the return of order and prosperity in the South as largely dependent upon "the rapidity with which the power of the politican is undermined by the gradual growth of the moneyed classes, whose pecuniary interests depend upon peace, and upon the respect and goodwill of the rest of the world, outside the South." Realizing that the racial upheaval in the postwar South resulted in "scarcity of capital" and "demoralized labor," Armstrong consistently called for racial peace and political stability, but nearly always at the expense of Southern blacks. He knew that the Northern capitalists would not eagerly invest in a region characterized by labor disorders and race riots. As he put it, "Liberalism must be organized into outward forms to induce northern men and capital to cross the border lines of the Southern states." He urgently demanded a quick resolution of political and racial conflict so that economic leaders could set in motion the wheel of material prosperity.[12]

Armstrong attempted to organize Hampton Institute as a model for the emerging Southern economy. Early on, he appealed for small businessmen to experiment with student and community labor. In December of 1877 he explored the idea of engaging the Hampton students in the manufacturing of cotton clothing for Northern markets. Armstrong instructed Charles Whiting, a white member of the Hampton staff, "to work up Negro labor, compete with New York labor in manufacturing for Northern markets." The students regularly performed hard labor for cheap rates in the school's workshops. According to the 1880 annual report, the school's Knitting Department produced "fifteen thousand dozen pairs of mittens for S. B. Pratt and Company of Boston, who sell them chiefly in the Northwest." Likewise, the young men in the Collis P. Huntington's Industrial Workshop were required to make products for the market economy. Advertising the new departure in the manufacture of doors, sashes, and blinds for the general market, Armstrong reported that the workshop did a prosperous business of "six thousand dollars a month, cutting over two million feet of lumber every year." On several occasions he invited entrepreneurs to take advantage of the "cheap labor in and out of the institution; students are paid from six to ten cents per hour."[13]

These work experiments extended beyond the typical industrial educational activities of the era. The Hampton model was more akin to the industrial training that first appeared during the 1820s in the reform schools established in New York City, Boston, and Philadelphia. Like the reformatories, in some cases Hampton contracted student labor to outside entrepreneurs who assigned the students routine and repetitive tasks like those done by unskilled factory or agricultural labor. Tileston T. Bryce, Hampton's financial agent, opened a meat packing and canning factory at the Institute in 1879. After two years he reported employing "hundreds of poor people" in "the large canning business," both student and community laborers. In a similar experiment, C. D. Cake, a white Virginia businessman, employed "ten colored and five Indian students" who "cut daily from six to eight thousand feet of yellow pine lumber." The Hampton staff observed the adaptation of black workers in these industries and developed theories which supported the extension of white dominance over black labor. After observing black workers in his canning factory, Bryce reported:

> I have found that the colored people, if the same chance be given them, work as diligently as the whites but not so intelligently. With intelligent direction they are admirable laborers, obeying orders and willingly; but when they attempt the direction of their own labor, it is apt to amount to but little.[14]

In an attempt to convince black leaders and workers to remain in the South as cheap and contented laborers, Armstrong and his associates propagandized that race prejudice which ranged against black participation in Southern politics, was not a barrier to black opportunity in the educational and economic arenas. He insisted that "There was no power and little disposition on the part of leading white conservatives to prevent the colored people from acquiring wealth and education." Indeed, he argued that "competition in the North" held back skilled Afro-American workers "more than prejudice at the South." Southern black mechanics, according to Armstrong, had "a fair field." Armstrong's propaganda in this area well illustrates the economic consciousness that he expected Hampton-trained teachers and leaders to model for the black community. Booker T. Washington, his prize student, often told black Southerners that "when one comes to business pure and simple, stripped of all ideas of sentiment, the Negro is given almost as good an opportunity to rise as is given to the white man." Like Armstrong, the Tuskegee principal forthrightly claimed that "the black man has a better chance in the South than in the North" for economic progress. Thus, "In spite of all talk of exodus," said Washington in 1885, "the Negro's home is permanently in the South." Washington epitomized the kind of black educator that Armstrong desired to train and in whom Armstrong wanted the black working class to place its trust. It is safe to say that the educational theory and method at Hampton were formulated to train an army of Booker T. Washingtons.[15]

Hampton's Educational Theory

The great educational question absorbing Armstrong's attention and intruding itself into every facet of Hampton Institute was the nature and role of teachers in shaping the social, economic, and political consciousness of the black masses. In Armstrong's view, the sociopolitical views embodied in the Hampton Idea would be primarily propagated among the black masses by black teachers. He conjectured that schools and churches were the best ways to socialize or "civilize" the black population. These institutions were viewed as agencies of amelioration and control, and they were the agencies under which most of the freedmen were organized. Therefore, said Armstrong, "Let us make the teachers and we will make the people." Surely the teachers and the people could be easily molded since they were "in the early stages of civilization." "Our students," stated Armstrong, "are docile, impressible, imitative and earnest, and come to us as a *tabula rasa* so far as real culture is concerned." Hampton was designed to build an ideological foundation upon these "blank minds" and return them to the outside world not as "polished scholars" but as "guides and civilizers, whose power shall be that of character and example, not of sounding words." To Armstrong, Hampton Institute had taken "a new departure" in the education of freedmen; it was a "civilizing power" that would encourage through its exemplars the "right ideas of life and duty."[16]

Armstrong's 1880 call, "Politicians to the background and schoolmasters to the front," echoed at once his disdain for the black politician and his vision of black teachers propagating the Hampton Idea of political economy throughout the Afro-American South. His was not merely another naive view of the ameliorative and modifying powers of common schooling. Armstrong's emphasis on the training of teachers or "guides" had even deeper roots in his awareness of the dependence of the black masses on the rising class of black teachers for the formation of ideologies. As he reasoned, black teachers were "usually the best educated of their society, are leaders of its thought, and give it tone by their superior wisdom and culture." Moreover, "The colored teacher is looked up to for his wisdom, is often chosen magistrate or other local dignitary, and is sometimes the only source of information from the outside world." Armstrong's concern with black teachers and their potential role in the black community led him to consider the forces which enhanced and threatened his aims. He feared the influence of black teachers and ministers who escaped the kind of ideological discipline that he propagandized. "The real trouble of the colored teachers," he complained, "is with a class of preachers, politicians, and editors of their own race who resent the introduction of intelligent ideas into religion and into the relations of life. They could easily be conciliated by substituting Latin for labor." Armstrong rejected the existing system of normal school training for blacks and campaigned relentlessly for the Hampton model.[17]

Armstrong sought to regulate the flow and quality of black teachers through avocating careful admissions processes and independent boarding schools. In 1881 he asked Virginia and other Southern public school officials to notify Hampton Institute of "worthy colored youth" that would make the right kind of teachers. Through this process the conservative whites could "do much to select wise leaders for the colored race." Such selection would bind the teachers to the white establishment and "any conflict of the races will be impossible." These recruits would be properly trained in independent boarding schools like Hampton. The "average Negro student," according to Armstrong, needed a boarding school so that his teachers could "control the entire twenty-four hours of each day — only thus can old ideas and ways be pushed out and new ones take their place." "When his whole routine of life is controlled," Armstrong believed, "the Negro pupil is like clay in the potter's hands." From this "clay" he intended to "create a class or guild who will be a nucleus of civilization," and one that would transmit the Hampton doctrines to the black race.[18]

As boarding schools were the institutional mechanisms for training teachers, Armstrong viewed his own brand of industrial education as the appropriate pedagogy to mold the economic and political consciousness of prospective black leaders and educators. Hampton's industrial education curriculum, therefore, was not intended primarily to create "small individualistic entrepreneurs" or to offer "Negroes the technical training necessary for effective competition in an industrial age." It was designed mainly to train black ideologues who were expected to model and transmit Armstrong's philosophy of Southern Reconstruction to the Afro-American working class. "The Negroes, who are to form the working classes of the South," he maintained, "must be taught not only to do their work well, but to know what their work means." But first it was necessary to condition the personality and attitudes of the teachers. Armstrong believed that "A teacher does more by virtue of what he is than of what he says; the most powerful constructive influence is indirect." He envisioned the Hampton students as the embodiment of "habits of living and labor, ... in order that graduates may be qualified to teach others these important lessons of life." To him, hard labor was the first principle of civilized life, and he drilled his students in manual labor routines so that they could effectively teach the value of routinized labor to the black masses. "If you are the right sort of man you will engage in any sort of labor, and dignify it," declared Armstrong. Indeed, "A man had better work for nothing and find himself than to spend his time in idling and loafing." Therefore, he instructed blacks to "Plow, hoe, ditch, grub; do anything rather than nothing." To be sure, Armstrong was not opposed to teaching trades to a few individuals, but he primarily sought to organize through his graduates a nonskilled or semiskilled black race that would shoulder the Southern economy. If the South was to achieve industrial and agricultural greatness, black workers needed to be taught to "love" labor and to understand the meaning of work more than they needed trade or technical skills. Consequently, Armstrong was almost exclusively concerned with the ideological value of industrial training.[19]

Routine and repetitive manual labor activities were developed to screen and condition certain types of students to serve as missionaries of the Hampton Idea. Armstrong held a life-long suspicion of highly educated blacks, believing that their aspirations were vain and dysfunctional to his views of Southern Reconstruction. His idealized student was a hard worker with elementary education and industrial training. He did not believe that highly educated blacks would remain as "civilizers" among the rural masses. "There is such a thing as over-education," he warned, "A highly educated Negro is as little likely as a highly educated white man to do a work against which his tastes and sensibilities would every day rebel." The highly educated could not serve as models for the masses who, according to Armstrong, were destined to plow, hoe, ditch, grub. Therefore, manual labor rather than scholarship became Hampton's chief criterion for social and ideological excellence. "One who shirks labor may be a fine mathematician," noted Armstrong, but "the blockhead at the black board may be a shining example in the cornfield." The idealized "blockhead" or "plodders," as they were called, became the standard by which all students were evaluated. In 1882 Armstrong reported: "A good labor record has often saved one from being dropped as incompetent while one brilliant in studies is sometimes sent away for inefficiency in the shop or farm." The students with good labor records were thought the best potential exponents of the Hampton Idea. Vice Principal H. B. Frissell, after visiting Hampton graduates in the field, reported in 1885 "that very frequently the dull plodder at Hampton is the real leader of his people toward better things, while the bright scholar who was our pride and delight at school, because of his mental acuteness, either yields to temptation or leaves school work for the more tempting offers of clerkships or political appointments." Similarly, Armstrong argued that "the plodding ones make good teachers."[20]

The Hampton Method

Hampton's industrial education system comprised three main areas: the academic program; the manual labor system; and a strict social discipline routine. The entire operation was systematically ordered to morally and intellectually discipline a conservative black teacher's corps; however, each division emphasized certain specifics. The academic program, aside from preparing students to teach grade school and to pass varied state teachers' certification examinations, was also planned for the ideological training of potential Hampton missionaries. The manual labor system, organized to shape attitudes and build character through steady, hard labor, was designed to connect the theoretical and practical lessons. The daily discipline routine served to rid the school of students at variance with the Hampton Idea.

The Hampton academic program consisted of an English course of study embracing reading and elocution, elementary mathematics, history, literature, moral science, and political economy. Armstrong excluded classical studies because he believed that such training stimulated "vanity" in black students, which propelled them toward high-flown notions of politics and professional life. Hampton sought to impress upon its students their "true" place in the Southern social order largely through courses in Political Economy, Civil Government, and Practical Morality. Whereas the other academic courses were taught by white women teachers, these courses were taught by Armstrong and Frissell with assistance from Tileston T. Bryce, a faculty member and the school's financial manager. Armstrong began the courses in the 1870s with triweekly talks on the important economic and political questions of the era. In 1882, he reported that Political Economy included the "discussion of labor, wages, money value, and the tariff." Political Economy was developed to promote proper relations between capitalists and laborers and the courses in Practical Morals and Civil Government were aimed at correcting the student's "wrong notions" regarding the "rights of persons and property, the origins of these rights, and how they may be violated."[21]

The *Southern Workman,* the main text in Political Economy, was used in all reading classes. Armstrong recommended the paper to other "colored normal schools and colleges." He was particularly satisfied with Tileston T. Bryce's series of articles on political economy that were eventually gathered into the Hampton textbook, *Economic Crumbs, or Plain Talks for the People About Labor, Capital, Money, Tariff, etc.* In 1878 Bryce initiated a series of essays that were structured around questions which appeared repeatedly on the student's senior examination in Political Economy. The Hampton students, examined annually by a committee appointed by the Board of Trustees, were required to answer the following questions in Political Economy: "What is labor? Who are the laboring classes? Show how all men are mutually dependent. What are wages? Who determines the price of wages? What is capital? Show the relationship of capital to labor. How are all men capitalists?" Bryce's essays on these questions were consistent with the basic premises of the Hampton Idea.[22]

To Bryce, no inherent or legitimate conflict existed between capital and labor. It was erroneous "to speak of the 'laboring classes' as distinct divisions of society" because "every man who puts forth any exertion, in order to obtain something in return, is a laborer." If the expression "laboring classes" had any distinctive meaning, it signified "free men as opposed to slaves." Bryce concluded that there were "no class feelings to irritate, no color line to fight over":

> The most pernicious quack, who peddles political nostrums, is he who attempts to excite the multitude by declaring that "all the ills that flesh is to heir" come from the employers of labor. People of this sort hold it as an axiom that there is an unending feud between capital and labor; and

that the former ever seeks to extinguish the latter. Some of these mischief-makers, assuming this statement to be true, are logical enough to declare that labor should try to extinguish capital. This is the doctrine of communism. Now if there be two things in this world between which the utmost amity should exist, and between which the most intimate reciprocal relations do exist, they are Capital and Labor.

Thus, labor unions were conspiracies to defy the laws of economics and to get something for nothing. Those who interfered with the workplace by violence or threats were labeled "either slave-catchers or thieves."[23]

"The bottom idea of capital," Bryce argued, "is that somebody has saved something." A man with only an "extra shirt" was "to that extent a capitalist." However, it was natural for some men to have more capital than others, and it was "no more unjust, than that one man should be stronger, taller, or more healthy than another." "The majority of people accept such as the natural state of things," contended Bryce, "and the minority, who decline to accept it, are found among the vicious, who have squandered all they had, the improvident, who never labor for more than mere existence." These views were supported by other Hampton textbooks.[24]

Armstrong was always pleased with the results of the senior class examination because "the students got a higher percentage of correct answers in Political Economy than in any other of the several branches." Black students came to Hampton, according to Armstrong, thinking "much of the rights of the laborers and little of those of the capitalist"; they viewed the two classes "as being opposed to one another." Clearly, such thinking diverged from the Hampton Idea, and the school's staff labored to "correct" such notions. There is no way of determining how many students were converted to Armstrong's doctrines of Political Economy. But the educational thought of the two most well-known Hampton graduates, Booker T. Washington and Robert R. Moton, parroted the Hampton doctrines.[25] Doubtless, other educators at the time, black and white, propagandized similar views of political economy. The point, however, is that Hampton was deliberately teaching prospective black leaders and educators economic values that were detrimental to the objective economic interests of black workers. Black domestics, sharecroppers, and factory laborers were not capitalists and their objective economic interests, as many of them realized, were fundamentally different than and opposed to Southern bosses and landlords who ruled over them. Thus, when Hampton trained leaders like Booker T. Washington to persuade blacks to remain in the South as cheap and contented agricultural and domestic laborers, it contributed to the development of a conservative Afro-American leadership which was at odds with the improvement of black employment opportunities and working conditions.

The relationship of black religious and moral development to the Southern social order was another major concern of the Hampton faculty. To Frissell and Armstrong, the "old-time" Negro religion hindered the development of a "new" political economy. It was too removed from questions of practical social responsibility. Armstrong commented:

> There is plenty of religion, such as it is, among both parents and scholars, but it is too often a religion that regards more the emotional part of the nature than the moral, and so aids little in the work of checking the evil tendencies of these growing lives.

In Armstrong's view, the separation of black religion from moral responsibility was nicely illustrated in the tale of the devout old "Auntie" who would attend church and not allow one poor old goose (that she had stolen) "come between her and her blessed Lord." In discussing black religion and moral strength in 1877, Armstrong told the American Missionary Association that "Pastors and deacons all sell whiskey and lead loose lives without scandal; an ex-jail bird returns to this former social positions; in politics and in society, character goes for little or nothing."[26]

Behind Armstrong's moral rationale lay more mundane considerations for political and economic reconstruction. He viewed black ministers as a class of leaders that eschewed hard labor in favor of political and professional life. He believed that "at least two-thirds" of the ministers were represented by one who, according to Armstrong, explained in a cotton field on a warm day, "O Lord, de work is so hard, de cotton is so grassy, and de sun am so hot, I b'leave dis darkey am called to preach." Such "exemplars" could not be expected to convey the Hampton doctrines of industry and hard labor to the black community. The Hampton staff, therefore, sought to train a corps of teachers that would counteract "the bad leadership of demagogues, whose chief temptation is to get a living by something else than hard work." Frissell attributed black conceptions of social responsibility to the slave experience: "Having been so grossly wronged, their thoughts have been fixed upon their dues from others more than on what is due others from themselves." To "correct their wrong notions," Frissell gave regular instruction on the importance of holding to a contract, on the origin and rights of property and person, and on the duties of citizenship. The Hampton staff labeled this course Practical Morals.[27]

As the academic courses were arranged to influence the students' political and economic ideology, the manual labor system was developed to reinforce consciousness through the formation of habits and character. The manual labor system was a central factor in admission and retention policy and in the students' day-to-day existence. Hampton advertised for "country youth who don't mind hard work." In order to acquire more "strong, able bodied young men" for the heavier farm and mill work, in 1888, Armstrong created a "special class" who "could not pass the entrance examination, but who were desirable from the work standpoint." Since the entrance examination was mainly a literacy test, it is reasonable to assume that many of these students were semiliterate. They were admitted mainly to work and after two years in the "Preparatory class" they entered the regular normal school curriculum. Meanwhile, brilliant students considered "indifferent and careless workmen," were "discharged from the farm and usually from the school in consequence." In the nineteenth century, Hampton graduated only one-fifth of its students and many of those dropped were disqualified for bad work habits and "weakness of character." The first three months of the school term were considered the "weeding out" session during which time approximately 20 percent of the new students were dismissed. During the entire three year's course, according to Armstrong, there were "frequent leaving of students for disciplinary, pecuniary, domestic, and other reasons."[28]

All Hampton students were required to work since nonworkers were viewed as "an aristocracy ruinous to manual-labor schools." The amount of work, however, varied according to the student's curriculum. Those who were admitted directly into the Normal school to qualify as teachers for graded schools, were required to work two ten-hour days every week during the three year's course. They were paid from seven to ten cents per hour or one dollar to one dollar and fifty cents per week. These earnings were credited to the students' accounts for the cost of board, washing, room rent, and tuition which amounted to approximately ten dollars per month. Thus, the students were invariably deficient and, to earn additional credit, they agreed to work any time "for any number of days not exceeding twelve." The trade students, generally about sixty male students in simple mechanical training, worked six ten-hour days every week for three years and then entered the Normal school for two additional years. Such students were also given a Normal school certificate until 1895 when Hampton began awarding trade certificates.[29]

The heart of Hampton's manual labor program was established in 1879 when Armstrong created the Night School with Booker T. Washington as principal.[30] It opened with 36 students who were required to labor ten hours per day, six days per week, eleven months per year for two years. Two years of night school work were equivalent to one year of the Normal school course. In their last two years of Normal school work the students had to study four days and work two days during each week. More than any other division, the Night School implemented Armstrong's social philosophy. By 1893, 305 of Hampton's 541 black students were enrolled in the Night School. The admissions to the regular or Day School declined significantly during the 1880s and, consequently, "the Night School became the main-feeder of the Day School." It functioned as a sifter for the Normal school by giving the Hampton staff ample opportunity to assess the students' character, industrial habits, and political attitudes before admitting them to the regular Normal school. To work from seven o'clock in the morning until six o'clock at night, and then study from seven o'clock until nine, was, as Booker T. Washington said, "an undertaking that few young men would be willing to stick to, through all the seasons of the year."[31]

Night School students were chiefly farm laborers, domestic servants, and mill hands. "Much of the labor that goes into our industries," reported Armstrong, "is neither skilled labor nor apprentice labor, but is made up of the great body of unskilled laborers who come here to work a year or two at whatever work the school may be able to give them." Male students worked in the sawmill, on the farm, in the kitchens as dishwashers and pantry boys, in the dining rooms as waiters, and in the cottages and smaller buildings as house boys. Female students received even less regular training and were encouraged to do little except "plain sewing, plain washing and ironing, scrubbing, mending, etc." In the words of the Hampton faculty, the undergraduates learned "how to work steadily and regularly, to attend promptly at certain hours to certain duties," and they "gained new ideas of the value of manual labor." As Armstrong put it in his last report, "We do not mean to say that much is not learned by every faithful student in these departments; he or she will be a better cook, laundress, or farmer, and surely much needed lessons in promptness, and thoroughness are inculcated, but still the object in view is not to teach a trade but to get the work done."[32] This manual labor system was designed to cultivate in Hampton students the industrial habits and a "love" for the lowest forms of labor that they were to impart to the black race. The emphasis on the morality and value of labor in contrast to technical development indicates the priority which Hampton placed on economic adjustment rather than economic advancement of the Afro-American South. Indeed, the work and trade programs at Hampton corresponded well with those typically found on Southern white plantations.

It seems that the Night School was established to produce the "dull plodders." The Hampton faculty described the students as "mostly grown men and women ... willing to spend their days in hard work on the farm or at the mill," for a chance to enter the Normal school curriculum. One Night School director, Anna G. Baldwin, reported that the students, most in their early twenties, were "often the best workers" but "the dullest scholars." The demanding work day undoubtedly retarded the students' academic progress. Armstrong, however, maintained that "nothing essential in study is lost, and much that is essential to success in life is gained." Yet, the teachers in the academic department constantly complained about low academic achievement. Some regarded it a "puzzling mathematical problem" as to how the Night School students could learn anything significant. Anna G. Baldwin recalled that an ambitious boy could "be overheard conjugating a verb while hoeing in the garden, or perched on a fence watching the cows, [and] meanwhile furtively study his reader." Similarly, Night School Principal Booker T. Washington reported that "One was noticed to carry a broken piece of slate about with him on which he could work examples while the wheelbarrow of dirt he had loaded, was being emptied." Washington, to illustrate the effectiveness of the Night School work routine, quite innocent of satire, stated "Their books were in their hands at every spare moment." Indeed, Armstrong had stood the educational process on its head; spare time was used for study and regular time devoted to hard labor.[33]

The "dull plodders" received praise and special treatment from the Hampton faculty. In the summer of 1885, approximately two hundred applicants were refused by Hampton's admission office. Many initial rejects were reconsidered, but only in favor of those physically able to take vacant positions in the saw mill and to do the heavier farm work. The Hampton staff certainly had good reason to announce, "There is a certain amount of grit and pluck needed for doing successful work in the night classes."[34] The survivors were held up as model students. In fact, as H. B. Frissell explained in 1885, Hampton gave special recognition to successful Night School students:

> There must always be here the double standard of judging students, by which their moral worth is taken into account even more than their intellectual advancement. What will this student do for the upbuilding of his race? is the question we are obliged to ask everyone placed under our care? During the past year, students have been asked to leave the school, whose scholarship was of the best, because it was felt that they lacked in moral earnestness.... At the last anniversary exercises, a young man spoke as the valedictorian of his class who by no means led his fellows in scholarship, but had notably taken the lead in Christian Manhood.[35]

Character or "moral earnestness," however, was judged in terms of the students' willingness to perform "ten hours' drudgery" in unskilled or semiskilled occupations. The study of mathematics or classical lore for hours on end was not considered an index of hard labor or moral strength.

Finally, for those students lacking in "moral earnestness," a rigid system of social discipline was instituted to remove the unfit. Armstrong established a "Daily Order of Exercises" which occupied nearly every minute of the students' time. They reported for morning inspection at 5:45; had breakfast and prayer from 6:00 to 6:30; worked or studied during the day having scarcely a half hour to themselves; went to supper and evening prayers from 6:00 to 6:45 P.M.; and, if in Night School, they retired to their dormitories thoroughly fatigued after evening study from 7 to 9. Male students were required to participate in military drill and to march to and from classes. Beret-Captain Henry Romeyn, who commanded the Hampton Cadets in 1878, stated clearly that the military drill was "not intended to make soldiers out of our students, nor to create a warlike spirit," but to "create ideas of neatness, order, system, obedience, and produce a better manhood." In Romeyn's view, the drill cultivated a "respect for order and properly constituted authority, that, in general, would do much to keep down the dangerously increasing communistic elements in the midst of the population of our country." All students submitted to a system of demerits for infractions of the social code. This routine enabled the teachers to observe the adaptation of students to the Hampton program. Many pupils were expelled for small infractions of the social code. One student was dismissed permanently after receiving reprimands for "using profane language," "not having room in order," "absence from church without permission," and "having light on after hours without authority." Another student, accused of "not rising during singing at morning prayers and causing disturbance by laughing," was suspended for the year of 1879. Many other students met a similar fate as Hampton sought to instill a respect for order and "properly" constituted authority.[36]

The Black Critique

The Hampton model of industrial education was viewed with suspicion and resentment in significant segments of the black community. An important critique was delivered by the black students who experienced the Hampton routine. Historians have failed to analyze the industrial education programs from this perspective. Yet, for Hampton, and probably for many other institutions, the most intimate assessment of industrial education, in practice, came from this group. Moreover, when it is considered that nearly all of Hampton's "rebel" students were probably dismissed during the "weeding-out" season, the protest of those who remained is particularly insightful and illuminating.

A significant number of the Hampton students attacked the school's industrial program at its most vulnerable points. Many came to Hampton with the understanding that they would learn skilled trades for future livelihood. Hampton was designed primarily to train conservative teachers or leaders and some students were disappointed with the low level of technical training. William W. Adams, having heard that "scholars could learn trades" at Hampton, entered the school in 1878 to learn the printing trade. Adams was appalled at the elementary character of the academic program and commented bitterly that he was "not learning anything," merely "going over what I had learned in a primary school." He was more disheartened, however, in discovering that no one would teach him the printing trade. He left in dismay and charged that the school was "greatly over-rated." Another student, ten years later, complained about the inadequate training in the printing division. As Thomas Mann wrote to Armstrong, "Bookbinding is a part of the printer's trade of which we get none.... As I wish to become a successful printer, I would like to learn all about the trade." Hampton was capable of offering better training in the printing trade as the school printed the *Southern Workman,* the *African Repository,* and operated the Normal School Press. But in 1878 there were no students in the printing trade and by 1890 only eight black students working in the printing office. However, the Hampton mission was to train teachers, not printers, or shoemakers.[37]

From the vantage point of the student, the technical instruction at Hampton was elementary and limited. A student in the blacksmith department complained in 1888 that there were "six blacksmiths and only two forges," which greatly restricted their practice in heating and hammering metals. John

Boothe, in his last year of training to become a shoemaker, wrote that he had not received "any instructions on cutting out and fitting shoes." J. F. Satter-white stated that the students were not trained to make boots, a product that brought significant profits to shoemakers. C. L. Marshall further criticized the shoemaking program for not teaching "sewed work" in the shop. Marshall, as Satterwhite, was displeased with his training in shoemaking. As he informed Armstrong, "The people do not want peg or nail work, but they want sewed work. Should I go home and attempt to set up a shoe shop without any knowledge of sewed work, I don't think I could earn my daily bread." Indeed, a shoemaker that could not make boots, cut, fit or sew shoes, was hardly worthy of the name.[38]

The "carpenters," like the shoemakers, were trained to be handymen rather than craftsmen or artisans. William M. Keffie was annoyed because he and fellow apprentices did not receive "enough practice in the way of building and framing houses." J. A. Colbert, another aspiring carpenter, worked "all day for six days each week" and was dissatisfied with the lack of training in "the use of timber." Apparently, Hampton's program in carpentry involved little more than teaching the students to make window sashes and frames. The students urged Armstrong to upgrade the work from essentially manual labor to advanced technical training. Perry Shields, writing to Armstrong in 1888, revealed much about the quality of the carpentry course.

> We the boys in the HIW [Huntington Industrial Workshop] need to learn how to build houses, the practice for which, we do not get in the mill. We work in the mill three years, after which we leave, giving others to think that we are carpenters. All of us can't find mills to get employ-ment, hence we will soon find out that building is the chief and only work of our branch by which we can earn a living. So you see that the only thing we learn in that direction is the use of tools and three years are too much time to spend learning merely to use tools. We draw buildings every week and if we had some of the work to do after drawing it we would become self-supporting mechanics. As it is, we begin with making window and door frames and have but few other jobs, but making frames.

Hampton's trade students were acutely aware of the Institute's shortcomings. O. H. Hawkins requested "more practical training or instruction pertaining to framing houses and how to get the different levels, angles, etc." Whether it was Jackson M. Mundy requesting mechanical drawing or George Johnson asking for improvements in the sawmill, trade students at Hampton were largely disappointed with their training.[39]

The students' resentment was eventually expressed in a petition of protest issued to the Hampton faculty in the summer of 1887. According to two students, Perry Shields and W. H. Scott, "every apprentice of the school signed his name" to the protest document. The faculty, however, ignored the petition and Shields responded to Armstrong; "We feel that we form a very insignificant part of the working class, from the fact that last summer a letter was written the faculty to which every apprentice of the school signed his name, and from that letter we have heard nothing, for nor against; from such points we lose interest." Likewise, W. H. Scott complained to Armstrong: "The petition put through by the trade-boys during the fall was seemingly ignored much to our disappointment." In the letters that followed the petition, the students protested against the menial level of training, hard labor, low wages, and poor working conditions. Realizing that very little educational benefit accrued from the industrial program, the students responded as a discontented working class. Dissatisfaction with overwork was a consistent and pervasive theme in their letters. John H. Boothe, who described the working conditions in terms suitable to characterizing convict labor, said that the students were "confined" in the shops "for a term of three years to work every day except legal holidays and Sundays." Hawkins viewed the students' training not as an educational program but as a process of "toiling at their trade through three years." W. H. Scott spoke for many of his fellow students in candid remarks about the work schedule: "It is to be remembered that four years at a trade like ours, working from 7 A.M. to 5:50 P.M., is enough to break down the constitution of a man, much less boys in the bloom of youth."[40]

Hampton's students understood that they were performing regular hard labor and some, like J. F. Satterwhite, stated simply, "I think we ought to get paid more." Similarly, Roberta Whiting, the mother of a Hampton student, questioned the school's manual labor program which operated at the expense of both trade and academic training:

> I received a letter from my son and he tells me that he has not attended day school since entering your institution. He also mentioned that his work was hard having to milk, and attend to a number of cows every day and that he has to get up at four A.M. to do this and the only time spent in school was at night. I have spoken to my physician and he thinks that amount of work detrimental to the health of a boy his age.

James C. Rollins also consulted his physician about the Hampton labor routine. Arriving at the school in "tolerably good health," he informed Armstrong that "My doctor has seriously cautioned me about overworking myself." George Johnson resented the harshness of his boss; Clayton Elks demanded better food; G. G. Spraggins complained of the rain which pierced his shop; and W. Z. Ruth pleaded for improved working conditions.[41]

Publicly, Armstrong propagandized that at Hampton "there was no begging except for more work." In contrast to his claims, however, the students actually asked for reduced work loads. J. H. Tucker, who may have understood Armstrong's passion for hard labor, could not comprehend why he had to continue painting in the dark merely to complete a ten hours' work routine. Male students particularly requested Armstrong to suspend work hours in Saturdays at four o'clock. According to Hawkins, they wanted the time "to engage themselves in such games, or local pleasures as they think best." Armstrong, however, believing that blacks had no "respect" for labor, insisted upon "the ten hours' drudgery" to put the students "in shape for the struggle of life." But, in the words of Perry Shields, "after working for a long time upon the same old thing in which there is no future," many students became disinterested in their training. In sharp protest against the constrictions on the students' intellect and creativity, Shields asserted, "the shop is cold and our minds are straying and our hands freezing — and we cannot retain any interests."[42]

In 1878, Hampton's newly formed Alumni Association petitioned the school's faculty regarding its policies and practices of racial subordination. The Alumni Association, which met at Hampton during the May commencement exercises, urged the faculty to "examine carefully" whether black visitors were accorded their proper respect. More specifically, the petition charged:

> That the graduates of this Institution have been insulted and have had our feelings mortified by public rumors and newspaper articles to the effect that the officers and teachers of this Institution have not, and do not accord to colored visitors the courtesies and hospitalities due them as a race.

The Hampton Alumni used their own experiences to charge the faculty with racial proscription. As the petition stated, "We the graduates of this Institution, after returning in compliance with the call of our Alma Mater, have had our feelings wounded most grievously by being barred from some of the privileges that ordinary white visitors enjoyed." Much of this protest remained within the confines of the Institute; nevertheless, it reveals important student perceptions of the Hampton program. Clearly, many of them perceived that Armstrong and his colleagues were trying to convince black people to accept a subordinate social position in the institution and in the society at large.[43]

Hampton's students and alumni were not alone in questioning the relevance of Armstrong's social philosophy to the interests and aspirations of the Afro-American South. Both Frissell and Armstrong acknowledge persistent black opposition to the Hampton Idea. In 1878, Armstrong declared that black criticism of the Institute was "no novelty" and in 1879 he admitted that objections to the Hampton program were "common in the colored papers." In 1888, Armstrong further stated: "During the first ten years of our school life our work was looked upon with disfavor by the Negro leaders as providing only a low grade of instruction...." H. B. Frissell recalled that "Negro conventions referred to Hampton as a 'slave pen and a literary penitentiary.'" The black Virginia *Star,* recommended "that the government make the place [Hampton] a National Reform School for her wards. It is admirably adapted for such, and it would prevent many unwary parents from sending their children there to equip them with a classical education." The *Christian Recorder* of the African Methodist Episcopal Church, after criticizing the conservative view of a

Hampton student in 1875, asked "Have Virginia conservatives captured Hampton?"[44]

Black criticisms of Hampton Institute received national attention in the Afro-American press during the late 1870s. In 1876, two black writers for the *People's Advocate,* which was edited in Alexandria, Virginia, by the prominent black journalist John Wesley Cromwell, characterized the Hampton program as an educational experience that sought to affirm the legitimacy of black subordination. After attending the 1876 commencement, one writer, struck by Hampton's pattern of race relations, reported that,

> On Commencement Day May 18th visitors were present, white and colored, but not one of the latter was to be seen on the splendid platform of Virginia Hall. The rudest and most ignorant white men and women were politely conducted to the platform; respectable and intelligent colored ladies and gentlemen were shown lower seats where they could neither see nor hear the exercises of the day with any pleasure. To speak in general the colored people and students are made to feel that they must forever remain inferior to their white brethren no matter what their attainments may be.

The reporter concluded that it was "Better, far better, yes infinitely better that we have no high schools and colleges, if our youth are to be brought up under such baneful influences." Several days later another reporter for the *People's Advocate,* who had also visited Hampton Institute, commented boldly: "I had rather my boy, should grow up ignorant of letters, than attend an Institution to be taught that Negroes, notwithstanding their acquirements, are and must forever remain inferior to the whites."[45]

This line of criticism continued in 1878 when the prominent black leader, Henry M. Turner, visited Hampton and reported his impressions of the school in the African Methodist Episcopal's *Christian Recorder.* In his weekly column, "Wayside Dots and Jots," Turner chastized Hampton for its Confederate orientation. He was struck immediately by the pictures of Andrew Johnson and General Robert E. Lee hanging on the walls of the school's chapel, and commented acidly: "What [they] had ever done for the colored people I could not tell." Turner attended an advanced class for seniors where the teacher purported to instruct the students in astronomy, and concluded that "the teacher knew comparatively nothing about it, and the class knew, if possible, less than nothing." He was convinced that Hampton deprived black students of intellectual development, particularly in "algebra, geometry, higher mathematics, Greek, Latin, and Science." He was most upset, however, with Hampton's policy of racial subordination. During his stay, "not a teacher asked me to sit down, made a solitary explanation, gave me a welcome look, nor showed me the civility of a visitor, while I was in the building." In contrast to the treatment he received, Turner observed that "when white visitors come in, chairs were offered them, etc." This differed from the cordial receptions he experienced at other black schools. Thus, he made the following assessment of the Hampton teachers and students:

> They are either in the whole ex-slave-holders themselves, or are pandering to the spirit of slavery. The graduates they send out cannot be called educated by any means, for they have not near the learning given by a respectable grammar school.... Besides, I think colored children are taught to remember "You are Negroes," and as such, "your place is behind."[46]

R. A. Green, editor of the Richmond, Virginia *Star,* reprinted Turner's editorial and informed his readers that he had received similar treatment while visiting Hampton Institute. A year later the *Louisianian* reported that "General Armstrong, the principal of Hampton Institute, does not seem to stand in high favor with the colored people of the east." The *Louisianian* declared that Armstrong was charged with "curbing the aspirations of his students" and with crushing the manhood of the male students by refusing to hire black professors. "To know and *feel* that he is indeed a man," argued the *Louisianian,* "the Negro should have the black professor side by side with his white brother. This manhood education can never come from white teachers alone, however competent." The *Louisianian* charged that Armstrong "by his educational policy, seems to think that we should only know enough to make good servants...."[47]

Even the more moderate wing of black educators and writers made specific criticisms of industrial education during the 1880s and 1890s. Black spokesmen like Harry Smith, Alexaner Crummell, and Calvin Chase questioned the motives of those who promoted industrial training as the educational model most suitable for Afro-Americans. Initially, it appeared that Crummell, the venerable and learned rector of Washington D.C.'s St. Luke's church, would support the Hampton-styled industrial education movement. In 1887, he published *Common Sense in Common Schooling,* which praised vocational education and stated that higher education was "ruinous [to] well-nigh half of the colored youth who graduate from high schools and colleges." The African Methodist Episcopals' *Church Review* criticized Crummell's position on the grounds that many whites would "refer to him as endorsing the position they hold, to wit, that the Negro only needs and should therefore only receive an industrial education." The editor of the *Church Review,* however, understood that Crummell only meant to emphasize the value of skilled trades and technical training and did not intend to encourage the popular Negro industrial education movement. Crummell confirmed this view when he later wrote that, "All the talk about 'industrialism' is with regard to the Negro and Negro education, and there is a lot of white men in the land who pity the Negro but who have never learned to love him, who take up this miserable 'fad,' and are striving by one pretext or another to put this limitation upon our brains and culture."[48]

In the 1890s, Harry Smith, editor of the Cleveland *Gazette,* and Calvin Chase, editor of the Washington *Bee,* continued to warn the black community about the dangers of the Hampton-Tuskegee industrial education movement. The *Gazette,* arguing that attainments in the industrial arts would not fit young blacks for the "higher duties of life," reported in 1890 that Hampton graduates were being employed as waiters and porters. While admitting to the necessity of trade training, the *Gazette* advocated higher and professional training for "the fullest development of the [Negro] mind." Likewise, the Washington *Bee* urged blacks to relegate industrial education to a secondary role and to place top priority on the training of lawyers, doctors, scientists, and varied professional persons. Much of the *Bee's* attack on industrial training focused on Booker T. Washington as the Tuskegeean became in the 1890s the symbol of black industrial education. In a typical editorial against Washington and the Hampton-Tuskegee Idea, the *Bee* remarked in 1896:

> It is a notorious fact, that the utterances of Mr. Washington are nothing more than to make himself rich by assuring the white people of this country that the negroes [*sic*] place is in the machine shop, at the plow, in the wash-tub and not in the schools of legal and medical professions; that he [the Negro] has no business to aspire to those places as they are reserved for the proud Caucasian.

Significantly, such criticisms, which started in the middle 1870s, long predated the Washington-DuBois debates of the early twentieth century, and represented a persistent strain of black protest against the Hampton-Tuskegee Idea for the training of black educators and leaders.[49]

The Hampton Idea and the Black Colleges

In 1888, Samuel C. Armstrong happily observed that there was a growing demand "for chances to learn trades, and evident appreciation of industrial education." "Authorities everywhere are coming to be of one mind in regard to the value of manual labor in schools; that is," wrote Armstrong, "it is almost universally acknowledged that some form of industrial training, some system by which the pupil may become grounded in one or another art or handicraft, is essential to true education." Indeed, a sharp increase occurred in industrial education courses in black colleges during the 1880s, and some important black and missionary educators promoted the curriculum innovations. Beginning with the creation of the John F. Slater Fund in 1882, which appropriated its capital exclusively for Negro industrial training, there emerged a sudden burst of enthusiasm for industrial education. As historian James M. McPherson has written, "Perhaps more than anything else this caused several schools to initiate vocational programs in the 1880s." During this period the Northern mission societies, particularly the American Missionary Association and the Freedmen's Aid Society, developed extensive industrial departments in some of their major black colleges and secondary schools. Both societies admitted that they established industrial courses in their schools, largely through gifts received from the Slater Fund.[50]

The sudden rise of industrial education in black schools during the 1880s has led some historians, particularly August Meier, to conclude that it became the "ascendant form of Negro education which temporarily eclipsed liberal and higher education." Yet a careful analysis of the curriculum reveals that industrial education was actually relegated to a subordinate role in most black colleges. In a useful and thorough study of the black colleges under mission societies, James M. McPherson demonstrates convincingly that the traditional liberal or classical curriculum remained dominant throughout the nineteenth and early twentieth centuries.[51] Most black colleges were under the direction of four major mission societies: the American Missionary Association; the Freedmen's Aid Society of the Methodist Episcopal Church; the American Baptist Home Mission Society; and the Board of Missions for the Freedmen of the Presbyterian Church in the U.S.A. A significant number of black secondary schools and colleges, however, were organized and controlled by black religious organizations. The African Methodist Episcopal Church, the Colored Methodist Episcopal Church, and the African Methodist Episcopal Zion Church established nearly all of the major colleges controlled by black organizations, and their combined voice largely articulated the educational policy of the black community. These institutions were never captured by the Hampton-Tuskegee pattern of black higher education and they gave low priority to industrial training. Consequently, at the close of the nineteenth century, the proponents of the Hampton Idea found little support for their model of industrial training. In fact, they faced powerful resistance, especially from important leaders in the mission societies.

The Northern mission societies generally accepted manual training courses such as printing, carpentry, blacksmithing, and the like, as areas for student work programs, the teaching of skilled trades, and character development, but tended to view such courses as relatively insignificant for intellectual and leadership training. The proponents of the Hampton model were never satisfied with the missionary interpretation of industrial training. Samuel Armstrong was one of the first to recognize that the industrial education concept left "a wide opportunity for difference of opinion as to the application of the principle, and these differences go deeper than the surface."[52] There were clear distinctions between the Hampton and the missionary model of industrial education. While Hampton established a system of menial labor, many leading missionary educators argued for high-level trade schools and departments of applied science and technology to train engineers, architects and industrial managers. At Hampton, industrial training was the core curriculum, while the mission societies maintained industrial education as an adjunct to the classical or liberal academic curriculum. The Hampton model was organized around a conservative sociopolitical ideology that advocated the political disfranchisement and economic subordination of the black race. The mission societies emphasized literary and professional training to develop a black intelligentsia that would fight for political and civil equality. Thus, there was far more discord than harmony between the two camps.

The missionary vanguard was headed by Thomas J. Morgan, Henry L. Morehouse, and Malcolm MacVicar of the American Baptist Home Mission Society, and Joseph E. Roy and William Hayes Ward of the American Missionary Association. Morgan, a colonel of the Fourteenth United States Colored Infantry during the Civil War and former Commissioner of Indian Affairs, served as executive secretary of the Baptist Home Mission Society from 1893 to 1902 and as editor of the Society's influential *Home Mission Monthly* for the same period. Morehouse was the executive secretary of the American Baptist Education Society. MacVicar, Superintendent of the Home Mission Society's Educational Department from 1890 to 1900, headed the Society's Virginia Union University from 1900 to 1904. Ward, one of the most vigorous defenders of black higher education, was for many years chairman of the American Missionary Association's executive committee, and was associate editor, 1868-1870; superintending editor, 1870-1896; and editor from 1896 to 1913 of the New York *Independent*. His colleague, Roy, was Field Superintendent of the American Missionary Association. The status of these men in missionary activities and in the larger society enabled them to form a powerful vanguard that stood clearly and unswervingly for black higher education and for the development of advanced technical schools to prepare blacks for executive and administrative capacities.[53]

This vocal missionary leadership objected to the Hampton model on the grounds that it undermined the democratic rights of blacks by assuming that black students were destined for a subordinate industrial role in the Southern economy. Following a conference on black education at the 1895 American Social Science Association, Morgan and Ward attacked the "reviving Negrophobia" which opposed the higher education of blacks and laid "special stress upon the necessity of Industrial training." Morgan, through the *Home Mission Monthly,* and Ward, in the *Independent,* "protest[ed] vehemently against any philosophy of education which will restrict the Negro schools to industrial training, or to rudimentary education." Moreover, they suspected "that the prime motive of the white men in the South who urge most strongly the industrial education of the Negroes, is the conviction in their minds that all the Negro needs to know is how to work. This proceeds upon the assumption that the race is doomed to servitude." The Negro industrial education concept, as Morgan and Ward understood it, was "based upon the denial of the humanity of a whole race" and was calculated to make the Negro "absolutely content with his lot as a servant." In contrast to the Hampton model of industrial training, Morgan urged the mission societies to create and endow technical schools "to develop among them [blacks] architects, artists, engineers, master mechanics, superintendents of mines, overseers of mills," etc. On another occasion, after politely stating his sympathy for Booker T. Washington, Morgan downgraded the manual training concept in favor of "the higher grade of industrial training proper, such as is now furnished in Pratt Institute and other similar institutions in the North."[54]

Generally, the missionary leaders were diplomatic in their handling of the industrial education movement, and they attempted to check its growth by vigorously defending the need for black higher education. "Neglect, if you will, the common school education in your missionary labor; neglect, if you must, the industrial education," advised Ward, "but never forget that it is your work to educate leaders." To the mission societies, leadership training meant, above all, higher literary education. According to Morehouse, the Home Mission Society believed in "the thorough humanity of the black man, with divine endowment of all the facilities of the white man; capable of culture, capable of high attainments under proper conditions and with sufficient time; a being not predestined to be simply a hewer of wood and drawer of water for the white race." Morehouse claimed that the black race would progress largely through the wise leadership of a gifted intelligentsia, and he, therefore, placed top priority on the higher education of the "talented tenth." Morgan also thought that black progress depended on the leadership of "noble and powerful minds raised up from their own ranks." Similarly, MacVicar argued for the highest form of liberal education because the mental development of the black man followed "precisely the same laws as in the case of the white man."[55]

Significantly, the views of the missionary vanguard were shared by white presidents who presided over the mission societies' black colleges and secondary schools. Henry S. DeForest, president of the American Missionary Association's Talladega College, contended "that while all should have the lower education, a great many should receive the higher." As he put it, "Every man may need silver, but the best commerce of the world requires that some should have gold, and a good deal of it." DeForest stated that Talladega had "not forgotten the industrial education"; however, the college's primary goal was to offer the black students "choice scholarship." George Sale, president of Atlanta Baptist College (Morehouse), informed the white Georgia State Teacher's Association that he objected to "the idea that the education of the Negro should be exclusively or distinctly industrial." If classical studies were valuable for whites, Sale asked, "Why should they not have the same value for Negroes?" E. C. Mitchell, president of Leland University in New Orleans, reasoned that it was purposeless to include industrial training in black colleges because "every village has its Negro mechanics who are patronized both by white and colored employers, and any who wish to learn the trade can do so." He viewed industrial training as a form of "class education" for blacks and argued that it did "not educate, even in trades." Likewise, Presidents Charles F. Meserve of Shaw University, George F. Genung of Richmond Theological

Seminary, and MacVicar of Virginia Union University, regarded industrial training as relatively insignificant to the higher education of black students.[56]

To be sure, many other college presidents were less adamant in their opposition to industrial training. In fact, most probably considered industrial education as a positive addition to the black students' general academic program. Even so, they relegated industrial training to a subordinate role in the curriculum. A. C. Osborn, president of Benedict College, saw some usefulness in industrial training, but as he clearly stated, "Benedict is not a trade or industrial school, in that it does not give the industrial work the foremost place." President L. G. Barrett of Jackson College also praised the positive aspects of limited industrial training while emphasizing that his college directed black students "on to higher study." In short, Ward spoke well for the missionary leadership when he said, "Industrial education is good, very valuable, and we give it as an adjunct, but it is not an important thing." Thus, the missionary idea of industrial education profoundly differed from the Hampton Idea.[57]

The conflicting ideologies of black education led to some significant confrontations between the missionary and Hampton camps in the late nineteenth century, and the outcome shaped the Hampton's advocates' course of action at the turn of the century. In 1890, following a suggestion of ex-President Rutherford B. Hayes, Quaker philanthropist Albert K. Smiley organized a conference at his Lake Mohonk resort hotel in the Catskills to discuss the "Negro Question." In order to be sure and get the Southern white men to come," wrote Armstrong, "he [Smiley] decided not to invite any colored people."[58] Modeled on the annual Indian conferences at Mohonk, the Negro conferences of 1890 and 1891 concentrated essentially on education. Samuel C. Armstrong, Hollis B. Frissell, Chairman Rutherford B. Hayes of the Slater Fund, and the like, argued strongly for the Hampton model as the best form of black education. Typical were the words of Armstrong: "The great mass of Negroes must be farmers and they need to be taught to farm intelligently." But, whether blacks were forced to be farmers or not, the missionary educators objected to the idea of imposing a unique form of second-class industrial training on the black race. Reverend Roy, Secretary of the American Missionary Association, after making a brilliant defense of the Negro's right to higher education, informed the Hampton supporters that it was "too late in the history of civilization to impose any repression upon any class of people." Similarly, William T. Harris, United States Commissioner of Education, admonished the conference that it was "not in the province nor in the power of one class to determine the metes and bounds of another class..." "I claim, therefore," said Harris, "the Negroes' right to an education from a, b, up to Syriac, from the multiplication table up to conic sections. Or, if there is anything higher than that, that higher thing, whatever it may be." Ward and MacVicar also supported higher education and equal rights for black people. Even though blacks were barred from the Mohonk conference on the Negro Question, the Hampton boosters failed to achieve a consensus in support of industrial Normal schools for training black leaders.[59]

Another debate regarding the "Instruction of the Colored Citizens" was held at the 1896 annual conference of the American Social Science Association. The major address was given by Hampton booster H. L. Wayland, the editor of the *New York Examiner,* who retired as president of the American Social Science Association in 1894. Wayland took great care to summon distinguished black supporters of the Hampton model, particularly Booker T. Washington and Hugh M. Browne, principal of a Washington, D.C., black high school. He wrote Robert C. Ogden, President of the Hampton Board of Trustees:

> On Tuesday evening, September 1, I shall read a paper at the Social Science, at Saratoga, on the higher education of the Southern colored, which will be followed by a debate. We hope to have Prof. Washington, who is heartily with us, and I shall ask Mr. Durham and one or two others.... Now what I want to say is this, will you not make it a point to be present.

Ogden did not attend the conference, but Wayland, Washington, and Browne gave an adequate defense of the Hampton Idea. To these men, as Wayland so aptly phrased it, the whole question of black education could be summarized in two words: "these two words are 'Hampton' and 'Tuskegee.'" But Morgan, Atlanta University Professor Silas X. Floyd, and Malcolm MacVicar were not persuaded by the arguments of the Hampton supporters. "I submit," replied Morgan, "that no form of industrial training yet devised can take the place of a college curriculum in giving breadth of knowledge, catholicity of sympathy, power of thought, constructive ability and fitness for leadership." Floyd and MacVicar joined Morgan in rejecting industrial training as an appropriate model of education for the black leadership. Wayland, in describing the results of the debate to Ogden, revealed that he was very much frustrated by the resistance to the Hampton Idea:

> Gen. Morgan and Dr. MacVicar held on to the old theory. I am surprised that they do not take counsel with common sense. Probably they would say, "The Colored people demand Greek and Latin, and if we do not give it to them, they will go elsewhere." But to that I would reply, "Both Hampton and Tuskegee have annually more applications than they can receive." And also it is our duty to give them what we conscientiously think best, and it is our right to do so since we pay for it ourselves.

It became increasingly clear to the advocates of the Hampton model that a powerful cadre of missionary educators, in addition to important black leaders, would never accept industrial training as the dominant form of black education. In 1895 and 1896, Wayland was sharply assailed for making rather caustic criticisms of black higher education. Even President William McKinley was chastised by Ward when, in 1898, the President praised Tuskegee for giving black students instruction in "practical industry" and for not "attempting the unattainable" by offering higher education. Ward replied acidly:

"What there is 'unattainable' to the Negro, or what school offers the unattainable, we do not know." The missionary vanguard met well the challenge of the Hampton ideologues and effectively blocked the spread of the Hampton doctrine in the mission schools; thus, at the close of the nineteenth century, the Hampton spokesmen found themselves cut off from the mainstream of black higher education.[60]

The Plan to Hamptonize

It is generally assumed that by 1895 industrial education had reached its zenith, and that Booker T. Washington entered the picture as the most widely recognized spokesman of a broadly accepted philosophy of black education. This half-truth, however, has obscured the critical distinctions between industrial education courses and the Hampton Idea. The varied groups supporting black education in the late nineteenth century understood these important differences. In his 1886 report to the Slater Fund, General Agent Atticus G. Haygood observed that most black colleges offered some form of industrial education. Spurred by such optimistic outlooks, some advocates of the Hampton model may have anticipated, momentarily, that the black colleges were on the brink of being converted to industrial Normal schools. Yet, two years later, Haygood reported sadly that "some of the best friends and supporters of the schools for Negroes in this country look with a degree of apprehension upon ... the industrial element in their work." When J. L. M. Curry became general agent of the Slater Fund in 1890, he soon called for "clearer ideas of manual training." Curry, a Hampton booster, noted correctly that for many persons manual training was "considered as accomplished, when a shop becomes an adjunct or an annex to a school, and a practical mechanic is put in charge of it, with little or no regard to the instruction as an educational discipline." Curry, whose conception of industrial training was consistent with the Hampton model, reported in 1894 that none of the black colleges measured up to the right idea of industrial training.[61]

Consequently, Curry, with the support of Frissell and Washington, reduced the number of schools supported by the Slater Fund and pursued a policy of concentration, designed to better equip Hampton and Tuskegee. In 1883, Hampton and Tuskegee received a combined 13 percent of the Slater Fund appropriations, but more than 50 percent by 1902. Washington explained this policy: "The matter of training leaders in the larger [industrial] institutions is not an experiment. The evidence of the wisdom and value of such concentration are apparent on every hand in the South." He was referring specifically to leaders like himself.[62]

By the close of the nineteenth century, Hampton supporters recognized that their model of industrial training was very subordinate in the scheme of black higher education. Yet they were determined to advance the Hampton program as the dominant educational model for the training of black leaders. In 1899, Frissell planned a tour of several Southern cities to convert important black leaders to the Hampton Idea. Frissell wrote: "Our trustees have felt strongly that it is important to stir up the colored people to an interest in industrial education." He had no illusions about the vogue of industrial education in the black community. "As you know," wrote Frissell to a friend, "there is a perhaps natural feeling among them against this form of instruction..." But, to the Hampton ideologues, their form of industrial training represented the best solution to the Southern race problem, and they launched a campaign to impose it as a regional system of black education. As Ogden, the president of the Hampton Board of Trustees, declared: "The main hope is in Hampton and Hampton ideas. Our first problem is to support the School; our second to make the School ideas national." Or, as Hampton Trustee Collis Potter Huntington put it, "The only question is, Where shall we get another Booker T. Washington for these other schools?..." William H. Baldwin, Jr., the president of Tuskegee Institute Board of Trustees, said to Washington: "I tell you again that your course is the only one, and the work must be organized in other states, and you must do it, and we must get the money."[63]

This dogmatic determination to spread the Hampton model throughout the Afro-American South set the stage for the early twentieth century struggle over the education of black people. Though many historians would come to view this struggle mainly as the Washington-DuBois debate, it is well to remember that the Hampton model was launched in 1868, the year DuBois was born. The Washington-DuBois controversy merely represented one of the last great battles in the long war to determine whether black people would be educated to challenge or accommodate the oppressive Southern political economy. DuBois and his colleagues, however, would face a far more powerful and well-organized Hampton movement than the missionary and black educators of the late nineteenth century. Beginning in 1898, the Hampton model constantly gained support among Northern businessmen-philanthropists and Southern whites. The Hampton supporters also picked up additional support in the black community. But the Hampton movement gained momentum not primarily because of a climate favoring industrial education, but mainly because its supporters waged a well-organized campaign to spread the Hampton doctrines.

NOTES

1. For traditional interpretations of black industrial education *see: Negro Thought in America, 1880-1915: Racial Ideologies in the Age of Booker T. Washington* (Ann Arbor: The University of Michigan Press, 1963), 1968 edition, pp. 85–99; James M. McPherson, *The Abolitionist Legacy, From Reconstruction to the NAACP* (Princeton: Princeton University Press, 1975), pp. 210–218; Henry Snyder Enck, "The

Burden Borne: Northern White Philanthropy and Southern Black Industrial Education, 1900–1915'' (Ph.D. Dissertation, University of Cincinnati, 1970); Clyde Hall, *Black Vocational and Industrial Arts Education: Development and History* (Chicago: American Technical Society, 1973).

2. Mark Hopkins et al., *Report Upon the Hampton Normal and Agricultural Institute* (Hampton, Virginia, 1870), p. 8; Samuel C. Armstrong, *Principal's Annual Report of Hampton Institute* (Hampton: Normal School Press, 1887), p. 6; For Hampton's first twenty classes, 604 of 723 graduates reported teaching in 1890. See Samuel C. Armstrong, *Twenty-Two Years' Work of the Hampton Normal and Agricultural Institute* (Hampton: Normal School Press, 1893), p. 293; For enrollment in trades and agriculture, *see Catalogue of the Hampton Normal and Agricultural Institute* (Hampton: Hampton Institute Press, 1900), pp. 109, 114.

3. Francis A. Walker, "Industrial Education," *Journal of Social Science*, No. 19 (December, 1884), pp. 117–131; Berneice M. Fisher, *Industrial Education: American Ideas and Institutions* (Madison: University of Wisconsin Press, 1967); Burt Powell, *The Movement of Industrial Education and the Establishment of the University, 1840–1870* (Urbana: University of Illinois Press, 1918); Calvin M. Woodward, "The Results of the St. Louis Manual Training School," *Journal of Proceedings and Addresses of the National Education Association*, Vol. 28 (Topeka, Kansas, 1889), pp. 73–91.

4. *Proceedings of the Trustees of the John F. Slater Fund for the Education of Freedmen, 1883,* p. 14 (Hereafter listed as Slater Fund Proceedings).

5. Samuel C. Armstrong to Robert C. Ogden (January 24, 1878), Robert C. Ogden Papers, Library of Congress, Washington, D.C. (Hereafter listed as the Ogden Papers); *Southern Workman* XI (January, 1882), p. 3; III (December 1874), p. 90.

6. *Southern Workman*, V (November, 1876), p. 82; (October, 1876), p. 74; III (October 1874), p. 74; (December, 1874), p. 90; VI (April, 1877), pp. 26–27; "Too Much Politics," VIII (April, 1879), p. 39; "Politics," I (July, 1872), p. 2.

7. *Southern Workman*, V (November, 1876), p. 82; VIII (April, 1879), p. 39; IX (January, 1880), p. 3; VI (December, 1877), p. 90; Samuel C. Armstrong, "Normal School Work Among the Freedmen," Paper read before the National Education Association, at Boston (August 6, 1872), reprint in Hampton Institute Archives, Hampton, Virginia (Archives hereafter listed as HIA).

8. Ibid., Harlan, pp. 58–61; Francis G. Peabody, *Education for Life: The Story of Hampton Institute* (New York: Doubleday, Page and Company, 1919), pp. 57–58; Edith Armstrong Talbot, *Samuel Chapman Armstrong: A Biographical Study* (New York: Doubleday, Page and Company, 1904), p. 155; *Southern Workman*, X (January, 1881), p. 3; As quoted in Talbot, *Samuel Chapman Armstrong*, pp. 137, 170–171; Peabody, *Education for Life*, pp. 83, 90–91, 54; Samuel C. Armstrong, "The Founding of Hampton Institute," *Old South Leaflets*, VI (1890), pp. 6–7.

9. Samuel C. Armstrong, "A.M.A. Paper on the Negro Question," *Southern Workman*, VI (December, 1877), p. 94; "Can the Negro Do Anything?" VIII (September, 1879), p. 91; X (April, 1881), p. 39; "Normal School Work Among the Freedmen," p. 4; Samuel C. Armstrong, "Average Negro," *Southern Workman*, XIV (April, 1885), p. 38; Henry A. Bullock, *A History of Negro Education in the South: From 1619 to the Present* (Cambridge: Harvard University Press, 1967), 1970 edition by Praeger Publishers, p. 76; Louis R. Harlan, *Booker T. Washington: The Making of a Black Leader, 1856–1901* (New York: Oxford University Press, 1972), 1975 edition, p. 58.

10. *Southern Workman*, X (June, 1881), p. 63; VI (December,1877), p. 90; Samuel C. Armstrong, "Politics," *Southern Workman*, I (July, 1872), p. 2; III (December, 1874), p. 90; *Southern Workman*, X (June, 1881), p. 63; Armstrong, "The Average Negro," p. 38.

11. Armstrong, "A.M.A. Paper on the Negro Question," p. 94; Armstrong, "Normal School Work Among the Freedmen," pp. 4–5.

12. *Southern Workman,* VI (May, 1877), p. 34; "To Northern Employers and Southern Workers," VIII (December, 1872), p. 2; "On Labor in Georgia," VII (April, 1878), p. 25; *Southern Workman,* IV (January, 1875), p. 2; IX (January, 1880), p. 3; V (October, 1876), p. 74; VI (March, 1877), p. 18; Ibid.; Armstrong, "Too Much Politics," *Southern Workman,* VIII (April, 1879), p. 39.

13. Samuel C. Armstrong to Robert C. Ogden (October 7, 1878); Charles E. Whiting to Samuel C. Armstrong (December 28, 1878), Ogden Papers; *Southern Workman,* IX (June, 1880), p. 63; Isabel C. Barrows, editor, *First and Second Mohonk Conferences on the Negro Question* (Boston: George H. Ellis, 1890–91), 1969 reprint by Negro Universities Press, p. 15; See *Annual Report* in *Southern Workman,* XIV (June, 1885); *Southern Workman,* VI (March, 1877), p. 18; I (January, 1872), p. 2; IV (January, 1875), p. 2.

14. *Southern Workman,* VIII (September, 1879), p. 103; (June, 1879), p. 63; (August, 1879), p. 87; X (July, 1881), p. 75; VIII (November, 1879), p. 98; (June, 1879), p. 63; Tileston T. Bryce, "Negro Labor," *Southern Workman,* IX (April 1880), p. 45; Robert L. Church, *Education in the United States: An Interpretive History* (New York: The Free Press, 1976), p. 194.

15. *Southern Workman,* V (December, 1876); X (June, 1879); Booker T. Washington, "Industry and Education," Address at the Smead School in Toledo, Ohio (June 5, 1903), Booker T. Washington papers, Library of Contress; Washington, "The Progress of the Negro" (January 16, 1893), Washington Papers; Washington, "The Educational Outlook in the South," *The Journal of Proceedings and Addresses of the National Education Association,* Vol. 23 (Boston: J. E. Farewell and Company, 1885), p. 127.

16. Samuel C. Armstrong, Address before the 1877 Anniversary Meeting of the American Missionary Association, printed in *Southern Workman,* VI (December, 1877), p. 94; Harlan, *Booker T. Washington,* p. 61; Op. cit., *Hampton Institute Catalogue, 1876,* pp. 36, 41; *Southern Workman,* III (November, 1874), p. 44; VI (December, 1877), p. 94.

17. *Southern Workman,* IX (January, 1880), p. 3; Samuel Armstrong, *Principal's Annual Report of Hampton Institute* (June, 1874); *Southern Workman* (June, 1878), p. 41; "Normal School Work Among the Freedmen," p. 10.

18. *Southern Workman,* X (September, 1881), p. 91; VII (January, 1878), p. 2; XI (February, 1882), p. 16; VI (December, 1877), p. 94; "Normal School Work Among the Freedmen," p. 4.

19. Meier, *Negro Thought in America,* p. 93; *Hampton Institute Catalogue, 1876,* pp. 35–37; Samuel Armstrong, "Nothing To Do," *Southern Workman,* III (April, 1874), p. 26; VI (December, 1877), p. 94; X (September, 1881), p. 91.

20. Armstrong, "Normal School Work Among the Freedmen," p. 4; *Southern Workman,* III (April, 1874), p. 26; VI (December, 1877), p. 94; X (September, 1881), p. 91.

21. *Southern Workman,* XI (June, 1882), p. 67; XII (June, 1883), p. 71; XII (June, 1884), p. 72; XIV (June, 1885), p. 75; XVII (June, 1888), p. 68; Armstrong, *Principal's Annual Report of Hampton Institute* (June, 1876), p. 37.

22. For the paper as classroom reader, *see Southern Workman* VIII (September, 1879), p. 90; Tileston T. Bryce, *Economic Crumbs, or Plain Talks For the People About Labor, Capital, Money, Tariff, etc.* (Hampton, Virginia: Normal School Press, 1879); For series of articles *see* Bryce, "Rights and Duties of Citizens VI," *Southern Workman,* VII (September, 1878), p. 69; "Labor," VII (October, 1878), pp. 76–78; "Capital," VII (November, 1878), p. 85; "Wages," VIII (February, 1879), p. 16; "Strikes and Lock-Outs," IX (May, 1880), p. 57.

23. Ibid., "Capital"; Harlan, *Booker T. Washington,* p. 74.

24. Ibid., "Labor," "Wages"; In addition to Bryce's textbook, *Economic Crumbs* and the *Southern Workman,* the students also use Richard R. Bowker, *Economics for the People, Being Plain Talks on Economics, Especially For Use in Business, in Schools, and in Women's Reading Classes* (New York: Harper and Brothers, 1886); and Jesse Macy, *Our Government: How It Grew, What It Does, and How It Does It* (Boston: Girn and Company, 1886).

25. Samuel C. Armstrong, *Principal's Annual Report of Hampton Institute* (June, 1885), p. 42; *Southern Workman,* XI (June, 1882), p. 67; XI (August, 1882), p. 84; The 60 seniors of the 1882 class received the following percentages of correct answers: Mathematics, 34.8; History, 66.5; Chemistry 62.1; English Literature 62.5; Political Economy, 78.5; Harlan, *Booker T. Washington* see "Great White Father" chapter.

26. Samuel C. Armstrong, *Principal's Annual Report of Hampton Institute* (June, 1886), pp. 28–29; *Southern Workman,* VI (December, 1877), p. 94.

27. Armstrong, "Normal School Work Among the Freedmen," p. 9; *Southern Workman,* VI (December, 1877), p. 94; XX (June, 1891), p. 207; XVI (June, 1877), p. 73.

28. Samuel C. Armstrong, *Principal's Annual Report of Hampton Institute* (June, 1874), p. 9; *Annual Report* (June, 1887), p. 5; *Southern Workman,* VIII (June, 1879), p. 63; X (September, 1881), p. 91; XVII (June, 1888), pp. 65–66, 70–71; Harlan, *Booker T. Washington,* p. 72.

29. Op. cit., "Normal School Work Among the Freedmen," p. 9; Hopkins et al., *Annual Report Upon Hampton Institute* (June, 1870), pp. 5–6; for a catalogue of significant changes in the Hampton curriculum see *The Hampton Bulletin,* XIV (May, 1918), "Some Facts Relating to Hampton's Growth in Fifty Years," Appendix; Also see Peabody, *Education for Life,* pp. 366–367.

30. *Southern Workman,* XXI (June, 1893), p. 93.

31. Ibid., (June, 1893), p. 93; BWT (Washington's Report), "The Plucky Class," *Southern Workman,* IX (November, 1880), p. 112; Armstrong, *Principal's Annual Report of Hampton Institute* (June, 1887), p. 3.

32. "Industries," *Southern Workman,* XIX (June, 1890), p. 71–73.

33. *Southern Workman,* XIV (June, 1885), p. 90; XI (June, 1882), pp. 64–67; *Catalogue of Hampton Institute* (June, 1886), pp. 25–30; Washington, "The Plucky Class," *Southern Workman,* IX (November, 1880), p. 112.

34. Ibid., *Catalogue,* 1886, p. 28.

35. *Southern Workman,* XIV (June, 1885), p.

36. Harlan, *Booker T. Washington,* p. 63; Samuel C. Armstrong to Mary Jackson (February 10, 1879), Letterbook, 1879, p. 257; to John Walker (February 11, 1879), Letterbook, 1879, p. 257; to Richard Bolding (February 13, 1879); to Mrs. Lenny Dennis (February 15, 1879); to Mrs. Susan Clark (February 15, 1879); to Archer Bolden (February 15, 1879); to Mrs. Harris (May 25, 1876); to Andrew Strong (May 5, 1876); to Edmund G. White (June 16, 1874); Also see student Discipline Books; HIA; *Report of Hampton Normal and Agricultural Institute* (Richmond: Clemmitt and Jones, 1878), p. 10; *Report of Hampton Institute* (Richmond: William Jones, 1880), p. 13.

37. William W. Adams to Samuel C. Armstrong (March 6, 1878); Thomas Mann to Samuel C. Armstrong (January 12, 1888), HIA.

38. S. G. Alexander to Samuel C. Armstrong (January 9, 1888); John H. Boothe to Samuel C. Armstrong (January 10, 1888); J. F. Satterwhite to Samuel C. Armstrong (January 9, 1888); C. L. Marshall to Samuel C. Armstrong (January 9, 1888); HIA.

39. William K. Kiffie to Samuel C. Armstrong (January 10, 1890); J. A. Colbert to Samuel C. Armstrong (January 6, 1888); Perry Shields to Samuel C. Armstrong (January 11, 1888); O. H. Hawkins to Samuel C. Armstrong (January 12, 1888); Jack-

son M. Mundy to Samuel C. Armstrong (January 12, 1888); George Johnson to Samuel C. Armstrong (January 9, 1888); HIA.

40. Ibid., Shields, Boothe, Hawkins, Satterwhite, Johnson; W. H. Scotte to Samuel C. Armstrong (January 6, 1888).

41. Roberta Whiting to H. B. Frissell (November 11, 1894); James C. Rollins to Samuel C. Armstrong (July 19, 1877); W. Z. Ruth to Samuel C. Armstrong (January 9, 1890); G. G. Spraggins to Samuel C. Armstrong (January 10, 1890); Clayton Elks to Armstrong (January 9, 1890); HIA.

42. *Southern Workman,* VIII (June, 1879), p. 63; J. H. Tucker to Samuel C. Armstrong (January 6, 1888); Ibid., Hawkins; Moses David to Samuel C. Armstrong (January 9, 1888); Armstrong quoted in Barrows, editor, *Mohonk Conference on the Negro Question,* p. 15; Ibid., Shields.

43. Article on the creation of the Alumni Association in *Southern Workman,* VII (March, 1878), p. 19, N. B. Clark was elected Chairman and O. M. McAdoo, Secretary; The Alumni Association of Hampton Normal and Agricultural Institute (Signed by O. M. McAdoo, Clerk, and N. B. Clark, Chairman) to the Faculty of Hampton Institute (May 22, 1878), HIA.

44. *Southern Workman,* VIII (May, 1879), p. 52; XVII (June, 1888), p. 64; H. B. Frissell, *"The Progress of Negro Education,"* *South Atlantic Quarterly,* VI (January, 1907), p. 39; *Virginia Star,* as quoted in *Southern Workman,* VII (May, 1878), p. 33; *Christian Recorder,* as quoted in *Southern Workman,* IV (December, 1875), p. 90.

45. The Alexandria, Virginia, *People's Advocate* (July 1, 1876) and (July 8, 1876).

46. Henry M. Turner, "Wayside Dots and Jots," *Christian Recorder* (May 2, 1878).

47. *Virginia Star* (May 11, 1878); *Louisianian* (May 10, 1879); Diary of John M. Gregory in Gregory Papers, Series 2/1/1, Box No. 5, University of Illinois Archives, Urbana, Illinois.

48. Alexander Crummell, "The Attitude of the American Mind Toward the Negro Intellect," *The American Negro Academy Occasional Papers,* No. 3 (1898); See the review of Crummell's *Common Sense in Common Schooling* in the *A.M.E. Church Review,* Vol. 3 (January, 1887), pp. 319-320; Alexander Crummell to Frazier Miller (July 28, 1898), Crummell Papers.

49. Cleveland *Gazette* (June 27, 1890) and (November 17, 1900); The Washington *Bee* (October 19, 1895), (October 26, 1895), and (March 28, 1896).

50. *Southern Workman,* XIV (March, 1885), p. 25; XVII (June, 1888), p. 64; McPherson, *The Abolitionist Legacy,* p. 213; *Freedmen's Aid Society, Twenty-Fifth Annual Report, 1891,* pp. 151, 164, 210; *Quadrennial Report of the Freedmen's Aid and Southern Education Society* to the General Conference of the Methodist Church Held in Omaha, Nebraska (May, 1892), p. 6; *American Missionary,* XLVII (May, 1894), "Industries Taught in Our Schools," pp. 189-192.

51. Meier, *Negro Thought in America,* p. 99; Ibid., McPherson, Chapter 12, "Detour or Mainstream? The Curriculum of Missionary Schools."

52. *Southern Workman,* XIV (March, 1885), p. 25.

53. McPherson, *The Abolitionist Legacy.*

54. "Limiting Negro Education," *American Baptist Home Mission Monthly,* Vol. XVIII (March, 1896), pp. 98-100, 205-209 (Hereafter listed as *Home Mission Monthly*); New York *Independent* (September 26, 1895); (October 17, 1895); Thomas J. Morgan, "The Education of the Negroes," *Home Mission Monthly,* vol. XVII (October, 1895), pp. 368-373; Thomas J. Morgan, "Negro Education," *Home Mission Monthly,* vol. XXII (January, 1900), pp. 3-4; Morgan, "Defects of Industrial Education," *Home Mission Monthly,* vol. XXII (July, 1900), pp. 197-206.

55. William Hayes Ward, "Higher Education," *Home Mission Monthly,* vol. XXII (November, 1900), p. 322; *Home Mission Monthly,* vol. XVIII (April, 1896), p. 123;

Thomas J. Morgan, "Negro Preparation for Citizenship," *Home Mission Monthly,* vol. XVII (December, 1900), pp. 334–337; "The Higher Education of Colored Women," *Home Mission Monthly,* vol. XVIII (May, 1896), p. 160; *also see* Morgan, *The Negro in America and the Ideal American Republic* (Philadelphia: American Baptist Publication Society, 1898); *Home Mission Monthly,* vol. XVIII (April, 1896), p. 123.

56. Henry S. DeForest, "Does Higher Education Befit the Negro," *American Missionary,* vol. XLI (March, 1887), p. 73; *American Missionary,* vol. XLVIII (July, 1894), p. 288; George E. Sale, "The Education of the Negro," *Home Mission Monthly,* vol. XX (October, 1898), pp. 346–349; "Education in Our Home Mission Schools," *Home Mission Monthly,* vol. XVIII (June, 1896), pp. 222–223; As quoted in Benjamin Brawley, *History of Morehouse College* (Atlanta, Morehouse College, 1917), p. 68; E. C. Mitchell, "Higher Education and the Negro," *Home Mission Monthly,* vol. XVIII (September, 1896), p. 308; Charles F. Meserve, "Shaw University," *Home Mission Monthly,* vol. XXI (August, 1889), p. 316; George F. Genung, "Richmond Theological Seminary," Ibid., p. 309–311.

57. A. C. Osborn, "Benedict College"; L. G. Barrett, "Jackson College," *Home Mission Monthly,* vol. XVI (August, 1889), pp. 319, 327; William Hayes Ward, "Higher Education," *Home Mission Monthly,* vol. XXII (November, 1900), p. 322; The Freedmen's Aid Society was more conservative than the American Missionary Association and the Home Mission Society. Thus, it gave industrial training a higher place in the schools under its control. *See* Freedmen's Aid and Southern Education Society, Report of the Board of Managers to the General Committee at the Annual Meeting, held in Philadelphia (November 13 and 14, 1899), p. 2. Of the 5,383 black students in the Society's schools, 2,640 were in manual training courses, while none of the 3,997 whites were enrolled in such courses.

58. *Southern Workman,* XIX (May, 1890), p. 49; (July, 1890), p. 84; McPherson, *The Abolitionist Legacy,* p. 137.

59. Barrows, editor, *Mohonk Conference on the Negro Question,* p. 68; Joseph E. Roy, "The Higher Education of the Negroes' No Mistake," Ibid., p. 91; William T. Harris, "Normal School Training for the Negroes," Ibid., p. 84.

60. H. L. Wayland to Robert C. Ogden (July 21, 1896), Ogden Papers; H. L. Wayland, "Instruction of the Colored Citizens," *Journal of Social Science,* no. XXXIV (November, 1896), pp. 78, 83; H. L. Wayland to Robert C. Ogden (September 10, 1896), Ogden Papers; *Independent* (September 26, 1895); (October 17, 1895); *Home Mission Monthly,* vol. XVIII (March, 1896), p. 98; Brawley, *Morehouse College,* p. 67; President William McKinley's address at Tuskegee Institute, December 18, 1898, printed in *John F. Slater Fund Proceedings,* 1899, pp. 41–44; McPherson, *The Abolitionist Legacy,* p. 219; *Independent* (December 22, 1898).

61. Meier, *Negro Thought in America;* Enck, "The Burden Borne," p. 38; *John F. Slater Fund Proceedings,* 1888, p. 44; Atticus G. Haygood, "A General Statement Concerning Tool Craft Among the Negroes," New York *Observer* (April 5, 1888); *John F. Slater Fund Proceedings,* 1894, pp. 10–11, 15.

62. Louis P. Harlan, editor, *The Booker T. Washington Papers,* Vol. 4 (Urbana: University of Illinois Press, 1975), pp. 141–145. J. L. M. Curry to Booker T. Washington; Washington to Frissell, and Washington to Daniel Coit Gilman; *John F. Slater Fund Proceedings,* 1883, p. 20; Meier, *Negro Thought in America,* p. 96.

63. H. B. Frissell to Rev. H. C. Potter (February 22, 1899), HIA; Ogden as quoted in Enck, "The Burden Borne," p. 52; Harlan, editor, *Washington Papers,* pp. 499, 526.

Northern Philanthropy and the Training of the Black Leadership: Fisk University, a Case Study, 1915–1930

James D. Anderson

The training of black leaders to mediate conflicts between Afro-Americans and the dominant society was a major mission of black higher education from the Reconstruction era until well into the twentieth century. The black leader's task, as perceived by the various elites who financed and presided over the development of black colleges, was to reason with the masses, to persuade, to convince them of one or another philosophy of the Negro's place in American society. Educational elites held various conceptions of Afro-America's place in the larger society, and ideological divergence led naturally to disparate educational policies. The Hampton-Tuskegee elite, as previously demonstrated, was interested in training an accommodationist black leadership that would encourage the masses to observe willingly the complicated system of Southern racial hierarchy. On the other hand, the mission societies recognized and fought for a more liberal black leadership that would struggle persistently for civil and political equality. The black educational elite, on balance, encouraged the development of a more radical intelligentsia. Many black leaders and educators called for an educated black vanguard to articulate the political and economic interests of the black masses and to keep the masses aware of points where their interests were at variance with those of the dominant society.

In vital respects, the intense concern of various elites over the training of black leaders reveals their belief in the indispensability of a black intelligentsia to the social transformation of the larger black population. Regardless of the actual capacity of black intellectuals to persuade the masses toward certain lines of social action, it was widely believed that a college-bred black leadership was an indispensable element in either maintaining the status quo or in

I wish to thank the Rockefeller Foundation for permission to quote from their manuscripts.

enhancing the rebellion of the masses. As Gunnar Myrdal wrote in *An American Dilemma,*

> When the white people want to influence Negro attitudes in one direction or another ... the natural device (besides the long-range one of "education") is to appeal to the "community leaders." These leaders are expected to get it over to the Negro masses, who are supposed to be rather passive.[1]

Hence, the controlling elites in black education were much concerned about the ideological function of black institutions of higher learning.

A central theme in the history of black higher education, therefore, is the struggle for intellectual hegemony by various elites who held, among other educational concerns, strong interests in education as a vehicle for shaping the political and economic consciousness of the emergent black intelligentsia. This theme is well illustrated in the conflict between missionary philanthropists and industrial philanthropists over the "right" training of the black leadership and its role in adjusting the black population to the Southern political economy. As revealed in this case study of philanthropy and Fisk University, black colleges underwent important changes due to the ebb and flow of different power elites.

The American Missionary Association, Freedmen's Aid Society, Presbyterian Board of Missions for the Freedmen, and the American Baptist Home Mission Society were the most important contributors to black higher education from 1865 to 1915. These Northern mission societies, with a fervor reminiscent of the antebellum abolitionist crusade, embraced liberal education as a panacea for black emancipation and began a campaign in the Reconstruction era which laid the foundation for black higher education. By 1915 missionary philanthropists had established over one hundred colleges and secondary schools for blacks, and these institutions enrolled approximately 7,773 secondary students and 2,517 college and professional students. Thus, missionary educators could (and often did) boast of impressive achievements for their campaigns to establish black higher education. Their efforts came at a critical time when public secondary schools for Southern blacks were almost nonexistent, and there was virtually no public support for black higher education. Even DuBois, who was not noted for romanticizing white missionaries, praised the mission societies for producing over "thirty thousand black teachers in the South" which wiped out the illiteracy of the majority of black people in America.[2]

The missionary philanthropists, basically equalitarian in their views of race relations, launched the movement for black higher education as a means to produce a college-bred black vanguard that would lead the race in its struggle for equal rights. The missionaries naturally offered the New England classical curriculum as the key to Southern black progress and were very self-righteous about their programs to assimilate blacks into the culture of white Protestant society. But to more conservative whites, both North and South, the equalitarian creed of the missionary colleges threatened to prolong the racial crisis in Southern society. Conservative white America was perturbed and fearful of the missionaries' push for racial equality and particularly of their efforts to train a black leadership that would demand the right to participate fully in the promise of American life.

The missionary philanthropists' defiance of Southern racism never reached its potential challenge. By 1900 they were poverty stricken, and their programs to establish and sustain independent black colleges were rapidly diminishing in scope and activity. In looking at the future of black higher education, the missionaries had many reasons to be downhearted. By any standards, the material and financial status of black colleges was bad. They were understaffed, meagerly equipped, and poorly financed. The combined efforts of the missionary and black organizations could not raise sufficient funds to meet annual operating expenses, to increase teachers' salaries, expand the physical plant, improve the libraries, or purchase new scientific and technical equipment. But more importantly, almost all of the missionary black colleges were totally without sufficient endowments to insure their survival. Cut off from the aid of the federal government and the Southern states, combined with the impoverished state of the mission societies, the black colleges entered the twentieth century starved for funds. Thus, they were in an extremely dependent position.

The decline of missionary philanthropy was accompanied by the ascendancy of industrial philanthropy which had been struggling to become a dominant force in Southern education since the establishment of the Peabody Fund in 1867 and the Slater Fund in 1881. As the abolitionists launched the campaign for equal rights after emancipation and sought to train a progressive black leadership to lessen the force of Southern racism, industrial philanthropists, backed by Northeastern capitalists, struggled to achieve black subordination, and attempted to develop a conservative black leadership that would encourage the race to submit willingly to a racial caste system.[3] Throughout the nineteenth century industrial philanthropists remained subordinate in the scheme of black higher education, concentrating their funds mainly on Hampton and Tuskegee to support an accommodationist black leadership which sought to retain blacks in the South primarily as unskilled and semi-skilled agricultural and domestic laborers. Moreover, the subordinate role of industrial philanthropy during the nineteenth century was due in large part to the more economically and politically powerful missionary movement that controlled virtually all of the significant black colleges.

But by 1901 industrial philanthropists cemented an important alliance with Southern white leaders which was ratified by the creation of two major educational foundations, the Southern Education Board in 1901 and the General Education Board in 1902. The Southern Education Board, intersectional in membership and financed largely by Northern philanthropists, was a propaganda organization that concentrated primarily on arousing Southern white support for universal education. The General Education Board, established in 1902 by John D. Rockefeller, served as a clearinghouse for industrial philanthropy and disbursed grants to institutions and educational agencies. The membership of both Boards was almost the same and, in 1914, the General Education Board absorbed the Southern Education Board. The General Education Board became a powerful philanthropic trust as Rockefeller supplemented his initial grant of $1,000,000 by others amounting to $53,000,000 by 1909. Moreover, the Board became an interlocking directorate of Northern philanthropy as its members directed the disbursements of the Peabody and Slater Funds and the Anna T. Jeanes Foundation which was established in 1907. As Louis Harlan so aptly put it, the Board assumed "virtual monopolistic control of educational philanthropy for the South and the Negro."[4]

The industrial philanthropists were more concerned with education as a means to economic organization and efficiency and political stability than with the civil and human rights of Southern blacks. Economically, they were similar to other twentieth century urban reformers who demanded an organized and efficient agricultural sector to supplement the emergent industrial nation.[5] Their concern for Southern agricultural prosperity was inextricably bound to black farm workers, especially in a period of declining rural population and rapid urban growth. To the philanthropists, the black worker was the last best hope to stimulate material prosperity in the South's agricultural economy. Thus, New York philanthropist Robert C. Ogden, president of the Southern Education Board, expressed the organization's philosophy in these words: "Our great problem is to attach the Negro to the soil and prevent his exodus to the city." In his view, "The prosperity of the South depend[ed] upon the productive power of the black man."[6] The industrial philanthropists comfortably embraced the idea that blacks should perform the lowest form of labor in the Southern economy. Railroad executive William H. Baldwin, president of the General Education Board, fittingly stated the philanthropists' policy of black economic servitude:

> In the Negro is the opportunity of the South. Time has proven that he is best fitted to perform the heavy labor in the Southern states. "The Negro and the mule is the only combination so far to grow cotton." The South needs him; but the South needs him educated to be a suitable citizen. Properly directed he is the best possible laborer to meet the climatic conditions of the South. He will willingly fill the mere menial positions, and do the heavy work, at less wages, than the American white man or any foreign race which has yet come to our shores. This will permit the Southern white laborers to perform the more expert labor, and to leave the fields, the mines, and the simpler trades for the Negro.

Despite the self-delusion of some reformers and the pronouncements of many historians, the industrial philanthropists' interest in Southern education, especially in black education, was not primarily out of compassion or a desire for

Negro advancement, but was based mainly on the belief that there could be no Southern economic revival, no consequent sound national economy, without a properly trained black work force. Most industrial philanthropists mirrored Ogden's and Baldwin's views of Southern educational reform.[7]

Their interest in harnessing the black race as the dominant laboring force for Southern agriculture motivated the philanthropists to organize a black leadership that would encourage the race to at least tolerate a subordinate status. At the dawn of the twentieth century they were optimistic that Hampton and Tuskegee would produce a conservative black vanguard that would convince the black masses to remain in the South as efficient servants and agricultural laborers. Ogden, who was at once president of Hampton's and Tuskegee's Board of Trustees, maintained that Tuskegee's "first and large work" was to produce "industrial leadership, especially in agriculture." Booker T. Washington, of course, typified this black industrial vanguard which pressed the race to seek its fortune in Southern agriculture. By 1905 the philanthropists, with Washington's assistance, had organized a vanguard to propagate the Hampton-Tuskegee Ideology. Included in this leadership was Robert Moton of Hampton Institute; Isaac Fisher, principal of the Colored Branch Normal College in Pine Bluffs, Arkansas; W. J. Edwards, principal of Snow Hill Institute in Alabama; Henry A. Hunt, principal of Fort Valley High and Industrial School; and William H. Holtzclaw, principal of Utica, Mississippi's Industrial and Normal School. Convinced that this type of leadership could achieve ideological hegemony over the black South, the industrial philanthropists largely supported the Hampton-Tuskegee pattern of black education from 1880 to 1915, and generally rejected higher education for blacks as having no immediate utility. As Baldwin put it, "Except in the rarest of instances, I am bitterly opposed to the so-called higher education of Negroes."[8]

Thus, industrial philanthropists took care to avoid giving grants to the missionary black colleges. Black and white equalitarians misperceived the philanthropists' actions as opposition to black collegiate education. Yet, the philanthropists were not as opposed to the idea of black higher education as they were to the type of black leaders which emerged from the missionary institutions. Industrial philanthropists, in contrast to the black and white equalitarians, believed that black opposition to the Southern racial hierarchy threatened to prolong the "Negro problem" and prevent the political and economic compromises prerequisite to bring the South abreast of Northeastern industrial standards. To the philanthropists, if black leaders would exhort their people to accept and be content with menial labor and a subordinate racial status, the South would achieve political stability and economic progress. They viewed the achievement of order and material prosperity more critical to the national welfare than the continued agitation of black and white liberals for equalitarian changes.

From the Reconstruction period until World War I, the industrial philanthropy relied primarily on certain black graduates of Hampton and Tuskegee to propagate its conservative ideology of racial subordination. Specifically, Hampton graduates Booker T. Washington, Robert R. Moton, and W. T. B. Williams were the leading ideologues of the accommodationist ideology. Later they were joined by graduates of Tuskegee such as Isaac Fisher and W. J. Edwards. To be sure, the accommodationist spirit was not confined to Hampton and Tuskegee, but its leadership was located in these centers and the Industrial philanthropists looked mainly to Hampton and Tuskegee to produce a conservative black leadership. The philanthropists were apparently satisfied with this arrangement during the time (1890–1915) of Washington's leadership. By 1915, however, as the more radical black intelligentsia increased in status and power, the philanthropists, in a desperate attempt to influence the ideological development of emerging black leaders, were forced to challenge the equalitarian traditions of the missionary black colleges. Thus, instead of ignoring the black colleges the philanthropists were suddenly compelled to attempt to control them in order to keep alive their efforts to win the ideological allegiance of influential black leaders.[9]

A confluence of shifting political circumstances and racial developments generated philanthropic interests in the black college. Significantly, they recognized that the Tuskegee machine was rapidly losing ground to the college-bred black vanguard. In 1911, Peabody admitted privately that the "large majority" of blacks followed DuBois.[10] This discovery broke forth with unprecedented force after World War I with the growing militancy of the young black intellectuals. The rising tide of this new mood was manifested in the emergence of a more radical black press, the regional and local expansion of the NAACP, and the literary tenor of the Harlem renaissance. Even more importantly, the rank and file black population was rapidly outstripping its intellectuals in resisting the subordinate status accorded the race. The nationalist politics of Marcus Garvey's incredible mass movement, and the race riots which spread across the nation from 1917 to 1919 demonstrated the increased politicization of the black community. Moreover, the migration of blacks from the South to the urban North, also a political reply of the masses, indicated the weakness of the accommodationist ideology which urged blacks to remain in the South principally as agricultural and domestic workers. What started in 1900 as largely a regional question had become by 1920 a national race problem. From the vantage point of the philanthropists, this situation increased the urgency to obtain the allegiance of the ascendant black intellectual class.[11]

The industrial philanthropists' first major attempt to control black higher education came in 1915 when the General Education Board decided to "take hold" of Fisk University and develop it as a model college for black youth. The pre-eminent Fisk University was founded and supported initially by the American Missionary Association. To the philanthropists, it was the "capstone" of black higher education. Wallace Buttrick, then president of the General Education Board, said "Perhaps the most promising of the academic institutions for the higher education of the Negro is Fisk University." Outside of

Howard University, Fisk had nearly twenty percent of the black college students enumerated in the Federal Report of 1917. Only two Southern black colleges had at that time one-fourth as many college students as Fisk. Thus, when the General Education Board held a private conference in 1915 to discuss the future of black higher education, Fisk University's President Fayette Avery McKenzie was invited as a key representative of black higher education.[12]

McKenzie, a sociologist at the Ohio State University before coming to Fisk in 1915, was quickly regarded by industrial philanthropists as the kind of leader that would help make Fisk a more conservative institution. More than any of his predecessors, McKenzie sought to make Fisk acceptable to the white South and urged its graduates to concentrate on the economic development of the region. In his inaugural address McKenzie paid homage to Fisk's liberal arts tradition but introduced a new concept of "service" education which promised that the college would help restore the South to economic prosperity. He maintained that,

> It was the function of Fisk to increase the material wealth of the nation ... Fisk University claims the right to say that it will be one of the chief factors in achieving larger prosperity for the South. Every dollar spent here in the creation of power may mean a thousand dollars of increase in wealth of the South within a single generation.

McKenzie attempted to persuade Fisks' students to forsake equalitarian principles and to work within the Southern racial hierarchy to improve the region's industrial efficiency and maintain interracial cooperation.[13] This policy pleased the industrial philanthropists and they hailed McKenzie's inauguration as a new and wise departure from the missionary tradition.

Consequently, as Raymond Wolters has demonstrated, McKenzie set out to convince the industrial philanthropists that "Fisk students were not radical egalitarians but young men and women who had learned to make peace with the reality of the caste system." To this end, McKenzie disbanded the student government association, forbade student dissent, and suspended the Fisk Herald, the oldest student publication among black colleges. He would not allow a campus chapter of the NAACP and instructed the librarian to excise radical articles in the NAACP literature. Student discipline was rigorously enforced, special "Jim Crow" entertainments were arranged for the white benefactors of the university and Paul D. Cravath, the president of the Fisk Board of Trustees, endorsed complete racial separation as "the only solution to the Negro problem." McKenzie would not allow certain forms of social intercourse such as dancing and holding hands, and he justified his code of discipline on the grounds that black students were particularly sensuous beings who needed to be subjected to firm control. In short, McKenzie attempted to repress student initiative, undermine their equalitarian spirit, and control their thinking on race relations in order to produce a class of black intellectuals that would uncomplainingly accept the Southern racial hierarchy.[14]

From the outset industrial philanthropists reinforced McKenzie's behavior by contributing their economic and political support to his regime. Philanthropists Julius Rosenwald, who visited Fisk at McKenzie's installation, was initially ambivalent about the possibility of transforming the college into an accommodationist institution. In revealing his "mixed feelings" about Fisk students to Abraham Flexner (the secretary of the General Education Board), Rosenwald stated, "There seemed to be an air of superiority among them and a desire to take on the spirit of the white university rather than the spirit which has always impressed me at Tuskegee." To Rosenwald and other industrial philanthropists, Tuskegee was training black leaders to maintain a separate and subordinate Negro society. They were primarily interested in supporting black institutions committed to this mission. Thus, Flexner assured Rosenwald that McKenzie, with the help of industrial philanthropy, was working to transform Fisk into an institution more acceptable to Southern white society. Toward this end, the General Education Board began appropriating in 1916 about $12,000 annually to help Fisk pay its yearly operating expenses. In 1917, the Board contributed $50,000 to Fisk for endowment and building purposes and persuaded the Carnegie Corporation to give the same amount. Still Fisk had no substantial endowment, was deeply indebted, its physical plant was deteriorating, and its faculty was poorly paid. According to Hollingsworth Wood, vice chairman of the Fisk Board of Trustees, "$1,600 has been the maximum salary of a professor at Fisk University. This has meant lack of food in some cases." Fisk authorities knew that the college could not really survive without a sizeable endowment, and sufficient money could be raised only from the industrial philanthropists. Under these circumstances, however, a certain amount of compromise was required. As McKenzie put it, "intimation has been made to me from several sources that if we continue to behave ourselves, if we are efficient in teaching and administration and continue to hold the right relationship to our environment, we can expect large and highly valuable financial aid in carrying out a great program at Fisk."[15]

The philanthropists' financial assistance to Fisk University was accompanied by a new coalition of Negro accommodationists, Southern whites, and Northern businessmen who took control of the University's administration from the old alliance of black and white equalitarians. McKenzie and the philanthropists restructured the Fisk Board of Trustees to reflect the new power realities. In October of 1915 Thomas Jesse Jones, director of the Phelps-Stokes Fund, informed Flexner of the new changes:

> The Board of Trustees is being strengthened. Governor Brumbaugh and two influential colored men have been added in the last few weeks. With Mr. Cravath and Dr. Washington as trustees and the constant attention which I can give to the institution, we have at least a guarantee of fairly sound educational policy.

By 1919 Jones was Executive Secretary of the Fisk Board of Trustees and one of five members on the Executive Committee. In 1920 the philanthropists, acting through the General Education Board, agreed to spearhead a campaign to obtain for Fisk a two-million dollar endowment and their strength on the University's Board of Trustees increased. William H. Baldwin, son of the General Education Board's first chairman, was appointed by the Board to chair the endowment committee. He was immediately appointed to the Fisk Board of Trustees and became in 1924 the chairman of the trustees' executive committee. Other conservatives were added as the philanthropists moved in a quiet and forceful manner to reorganize the school's administration. In May of 1920, Fisk University's trustee Hollingsworth Wood notified the president of the General Education Board that,

> Dr. Moton of Tuskegee is now on the Board; Miss Ella Sachs, daughter of Samuel Sachs, and a close friend of the Rosenwalds, is an eager new member; and Mrs. Beverly B. Mumford of Richmond, Virginia adds an excellent influence from the Southern viewpoint.

The traditional missionary egalitarians were gradually pushed off the Fisk Board of Trustees. They were replaced mainly by Northern businessmen and a few conservative Negroes who were virtually hand-picked by industrial philanthropists. The philanthropists were actually raising an endowment for a new Fisk that was largely controlled by their agents and supporters.[16]

The philanthropists no doubt hoped that their economic and firm political hold on Fisk would squelch the school's equalitarian tradition and allow them to develop a more conservative black professional class. In 1923 the General Education Board generated a memorandum on the Fisk endowment campaign which emphasized the urgent need to train "the right type of colored leaders" who would help make the Negro "a capable workman and a good citizen." The philanthropists recognized that they were facing a new situation between the races. "How the Negro is going to get on in this country and what his relations are to be with the whites, are no longer problems of a single section; they are national," the memorandum stated. To the philanthropists, this new situation, in the context of growing race friction, increased the necessity of training "the right kind" of black leaders. The report maintained that,

> Due to various experiences during and since the World War, there is a growing disposition among the Negroes to suspect all white men and their motives and therefore to break all contacts with them and go it alone. Because such a movement by ten percent of the population is obviously futile, is no reason to overlook the fact that ten percent is a large enough proportion to cause considerable harm if permitted to go off at a tangent from the general interest. This very real menace to the public welfare makes the strengthening of school facilities for Negroes a matter of national significance.

The philanthropists reasoned that they could define and generally direct the socio-political paths of the black race by controlling its professional class.

> The Negro has become extremely race-conscious and turns to his teachers, preachers, newspapers, doctors, and professional men and women for leadership. The training of these persons, because of their leadership, thus becomes of primary importance to the future of the Negro and to the general welfare of the nation.

It was on the basis of such considerations that industrial philanthropists were motivated to "select a leading Negro college for proper development." This development, as the memorandum stated, was aimed primarily at "helping the Negro to the sane and responsible leadership that the South wants him to have." To the white South, "sane" Negro leadership was that type of guidance which sought to make the race content with servile living and working conditions. The philanthropists, in their efforts to restore the South to political order and economic prosperity, urged black leaders to advocate industrial efficiency and non-resistance to the region's racial hierarchy.[17]

By 1920, however, there was no powerful segment of the black intelligentsia that would cooperate with the philanthropists in their efforts to settle the "Negro problem" by compromising the fundamental rights of American blacks. In March of 1920, the *Crisis* published a revealing article by Harry H. Jones which essentially argued that, except for R. R. Moton, few black leaders accepted the Washington philosophy of accommodation. The liberal and radical wings of the black intelligentsia were the ascendant political voices in the black community and the philanthropists understood the meaning of this change to their own political program. Philanthropist George Peabody, having read the Jones' article, apprised Hampton's principal James Gregg of its implications:

> It is clear to me, with the Negro people having found themselves in a general way, during the war excitement, there is some danger of sharp definitely conscious line of division. We must, I think, give great weight in the present temper of susceptibility to the advertising influence of the *Crisis* and other publications, including James Weldon Johnson in The New York *Age.*

The problem then, for the philanthropists, was how to secure an articulate black conservative wing with sufficient status within the race to counter the influence of men like DuBois, Trotter, and Johnson.[18]

Peabody wanted a conservative black leader to "write the most effective reply, which I have in mind, to the article in the March issue of the *Crisis.*" Significantly he did not believe that Moton or Fred Moore, the New York *Age's* editor who sympathized with Moton's accommodationist philosophy, had sufficient status as black leaders to challenge Johnson and DuBois. In fact, Peabody could only think of Isaac Fisher as a potentially effective ideologue of the industrial philanthropic view. Interestingly, Fisher, a Tuskegee graduate who took his ideology from Washington, was appointed to the Fisk administration shortly after McKenzie became president. When McKenzie suspended the student operated *Fisk Herald* he established the conservative *Fisk University News* and made Fisher its editor. Following the bitter race riots of 1919, in a period of rising black militancy, Fisher called for the return of the "conservative Negro." He castigated the liberal and radical segments of the black intelligentsia which he claimed had "muzzled" the voice of the conservative Negro, and taken away his "mandate to speak for his race." Fisher defined the conservative Negro leader as one who urged his people to lay a foundation in economic efficiency, to submit willingly to the laws and customs of the South, and to work for better race relations through the guidance of the "best white South." Toward this end, he instituted at Fisk in 1917 a seminar on "Race Relations" and later became a member of the Southern white dominated Commission on Interracial Co-operation. Yet such conservatives as Fisher and Moton could not really challenge the intellectual hegemony which the liberals and radicals had achieved over the black community by 1917. DuBois probably expressed the dominant black view of the conservative wing when he informed the Commission on Interracial Co-operation that, "Isaac Fisher represents nothing but his own blubbering self. Major Moton is a fine fellow, but weak in the presence of white folks." To DuBois and many other black leaders who demanded full American rights for blacks, Moton and Fisher were "the sort of Colored men that we call 'White Folks' Niggers.'"[19]

But despite the protest of independent intellectuals like DuBois, Trotter, and Johnson, the private black college shouldered the main burden of educating the emerging black intellectual class. Southern white institutions would not accept black students and Northern white institutions would only allow token black representation. The black state and Federally supported schools generally were not allowed to offer liberal arts degrees. Outside of Howard University, which enrolled 1,053 college students, in 1917, the 27 black land grant and state institutions enrolled only 52 college students. The philanthropists understood this reality and black private schools were told to accommodate to philanthropic interest or starve. As Flexner put it, the philanthropists would "not try to suppress them or consolidate them, but just let them 'sweat.'" For a long period the black college paid dearly for its independence and equalitarianism but was forced by economic circumstances to eventually compromise with industrial philanthropy. Even the most equalitarian black leaders understood this dilemma. President John Hope of Morehouse, a courageous and dedicated leader for black equal rights, was compelled to turn to Washington for economic support in 1910. Hope especially wondered if his friend, DuBois, would understand the compromise and he took care to point out that he had not abolished his radical principles:

> You may remember too, that while some may have answered the call to that seemingly radical meeting in New York last May, I was the only president, colored or white, of our colleges that took part in the deliberations of that meeting. I cite this to show that I have dared to live up to my views even when they threw me in the midst of the most radical.

DuBois understood that Hope's actions merely indicated the extent to which the black college was "tongue-tied and bound." "I must say frankly that I do not see any other course of action.... In your position of responsibility your institution must stand foremost in your thought."[20]

The industrial philanthropists, acutely aware of the black college dilemma, pushed ahead with their campaign to endow Fisk. By 1917 Fisk enrolled 188 of the 737 college students in private black institutions and Virginia Union University, with 51, had the next largest enrollment. The philanthropists no doubt understood the importance of conquering Fisk in their efforts to achieve hegemony over black higher education. By June 1924 they had successfully conducted a campaign for Fisk's million dollar endowment. The following pledges were then in hand: $500,000 from the General Education Board; $250,000 from the Carnegie Corporation; and $250,000 secured elsewhere, including sizeable pledges from such philanthropists as Julius Rosenwald and George Peabody. This endowment fund was not, however, collectable until the deficits, which Fisk had accumulated, were met. The outstanding indebtedness of that date was $70,000. To meet this indebtedness a special campaign by Nashville's white citizens for $50,000 was successfully completed by June 1924. This campaign was led by Nashville's Commercial Club which included Tennessee's governor, Nashville's mayor and many of the city's leading businessmen. From 1915 to 1924, Fisk had become so conservative that the Commercial Club was inspired to call Fisk "the key" to interracial cooperation and understanding in the South. "He came into our midst unknown," the Commercial Club said of McKenzie, "and by his wise administration and official methods won our hearty co-operation." With such backing, plans were perfected for raising the money to eliminate the school's deficits and thereby secure the endowment for Fisk's financial rehabilitation.[21]

At this juncture, however, McKenzie's conservative administration was attacked by black students, intellectuals, and community organizations. Led by DuBois, the Fisk Alumni attacked McKenzie's Draconian code of student discipline and were outraged by the humiliation and insults perpetrated on the University's students. DuBois openly challenged the school's administration in 1924 when he was invited to give the commencement address. He especially criticized the administration's campaign to suppress Fisk's egalitarian tradition in order to obtain economic support from industrial philanthropy. The students, long dissatisfied with McKenzie's regime, were reinforced by Alumni support and escalated their protest against the school's repressive policies. In January of 1925, the *New York Times* reported that Fisk's Alumni was organizing in "all sections of the United States to agitate for the removal of Dr. Fayette McKenzie, the white president of the University." The following month the students went on strike against McKenzie's administration, and as Wolters has shown, they were backed in their protest by the alumni, the black press, and the local black community. On the day following the student rebellion more than 2,500 black citizens of Nashville convened and formally declared that McKenzie's "usefulness as president of Fisk is at an end." This protest forced McKenzie to resign in April of 1925.[22]

DuBois praised the students' victory over McKenzie and hailed them as the new breed of black intellectuals necessary to challenge the power of industrial philanthropy:

> God speed the breed! Suppose we do lose Fisk; suppose we lose every cent that the entrenched millionaires have set aside to buy our freedom and stifle our complaints. They have the power, they have the wealth, but glory to God we still own our own souls and led by young men like these at Fisk, let us neither flinch nor falter, but fight, and fight and fight again.

But many black intellectuals, especially those responsible for black colleges, could not easily afford to attack the policies of industrial philanthropy. After the Fisk rebellion, the General Education Board withheld the endowment pledges on the grounds that they were not collectable until Fisk eliminated all of its deficits. The Nashville Commercial Club, which was expected to raise the capital to cover the deficits, withdrew from the campaign following McKenzie's resignation. Convinced that McKenzie's successor, Thomas Elsa Jones, did "not conceive himself to be a leader or an emancipator of the Negro group," the philanthropists eventually granted Fisk the endowment. Fisk, however, was still dependent on industrial philanthropy. From 1915 to 1960, the General Education Board alone disbursed over $5,000,000 to Fisk. During the same period it also granted over $5,800,000 to Atlanta University; $1,900,000 to Morehouse; $2,150,000 to Dillard University; $3,500,000 to Spellman; and $1,100,000 to Clark College. In all the General Education Board's expenditures to black higher education, from 1902 to 1960, amounted to $41,410,399. Thus, given the philanthropists' demand for a conservative black leadership, especially in the 1920s and 1930s, a certain amount of compromise was inevitable. This undoubtedly affected the ability of black colleges to deal squarely with the economic and political exploitation of black people. Few black college leaders could afford to challenge, as DuBois did, the "power in high places, white power, power backed by unlimited wealth." But many black college leaders, under extremely difficult conditions, made some compromises in order to maintain black higher education without abolishing its vital thrust toward the establishment of an independent black intelligentsia. Educators, like John Hope, held together the college system while more independent social critics, like DuBois, reminded the emerging black intellectuals of the essential struggle: "Let us never forget that the arch enemy of the Negro race is the false philanthropist who kicks us in the mouth when we cry out in honest and justifiable protest."[23]

NOTES

1. Gunnar Myrdal, *An American Dilemma* (New York: Harper and Row, Publishers, 1944), McGraw-Hill Paperback Edition, p. 711.

2. James M. McPherson, *The Abolitionist Legacy: From Reconstruction to the NAACP* (Princeton: Princeton University Press, 1975), pp. 143, 148, 152, 205-206, 223, Appendix B.

3. James D. Anderson, "Education as a Vehicle for the Manipulation of Black Workers," in Walter Feinberg and Henry Rosemont, Jr., editors, *Work, Technology, and Education, Dissenting Essays in the Intellectual Foundations of American Education* (Urbana: University of Illinois Press, 1975), pp. 15-40; Anderson, "Education for Servitude: The Social Purposes of Schooling in the Black South, 1870-1930" (University of Illinois, Ph.D. Dissertation, 1973), *see* especially Chapters 4 and 5.

4. Raymond B. Fosdick, *Adventure in Giving: The Story of the General Education Board* (New York: Harper and Row, 1962); Louis Harlan, *Separate and Unequal: Public School Campaigns and Racism in the Southern Seaboard States 1901-1915* (Chapel Hill: University of North Carolina Press, 1958), 1968 Atheneum edition, p. 86-87.

5. For an excellent treatment of urban interest in organizing American agriculture see David Byers Danbom, "The Industrialization of Agriculture, 1900-1930" (Stanford University, Ph.D. Dissertation, 1974).

6. Robert C. Ogden to Mrs. Arthur Gilman (May 12, 1903), Box 6, Robert C. Ogden papers, Library of Congress, Washington, D.C. (hereafter listed as Ogden Papers); Ogden, "Speech on Negro Education" (1900), Box 22, Ogden Papers; *See* especially James D. Anderson, "The Southern Improvement Company: "Northern Reformers' Investment in Negro Cotton Tenancy," *Agricultural History* (January 1978).

7. William H. Baldwin, "The Present Problem of Negro Education in the South," *Proceedings of the Second Capon Springs Conference for Education in the South* (Raleigh: Edwards and Broughton, 1899), pp. 94-100, 106; For similar philanthropic views *see* Henry S. Enck, "The Burden Borne: Northern White Philanthropy and Southern Black Industrial Education" (University of Cincinnati, Ph.D. Dissertation, 1970), pp. 152-164; Anderson, "Education as a Vehicle for the Manipulation of Black Workers," pp. 31-38; Robert Jay Rusnak, "Walter Hines Page and *The World's Work* 1900-1913" (University of California, Santa Barbara, Ph.D. Dissertation, 1973), Chapters 7 and 8.

8. Robert C. Ogden to Mrs. Arthur Gilman (May 12, 1903), Box 6, Ogden Papers; Booker T. Washington, editor, *Tuskegee and Its People: Their Ideals and Achievement* (New York: D. Appleton and Company, 1905); Baldwin quotation from Fosdick, *Adventure in Giving,* p. 11; Washington quotations from Anderson, "Education for Servitude," p. 176.

9. George F. Peabody to W. E. B. DuBois (August 26, 1911); DuBois to Peabody (August 28, 1911); Peabody to DuBois (September 1, 1911), Box 6, Ogden Papers.

10. George F. Peabody to Edgar Gardner Murphy (October 14, 1911), Box 1, George F. Peabody Papers, Library of Congress, Washington, D.C. (hereafter listed as Peabody Papers).

11. Harry H. Jones, "The Crisis in Negro Leadership" *Crisis,* 19 (March, 1920), pp. 256-59; Robert H. Brisbane, *The Black Vanguard: Origins of the Negro Social Revolution, 1900-1960,* Ch. 2-4 (Valley Forge: Judson Press, 1970).

12. Thomas Jesse Jones, editor, *Negro Education: A Study of the Private and Higher Schools For Colored People in the United States,* Vol. I (Washington: Government Printing Office, 1917), pp. 310, 314-15; Howard enrolled 1,001 of the 1,053 college students in black public colleges and Fisk enrolled 188 of the 737 students in the

college curriculum at black private institutions; The General Education Board's Conference on Negro Education (November 29, 1915), G.E.B. Files.

13. Fayette A. McKenzie, *Ideals of Fisk* (Nashville: Fisk University Press, 1915), p.
7; Herbert Aptheker, editor, *W. E. B. DuBois: The Education of Black People*
(Amherst: University of Massachusetts Press, 1973), pp. 52–57; DuBois, "Fisk,"
Crisis 28: 251–252; Raymond Wolters, *The New Negro On Campus: Black College
Rebellions of the 1920s* (Princeton: Princeton University Press, 1975), pp. 35–39.

14. The most thorough study of McKenzie's repressive educational practices is
Wolters, *The New Negro,* chapter 2, "W. E. B. DuBois and the Rebellion at Fisk University," pp. 29–69.

15. Julius Rosenwald to Abraham Flexner (January 15, 1917), Box 138, General
Education Board Files, Rockefeller Foundation Archives (hereafter listed as G.E.B.
Files); Flexner to Rosenwald (January 17, 1917), Box 138, G.E.B. Files; Flexner to
Harold H. Swift (April 2, 1917); Stewart B. Appleget to H. J. Thorkelson (June 12,
1928), "Appropriations Made by the General Education Board to Fisk University";
For endowment contributions *see* report of William H. Baldwin to General Education
Board (October 6, 1924); L. Hollingsworth Wood to the General Education Board
(May 6, 1920); Box 138, G.E.B. Files; *Fisk University News* (December, 1924), p. 20.

16. *Fisk University News* (April), 1923, p. 7; *Fisk University News* (October, 1920),
p. 21; Thomas Jesse Jones to Abraham Flexner (October 4, 1915); L. Hollingsworth
Wood to Wallace Buttrick (May 6, 1920); H. J. Thorkelson to L. Hollingsworth Wood
(November 5, 1926), Box 138, G.E.B. Files. For the philanthropists' role in actively
recruiting trustees *see* Abraham Flexner to Julius Rosenwald (January 8, 1917); Rosenwald to Flexner (January 13, 1917); Flexner to Rosenwald (January 17, 1917); Flexner
to Harold H. Swift (April 2, 1917); Flexner to Harry Pratt Judson (March 27, 1917);
Judson to Flexner (March 30, 1917); Judson to Flexner (April 13, 1917), Box 138,
G.E.B. Files.

17. Flexner, Memorandum on the Fisk Endowment Campaign (May 25, 1923), Box
23, G.E.B. Files.

18. Harry H. Jones, "The Crisis in Negro Leadership" *Crisis,* 19 (March, 1920),
pp. 256–59; George F. Peabody to James E. Gregg (April 5, 1920), Box 58, Peabody
Papers.

19. Peabody to Gregg, Ibid.; *Fisk University News* (September, 1919), pp. 2–4;
W. E. B. DuBois to Robert B. Eleazer (March 12, 1926), Commissionon Interracial
Cooperation Collection, Trevor Arnett Libraries, Atlanta University.

20. Jones, editor, Negro Education, pp. 310, 314–15; Flexner quoted in the General
Education Board's Conference on Negro Education (November 29, 1915), p. 130,
G.E.B. Files; Hope and DuBois letters in Herbert Aptheker (Ed.), *The Correspon-
dence of W. E. B. DuBois, Volume I: Selections, 1877-1934* (Amherst: University of
Massachusetts Press, 1973), pp. 166–67.

21. "Fisk University," a 1926 Memorandum in Box 138, G.E.B. Files; "Fisk
Endowment Drive in Nashville," *Fisk University News* (May 1924), pp. 31–32; "First
Million-Dollar Endowment for College Education of the Negro in the History of
America," *Fisk University News* (October, 1924), pp. 1–13; The Commercial Club of
Nashville to the General Education Board (January 24, 1920), Box 138, G.E.B. Files.
Jones, editor, *Negro Education,* pp. 314–15, 320–21.

22. Wolters, *The New Negro On Campus,* pp. 34–40, 49; *New York Times* (February
8, 1925), 2: 1.

23. DuBois quoted in Wolters, *The New Negro On Campus,* pp. 62–63; "Fisk University," A 1926 memorandum in Box 138 G.E.B. Files; For General Education
Board's contributions *see* Fosdick, *The General Education Board,* pp. 329–332; "Fisk
University," Report by Thomas E. Jones to the General Education Board (September
27, 1928) and (September 28, 1928), Box 138, G.E.B. Files.

In Pursuit of Freedom:
The Educational Activities of Black
Social Organizations in Philadelphia,
1900–1930

Vincent P. Franklin

The slave background of the Afro-American has had a profound influence upon many aspects of the contemporary black culture. The experience of slavery was a major component in the development of the rich and in many ways unique religious tradition of black Americans. The oral tradition in the form of folktales and spirituals had its roots in the not-so-peculiar institution.[1] At the same time, the fact that blacks were brought to this country as slave laborers to a large extent has defined the perceptions of other Americans about the character and capacities of black men and women. This twisted legacy is still with black Americans in the form of the recent attempts to define the progeny of the slave laborers as "culturally deprived."[2]

The quest for freedom from slavery has also helped to shape several important black cultural traditions. When one examines the literature of black Americans, one cannot help but be struck by the recurrent themes of protest and liberation.[3] Education which was often denied the slave by tradition and later through legislation assumed a great importance to black Americans as a means through which one became liberated or liberated the minds of others. The three most important literary works by black Americans in the nineteenth century, David Walker's *Appeal,* Frederick Douglass' *Narrative of His Life,* and

An earlier version of this essay was presented at the 61st Annual Meeting of the Study of Afro-American Life and History, Chicago, 1976. I would like to acknowledge the financial assistance of a Spencer Postdoctoral Fellowship from the National Academy of Education in the completion of this essay.

Booker T. Washington's *Up from Slavery,* all echo the theme of freedom through education. Schooling, both formal and informal, was judged to be the main thoroughfare by which blacks could leave "Babylon" and reach "Canaan-Land."[4]

For blacks in the North the slave background did not last as long as it did for their brothers in the South, thus the quest for freedom through education began in the early part of the nineteenth century. The possibility of receiving an education allowed these northern blacks to develop educational institutions which would be instrumental in the pursuit of freedom for blacks throughout the nation. Thus we find in the city of Philadelphia in the 1820s and 1830s not only public and private schools for blacks, but also many community educational agencies and social organizations that were about the task of "freeing" black Philadelphians. In her study of the educational activities of black literary societies in the first half of the nineteenth century, Dorothy Porter provided a number of insights into the functioning of these organizations. Literary and debating societies, reading rooms, and lyceums sponsored lectures, published newsletters and antislavery tracts, and provided reading materials for their members and for the Philadelphia community at large.[5] Many of these societies were founded by and for women who were interested in the dual issues of black advancement and the general moral reform of the community.[6] Although most of the societies were short-lived, they did serve a useful purpose in providing educational materials and activities for the Philadelphia black community.[7]

As the black population in Philadelphia increased between 1870 and 1900 there was a proliferation in the number of social organizations and institutions in the black commuity. DuBois described many of these social, secret, and cooperative associations in *The Philadelphia Negro.* He discussed the general activities of the benevolent and fraternal organizations, the literary societies, and political clubs, but did not describe the "community service" and community education programs sponsored by these groups.[8] In this essay the community-wide educational activities of black social organizations and institutions in black Philadelphia between 1900 and 1930 will be examined. Many of the organizations active during these decades were also functioning in the 1890s when DuBois was conducting his monumental study. The hundreds of lectures, exhibitions, conferences, and public meetings which took place dealt with a wide variety of topics and issues. However, these educational activities generally fall into three overlapping areas of concern: education in the black heritage, education for individual and community development, and education for black social and political advancement. Through an examination of the organized educational activities of the black social organizations we are able to determine just how black Philadelphia educated itself during the first three decades of this century.

Education in the Black Heritage

Many of the black social organizations and institutions to be discussed were active in the discovery and rediscovery of black History. Since the exploits of blacks and their contributions to the development of the nation were often not integrated into "American" History, it became necessary for black Americans to preserve and document their own history in the United States. Just as the rise of the black newspaper has been interpreted as a development that came about in order to fill a definite need of the black community, the rise of historical societies and organizations can be seen as an attempt to fill a gap in the black community's knowledge of itself.[9]

The earliest black historical organization in Philadelphia was the Reading Room Society founded in March, 1828. This was followed by the Benjamin Bannaker Institute in 1854. Both of these societies were primarily involved in providing reading materials for the "mental improvement" of the Philadelphia Negro.[10] The most ambitious and important historical undertaking of blacks in Philadelphia in the late nineteenth and early twentieth century was the formation of the American Negro Historical Society in October, 1897. Meeting at the Church of the Crucifixion, Robert Adger, Rev. Matthew Anderson, Rev. Henry L. Phillips, and several other prominent persons started the Society in order to "collect relics, literature and historical facts in connection with the African Race, illustrative of their progress and development."[11] Coming together on the fourth Tuesday of every month, the members discussed historical materials unearthed by the individuals in the group. On December 28, 1897, a committee on the celebration of the Emancipation Proclamation reported on the preparations for the first public lecture to be sponsored by the Society. It took place on January 3, 1898, at Allen Chapel, Lombard Street above Nineteenth. Rev. J.C. Brock, a member of the group, spoke on "The Dawning of Liberty"; Rev. Matthew Anderson discussed "The Achievements of the Colored People in 25 Years of Liberty"; and Mr. William Baugh related the exploits of "The Colored Soldier."[12]

The public lectures of the American Negro Historical Society were to become an important forum for the education of Philadelphians into the black heritage from 1898 to 1923, when the Society ceased activity. During that period such illustrious black Philadelphians as Bishop Levi J. Coppin, John C. Asbury, Jessie Fauset, and William C. Bolivar were to lecture on historical and contemporary topics under the auspices of the Society.[13]

During and after the primacy of the American Negro Historical Society, several church and literary societies in black Philadelphia sponsored free lectures on various historical topics. The largest and most active of these groups were listed in the Philadelphia Colored Directories for 1908, 1910, and 1913.[14] These literary societies were usually made up of interested communicants from the various black churches in the city. For example, the J.C. Price Literary Society was organized by the members of the Wesley A.M.E. Zion Church, and the Douglass Literary Society was associated with the Union A.M.E. Church in Philadelphia.[15] Other groups were not directly connected with churches, as was the case with the Paul Lawrence Dunbar Literary Society, and the Phillis Wheatley Literary Society, founded by Rev. Richard Robert Wright, Jr., who for many years was editor of the *Christian Recorder,* an official publication of the African Methodist Episcopal Church.[16]

One can gauge the amount and type of activities of these societies through a perusal of the *Philadelphia Tribune,* the most important black newspaper in the city from the late 1880s to the present day. The *Tribune* usually published a great deal of information on the activities of these groups in its religious and community affairs columns.[17] One of the most active of these church literary societies during the period 1920 to 1928 was the Pinn-Memorial Literary Society. This organization not only sponsored lectures by its membership and other black Philadelphians, but also worked with other groups to bring speakers to the city to give free public lectures, especially for the various celebrations of the black heritage.[18]

Commemorative celebrations of persons and events of great importance to black Americans were very successful educational activities in the black community of Philadelphia. Beginning with Emancipation Day, January 1, these celebrations were times when speeches and lectures informed the black community of its heritage and made clear the relationship between the past event and contemporary conditions. In the period 1920–1930, the Citizens Committee of Allied Organizations worked to make Emancipation Day one of the most eventful of the entire year. Audiences of five hundred to five thousand were assembled at the Philadelphia Academy of Music or Tindley Temple, and heard such prominent speakers and musicians as Carl Diton (1920), James Weldon Johnson (1921), Emmett J. Scott (1924), Marian Anderson (1925), and Hallie Q. Brown (1926).[19]

The month of February was particularly eventful because of the celebrations of the birthdays of Abraham Lincoln (the twelfth) and Frederick Douglass (the fourteenth). Activities took place throughout the city and usually included public lectures and speeches on the contributions of these two great men to America.[20] Beginning in 1926, Negro History Week subsumed both of these dates under a more general celebration of black History. With the formation of the Philadelphia chapter of the Association for the Study of Negro Life and History in 1927, a coordinated program of lectures and exhibits was available to Philadelphians in the public schools and other locales during the second week of February.[21]

Longer celebrations of the black American heritage took place in Philadelphia in 1913 and 1926. In 1913 the entire month of September was designated as a time to commemorate the "Fifty Years of Progress" of black Americans. An exposition was opened which emphasized the religious, economic, and political advancements of blacks since the signing of the Emancipation Proclamation. Literally thousands of persons participated in the festivities which were planned and coordinated by blacks in Pennsylvania.[22] As part of the celebration of the Sesquicentennial of the United States, which took place in Philadelphia during the summer of 1926, blacks played an active role in the planning and development of exhibits and educational programs. Although several problems arose, such as the threat of official segregation at exhibits and facilities and the lack of sufficient state and local funding, on the whole, black Philadelphians were pleased with the recognition which they and all black Americans received through participation in this important exposition.[23]

The 1920s also witnessed a resurgence or "renaissance" in black cultural and literary expressions. Centered in Harlem, young black writers and artists plummed black historical and cultural traditions in order to reveal the unique "black aesthetic." Black Philadelphians participated in the "New Negro" creative mood of the decade in New York and in Philadelphia. Black authors and artists in Philadelphia were involved in many literary activities and published their own literary journal in 1927 entitled *Black Opals*. Through this magazine and other popular journals of the era blacks in Philadelphia were exposed to the latest cultural expressions of Afro-American artists.[24]

Education for Individual and Community Development

While the historical and literary societies concentrated most of their educational activities on the general social and historical development of Black America, the black social, religious, and fraternal institutions in Philadelphia were primarily involved in education for self-improvement and home and community development. For example, the various women's clubs and organizations not only sponsored lectures on such topics as "The Accomplishments of Negro Womanhood" and "The Industrial Labor Problems of Colored Women," but also worked closely with the various social welfare agencies serving the black community. The Colored Women's Society for Organized Charity, The Allied Social Agencies Aid, and the most important group, The City-Wide Federation of Colored Women's Clubs, were intimately involved in the improvement of the social conditions of blacks, especially black youth, in Philadelphia through the sponsoring of educational programs and other charitable works.[25] Many of the members of the women's clubs worked with the community centers and settlement houses in the black neighborhoods. The Eighth Ward Settlement House, St. Simon Settlement, and later the Wharton Settlement House were very active in assisting new arrivals from the South during the Great Migration and sponsored educational and recreational programs which helped to ease the adjustment of the black migrants to "life in the big city."[26] Though many of these community centers were financed by the municipal government or philanthropic agencies in the city, the staffs were often made up of blacks with the knowledge and experience necessary to formulate a meaningful program of activities.[27]

The Sunday schools of the black churches were active in passing on the religious traditions of the various denominations to the children in their congregations. Teachers who usually had special training in the instruction of religious dogma held classes in the churches each Sunday morning. We have a very complete picture of the activities of these schools from the *Philadelphia Tribune* for the period 1912–1930. In its column on religious news called "Churches and Their Pastors," the *Tribune* published information on the activities of these classes which was usually provided by the teachers or the pastors of the churches.[28] Beginning in June, 1924, the *Tribune* began publishing a weekly "Sunday School Lesson" prepared by Arthur Huff Fauset, then Principal of the Singerly Public School. This lesson usually consisted of a Bible story followed by a short religious commentary.[29] Special events which involved the Sunday schools, such as the Annual Sunday School Congress, were generally reported in the religious section of the *Tribune*.[30]

The most thoroughly reported educational activities of the black religious community of Philadelphia, however, were those of the Young Men's Christian Association (YMCA) and the Young Women's Christian Association (YWCA). The YMCA movement which began in England in 1844 was imported into the United States in 1852. The first Association for Negroes was started in Washington, D.C. in 1853. In the early years the activities of the organization centered on evangelism (preaching and sermons), Bible classes, and other religious observances for young adults. In later years (after 1885) the YMCA developed a four-fold purpose: to improve the physical, intellectual, social, and religious life of young men and boys.[31]

The earliest YMCAs for Negroes were mostly social and religious gatherings because they had no separate buildings and were usually confined to what was offered by the various churches in the communities. Beginning in 1912, however, several northern cities began to plan the building of colored YMCAs and were aided in this endeavor by generous contributions from the Julius Rosenwald Fund. As a result, by 1938 there were forty-six separate Associations for blacks which were basically of two types: YMCAs with buildings and "non-equipment" YMCAs which carried on activities in local churches. Besides the various recreational and physical activities provided by the Ys, they also had extensive programs in adult education, crafts, Negro heritage clubs, Bible schools, art classes, and glee clubs. Many Negro YMCAs had important "extension programs" in order to provide activities for young men and boys who were not in close proximity to the main (Negro) branch.[32]

In Philadelphia the Negro YMCA began functioning in 1889. By 1896, however, the disadvantages of not having a separate building had become apparent. W.E.B. DuBois found that "the colored Y.M.C.A. has been virtually an attempt to add another church to the numberless colored churches in the city, with endless prayer-meetings and loud gospel hymns in dingy and uninviting quarters. Consequently the institution is now temporarily suspended. It had accomplished some good work by its night schools and social meetings."[33]

The campaign to erect a separate building for the Negro YMCA was carried out during the first decade of this century. With assistance from the Rosenwald Fund, Rev. Henry L. Phillips and others were able to purchase a lot in South Philadelphia and construction of the building began in April, 1912.[34] Completed by January, 1914, the Southwest Branch (Christian Street) YMCA not only provided much needed recreational and educational activities for the large black community in South Philadelphia, but also served as social center and meeting place for black organizations from all over the city.[35] Under the leadership of Rev. Henry Porter, the Christian Street YMCA was one of the most important educational agencies in the black community throughout the period 1914–1930.[36]

The history of the Young Women's Christian Association (YWCA) to a very great extent parallels that of the YMCA. First established in England in 1855, the YWCA began operation in the United States in 1858 in New York City. By 1900 there were hundreds of Associations throughout the country and a national organization was formed in 1906. The first "colored" YWCA was opened in Dayton, Ohio, in 1893. After the formation of the national organization, a colored Secretary was appointed in 1913. The YWCAs also sponsored a number of activities to promote interracial understanding and cooperation.[37]

In Philadelphia the work of the YWCA among colored women began in 1902. Within a few years the organization acquired a separate building on Fifteenth Street in South Philadelphia.[38] The Southwest YWCA provided educational and recreational activities for women, and offered classes in various industrial and domestic arts, including dressmaking, millinery, crocheting, and knitting.[39] In addition, the Southwest YWCA acquired a building for the lodging of single women and was active in seeking employment for its membership.[40] The Metropolitan (main) Branch in the city exercised a good deal of financial control over the Southwest YWCA and on several occasions conflicts arose.[41] After 1921, however, the Southwest branch launched campaigns to raise funds to allow it to remain relatively independent of the control and interference of the main branch in the city. As was the case with the YMCA, the Southwest YWCA served as a social and convention center for the Philadelphia black community and sponsored numerous lectures and exhibits on black womanhood, black religious traditions, black artistic achievements, and many other popular topics.[42]

The various secret and fraternal organizations in black Philadelphia also played a significant role in the education of the community. The Knights of Pythias, the Odd Fellows, and most importantly the Improved Benevolent and Protective Order of Elks of the World (the Elks), sponsored educational activities such as public lectures and debates, not merely for their membership, but for the community at large.[43] In August, 1925, the Grand Lodge Session of the

Elks passed a resolution "to provide scholarships for deserving Negro youths in the various Schools of Higher and Secondary Education.... In order to provide the funds necessary to granting of these scholarships ... every subordinate lodge shall pay annually into the Educational Fund twenty-five cents for every member carried on its rolls."[44] These Elks scholarships were an extremely important source of financial aid for many black students even to the present day.[45]

Beginning in 1926, the Elks began to sponsor an "Educational Week" in which meetings were held and programs were presented in the Elks lodges throughout the country for the purpose of encouraging Negro youth to stay in school. At the second annual Educational Week in 1927, the Elks inaugurated the National Oratorical Contest in which cash prizes and scholarships were given to young black men and women who presented the best orations on the topic, "The Constitution of the United States."[46] The various Elks lodges in Philadelphia participated in the local and regional oratorical competitions and received a great deal of enthusiastic support from the rest of the black community. Philadelphians were particularly pleased when a local boy, William Harvey III, was able to triumph over representatives from all over the nation in the oratorical contest for 1929.[47]

Delta Sigma Theta sorority and Alpha Phi Alpha fraternity were also active in promoting the schooling of black youth and in providing educational activities for the Philadelphia black community. The Deltas brought speakers to the city for free lectures and sponsored an annual Education Week similar to that of the Elks.[48] The annual "Go to High School — Go to College" campaign of Alpha Phi Alpha fraternity received a great deal of support from the membership of the organization in the various cities and towns throughout the country. The campaign in Philadelphia usually consisted of a week of activities for children and their parents stressing the benefits of secondary and higher education. Such prominent persons as A. Philip Randolph, Carter G. Woodson, Raymond Pace Alexander, and W.E.B. DuBois spoke in the city during these educational campaigns.[49] There were, of course, many other social, religious and fraternal groups that sponsored educational activities for the black community during the period 1900–1930, however, this sampling of activities and organizations should provide some indication not only of the commitment of these groups to the passing on of their individual traditions to their membership, but also of their efforts to improve the entire black community through the sponsoring of organized educational activities.

Education for Black Social and Political Advancement

Along with their regular social and political activities, many of the social improvement organizations of black Philadelphia involved themselves in community-wide educational activities.[50] "The Philadelphia Association for the Protection of Colored Women" began in 1905 working with newly-arrived southern women interested in living and obtaining employment in the city. Although the primary objective of the Association was to support and protect these women from the "immoral influences" of the city, it also attempted to educate women intending to leave the South in such matters as industrial conditions, wages, opportunities, and competition that they would meet in northern cities.[51] Thus "education" was one of the specific goals of this organization for black social advancement. The community at large was informed, almost on a monthly basis, of the activities of the organization through the *Tribune,* and rallies were held throughout the city in order to raise funds for its endeavors. At these meetings speakers from all over the nation would discuss efforts of this group at self development and other issues pertinent to the social and moral improvement of black America.[52]

The Armstrong Association of Philadelphia, an interracial organization concerned primarily with the industrial and employment conditions for blacks in the city, often sponsored activities that not only informed the community of its work and progress, but also educated Philadelphians as to the general industrial conditions of the nation.[53] In 1912, for example, the Armstrong Association participated in a number of public meetings with the Legal Aid Society, Children's Aid Society, the Colored Methodist and Baptist Churches; and sponsored a series of rallies to raise funds for Tuskegee Institute which brought Booker T. Washington to the city.[54]

In 1926 the Association organized classes in trade education at the Christian Street YMCA in order to prepare blacks for jobs in the skilled trades and construction industry in the city and sponsored "Negro in Industry Week" which was a drive to open up industries in the city to blacks.[55] The Association also worked as a liaison between the Municipal Courts and Negro youths who were in trouble with the law and cooperated with social workers in dealing with many of the problems facing blacks in the city.[56] As National Urban League affiliate in Philadelphia, the Armstrong Association planned and coordinated the national convention of that organization when it was held in the city in 1928. Thus Philadelphians participated in the national efforts to inform Americans of the industrial conditions of the black population.[57]

The Philadelphia Branch of the National Association for the Advancement of Colored People (NAACP) through its annual membership drives and special lectures and conferences was one of the most important agencies for the education of the Philadelphia community, especially the black community, in the contemporary legal, political, and social conditions of black Americans. Organized in 1913, the Phladelphia Branch brought many speakers to the city to address audiences assembled at the Southwest YWCA, the Christian Street YMCA, and various black churches throughout the period 1913-1930.[58] Although it was not politically active before 1920, during the decade of the twenties the local NAACP participated in activities to protect the civil rights of black citizens and worked to bring an end to discrimination against blacks in the public schools, hotels, and other public places.[59] With the Citizens Republican Club, the Armstrong Association, and other organizations, the Philadelphia NAACP engaged in many activities for the social, political, and educational benefit of the black community.[60]

The separate public and Catholic schools for blacks in Philadelphia in spite of their many inadequacies did benefit the black community by serving as "social centers" and meeting places for black organizations. The Durham Public School and St. Peter Claver Catholic School in South Philadelphia and the Reynolds Public School in North Philadelphia opened their doors to a large variety of activities for community improvement.[61] One of the most successful annual events sponsored by the black public schools was "Negro Health Week." Exhibits were set up in the schools which stressed the benefits of a nutritional diet and dental hygiene. Mothers were advised about the care of their families and their homes, and, most importantly, doctors were available in the schools to give free checkups for tuberculosis and other diseases.[62] Also, the parent-teacher organizations of the black schools and the Citizens Committee for Regular School Attendance sponsored an annual "Friendship Week" which fostered interracial cooperation in the schools and throughout the community. In the first annual celebration in 1925, George Washington Carver came to Philadelphia and discussed his famous agricultural experiments at Tuskegee Institute.[63]

A great part of the above discussion of the educational activities of the black social institutions and organizations is based on reports of these events in the *Philadelphia Tribune,* but it should also be noted that the newspapers in general and the *Tribune* in particular were very important educational agencies for the black community. Although it began publishing in 1884, one can get some understanding of the *Tribune's* emphasis on education and black social and political advancement by perusing the pages of the newspaper for the years that have survived (1912 to the present). Under the leadership of Chris J. Perry, the founder and publisher, G. Grant Williams, managing editor, and later E. Washington Rhodes, editor, the *Tribune* actively participated in the various campaigns to improve the social, political, and educational conditions in the black community.[64] The newspaper sponsored public meetings and disseminated information on what occurred at these meetings through editorials, articles, and special features. The *Tribune* published columns on "Negro History and Heroes," "School and Community News," "Health Problems," and other topics relevant to black social advancement. The paper also supported and publicized the candidacies of black politicians in Philadelphia. The *Tribune* was usually at the forefront of the various campaigns for the social and political advancement of black Philadelphians.[65]

There were clearly a wide variety of black social organizations and institutions active in providing community education programs in black Philadelphia between 1900 and 1930. Thus it is very likely that most blacks in the city came into contact with these educational programs either as a member of a sponsoring organization or as attendants at one of the educational programs. Although some of the organizations had small memberships, the activities sponsored by these groups reached a much larger audience. Thus the fifteen black members of the committee on the "Fifty Years of Progress" of the Afro-American since the signing of the Emancipation Proclamation, were instrumental in the planning and coordinating of an exposition attended by thousands of persons, black and white. The various committees and organizations active in assisting the adjustment of southern blacks to the city did not have many members, but there is evidence that their work affected large numbers of southern blacks in need of housing and employment during the Great Migration.[66]

In previous examinations of social organizations in urban black communities, researchers have discussed only certain aspects of the functioning of these groups.[67] Thus literary and debating societies and historical associations were viewed as "middle class organizations" which served as little more than "social clubs" for enhancing the status of the membership. These types of organizations were then contrasted with race betterment or "race conscious" organizations which were primarily interested in the advancement of the race as a whole. The National Urban League, the NAACP, the Universal Negro Improvement Association would be considered "race conscious" organizations.[68] This dichotomization of black social organizations may provide some information on the differences among the various groups, but it has also tended to obscure their similarities. In black Philadelphia between 1900 and 1930 both race and status conscious organizations were active in sponsoring community-wide educational programs which were not aimed solely at the "middle class" members of these social organizations, but focused upon issues which affected not just "middle class" or "lower class" blacks, but all blacks in Philadelphia. Thus the various public meetings, newspaper articles, and conferences on the segregated public schools, job discrimination, and related issues dealt with issues which had ramifications for the entire community of blacks in the city. The various celebrations of the black heritage served to educate both upper and lower status blacks about their history in this country and throughout the world.

In previous historical investigations the educational efforts of black social organizations have been generally ignored in assessments of the "black urban condition." However, this examination of the educational activities of the black social organizations in Philadelphia suggests that organized educational activities were an important part of the social environment of blacks in urban America.

NOTES

1. For an excellent discussion of the relationship between the slave experience and contemporary black culture, *see* John W. Blassingame, *The Slave Community: Plantation life in the Antebellum South* (New York: Oxford University Press, 1972), pp.

41–76. *See also* Houston A. Baker, Jr., *Long Black Song: Essays in Black American Literature and Culture* (Charlottesville: University of Virginia Press, 1972).

2. For discussion of these issues, *see* William Ryan, *Blaming the Victim* (New York: Vintage Books, 1971), pp. 30–60, 112–36.

3. For a discussion of the themes of protest and freedom in black writing, *see* Abraham Chapman, "Introduction," in *Black Voices: An Anthology of Afro-American Literature* (New York: Mentor Books, 1968), pp. 21–49; Arthur P. Davis, *From the Dark Tower: Afro-American Writers, 1900–1940* (Washington, D.C.: Howard University Press, 1974). Cf. James Baldwin, "Everybody's Protest Novel," in *Notes of a Native Son* (New York: Beacon Press, 1955), pp. 9–17.

4. In his essays, "Revolution and Reform: Walker, Douglass, and the Road to Freedom" and "Men and Institutions: Booker T. Washington's Up From Slavery," Baker discusses the theme of education and freedom, *see* pp. 58–95.

5. Dorothy Porter, "The Organized Educational Activities of Negro Literary Societies, 1828–1846," *The Journal of Negro Education*, V (October, 1936), 555–74.

6. One gets some idea of the concerns of these groups from their names, for example, in Philadelphia there was the Female Literary Society (1831), the Library Company of Colored Persons (1833), and the Philadelphia Association for the Moral and Mental Improvement of the People of Color (1835); *see* Ibid., pp. 557–64.

7. *Ibid.; see also,* Leon Litwack, *North of Slavery: The Negro in the Free States, 1790–1860* (Chicago: University of Chicago Press, 1961), pp. 181–86.

8. DuBois, *The Philadelphia Negro: A Social Study* (1899, reprinted New York Schocken Press, 1967), pp. 221–34. According to U.S. census reports, in 1900 there were 62,613 blacks in Philadelphia, making up almost 5 percent of the population; by 1930 there were over 219,000 blacks in the city, and they made up over 11 percent of the residents.

9. For a discussion of the reasons for the rise of the Negro press, *see* I. Garland Penn, *The Afro-American Press and Its Editors* (1891, reprinted, New York: Arno Press and the New York Times, 1969), pp. 25–31.

10. Porter, pp. 557–64; James Spady, "The Afro-American Historical Society: The Nucleus of Black Bibliographies, 1897–1923," *Negro History Bulletin*, XXXVII (June-July, 1974), 254–55.

11. Minutes of the American Negro Historical Society, October 25, 1897, MSS Box 10G, Leon Gardiner Collection, Historical Society of Pennsylvania (HSP).

12. *Ibid.,* December 28, 1897; January 3, 1898.

13. The public lectures offered by the American Negro Historical Society were often publicized in the *Philadelphia Tribune, see* February 17, 1912, n.p.; February 15, 1913, p. 2; March 8, 1913, p. 1; January 31, 1914, p. 5; August 8, 1914, p. 4; July 24, 1920, p. 1; July 31, 1920, p. 1; August 7, 1920, p. 1.

14. *The Philadelphia Colored Directory — A Handbook of the Religious, Social, Political, Professional, Business and Other Activities of Negroes in Philadelphia, 1908* compiled by R. R. Wright and Ernest Smith, 1908, pp. 28–50; *The Philadelphia Colored Directory,* 1910, pp. 20–35; *The Philadelphia Colored Directory,* 1913, pp. 18–23 (HSP).

15. *See,* for example, *The Philadelphia Colored Directory,* 1908, p. 43.

16. See *The Philadelphia Colored Directory,* 1910, p. 34.

17. For discussions of these churches and literary societies, *see* the *Philadelphia Tribune,* January 27, 1912, p. 1; July 17, 1915, p. 1; June 10, 1916, p. 1; January 31, 1920, p. 9; September 25, 1920, p. 1.

18. For information on the lectures of the Pinn-Memorial Literary Society *see* the *Philadelphia Tribune,* October 16, 1920, n.p.; March 7, 1925, n.p.; February 16, 1928, p. 2. This society was sponsored by Pinn-Memorial Baptist Church.

19. *Ibid.,* January 10, 1920, p. 1; January 1 and 8, 1921, p. 1; January 5, 1924, p. 1; January 10, 1925; p. 1; January 9, 1926, p. 1.

20. *Ibid.,* March 3, 1917, p. 1; March 1, 1919, p. 1; February 12, 1921, p. 1; February 19, 1921, p. 2; February 27, 1926, p. 15; February 19, 1927, p. 7.

21. *Ibid.,* February 20, p. 1. For the information of the Philadelphia Branch of the Association for the Study of Negro Life and History, *see* the *Tribune,* November 17, 1927, p. 2. Negro History Week activities may be found in the *Tribune* on the following dates: January 12, 1928, p. 5; February 2, 1928, p. 16; January 23, 1930, p. 13.

22. For coverage of the activities of the Exposition, *see* the *Tribune* July 12, 1913, p. 1; September 6, 1913, p. 1; September 20, 1913, p. 1; October 4, 1913, p. 1; October 18, 1913, p. 1.

23. For black participation in the Sesquicentennial Celebration (1926), *see* the *Tribune,* February 13, 1926, p. 9; June 5, 1926, p. 5; June 12, 1926, p. 15; September 18, 1926, p. 5. *See also,* W.E.B. DuBois, "The Sesquicentennial Exposition," *The Crisis,* XXXIII (December, 1926), 65.

24. The first issue of *Black Opals* (Spring, 1927) was entitled "Hail Negro Youth," and presented the poetry and prose of a number of young black writers in Philadelphia. One of the leading black writers of the Harlem Renaissance was a Philadelphian, Jessie Fauset. Ms. Fauset served as a literary editor of *The Crisis* magazine throughout the 1920s. *The Crisis* and *Opportunity* magazine published many of the important black literary works of the decade.

25. *Philadelphia Tribune,* February 12, 1921, p. 1; April 19, 1924, p. 1; May 24, 1928, p. 3. *See also* Gerda Lerner, editor, *Black Women in White America — A Documentary History* (New York: Pantheon Books, 1972), pp. 440–58; For a five-year review of the activities of the Colored Women's Clubs in Philadelphia, see the *Tribune,* April 10, 1915, p. 2; May 8, 1915, p. 2. For the activities of the City Federation of Colored Women's Clubs, see February 24, 1917, p. 1; July 5, 1919, p. 1; July 12, 1919, p. 1; March 6, 1920, p. 5; November 6, 1920, p. 1.

26. For specific information on the educational activities of the various community centers, *see* the *Tribune,* November 16, 1912, p. 1; March 8, 1913, p. 1; January 10, 1925, p. 3; May 16, 1925, p. 9.

27. A very good example of this situation was the Wissahickon Boys Club, which worked with young men and boys in the black community and had a black staff led by William T. Coleman, but was financed primarily by members of the white community. *See* the *Philadelphia Tribune,* April 19, 1919, p. 1; April 2, 1927, p. 7. *See also,* Eugene Beaupre, "Negro Boy's Activities at Wissahickon (Boys Club)," *Southern Workman,* LVIII (September, 1929), 405–14.

28. For the column on Church News, *see* the *Tribune,* January 6, 1912, n.p.; ("Churches and Their Pastors,") and February 10, 1912, p. 3; and for the "Church Directory," *see* February 15, 1913, p. 2. They were edited by Rev. Robert H. Peerce.

29. *Ibid.,* June 7, 1924, p. 9.

30. *Ibid., see,* for example, January 27, 1912, n.p.; February 17, 1912, p. 4; March 16, 1912, p. 4; July 13, 1912, p. 6; August 10, 1912, p. 1.

31. Jesse E. Moorland, "The Young Men's Christian Association Among Negroes," *The Journal of Negro History,* IX (April 1924), 127–38; George Arthur, "The Young Men's Christian Association Movement Among Negroes," *Opportunity,* I (March 1923), 16–18; John Hope, "The Colored YMCA," *The Crisis,* XXXI (November, 1925), 14–17.

32. *Ibid.;* Campbell C. Johnson, "Negro Youth and the Educational Program of the Y.M.C.A.," *The Journal of Negro Education,* IX (July, 1940), 354–62.

33. DuBois, *The Philadelphia Negro,* p. 232.

34. *Philadelphia Tribune,* April 20, 1912, p. 2.

35. *Ibid.,* January 24, 1914, p. 1; *see also,* May 7, 1921, p. 6.

36. The activities of the Christian Street YMCA were reported in the *Tribune* almost weekly throughout this period; however, detailed information may be found on the following dates: November 29, 1924, p. 1; October 31 1925, p. 1; November 7, 1925, p. 1.

37. Lerner, pp. 458-97; Channing Tobias, "The Work of the Young Men's and Young Women's Christian Associations with Negro youth," *The Annals of the American Academy of Political and Social Science,* CXL (November, 1928), 283-86; Marion Cuthbert, "Negro Youth and the Educational Program of the Y.W.C.A. *The Journal of Negro Education,* IX (July, 1940), 363-71.

Most of the above sources make note of the fact that the YWCA was more "interracial" than the YMCA, but no reason was given as to why this was the case. It probably was related to the fact that there was less competition and thus less possibility of conflict among whites and blacks in the YWCA. There were advantages to this situation for black women in that they had access to greater funds through its connection with the "white" officials. However, the disadvantage was increased control of the white administration over its activities. In Philadelphia this situation caused several problems; *see* the *Philadelphia Tribune,* October 18, 1913, p. 4.

38. *The Philadelphia Colored Directory,* 1908, p. 47.

39. *Philadelphia Tribune,* November 20, 1920, p. 7.

40. *Ibid.,* November 6, 1920, p. 3; November 27, 1920, p. 1.

41. The conflict with the Metropolitan Branch of the YWCA in Philadelphia was covered in the *Tribune* on the following dates: January 15, 1921, p. 1; January 22, 1921, p. 1; January 29, 1921, p. 1; October 1, 1921, p. 1.

42. As was the case with the YMCA, the activities of the Southwest YWCA were reported on almost a weekly basis in the *Philadelphia Tribune.* But more detailed information may be found on: May 21, 1921, p. 8; June 4, 1921, p. 9; May 17, 1924, p. 1; and July 25, 1925, p. 4.

43. The *Tribune* has several columns of almost every issue devoted to the activities of the fraternal organizations in the city, *see,* for example, January 6, 1912, n.p.; January 27, 1912, n.p. *See also,* DuBois, *The Philadelphia Negro,* pp. 221-26; Clara A. Hardin, *The Negroes of Philadelphia: The Cultural Adjustment of a Minority Group* (Bryn Mawr: Bryn Mawr College, 1945), pp. 130-32.

44. Quoted in William C. Hueston, "A Forward Step in Fraternalism," *The Crisis,* XXXIV (July, 1927), 149.

45. Scholarships for black students in Philadelphia, for example, were given out by the Fez Club of the Elks formed in 1949 by Florence C. Franklin and are still being offered; *see* "Twenty-fifth Anniversary of the Philadelphia Fez Club, October 20, 1974" (pamphlet in possession of the writer).

46. *Philadelphia Tribune,* June 9, 1927, p. 1; June 16, 1927, p. 1; July 7, 1927, p. 1.

47. *Ibid.,* April 25, 1929, p. 7; May 30, 1929, p. 1; September 5, 1929, p. 1.

48. *Ibid.,* May 7, 1921, p. 1; May 28, 1921, n.p.; May 23, 1925, p. 9.

49. *Ibid.,* April 12, 1924, p. 9; April 26, 1924, p. 9; July 19, 1924, p. 5; May 23, 1925, p. 5; May 30, 1925, p. 1; May 9, 1929, p. 1; May 16, 1929, p. 16.

50. In the larger study of the overall education of the Philadelphia black community between 1900 and 1950 from which this essay is derived, the participation of black social improvement organizations in activities to bring about a *change* in the social, economic, and political conditions of black Philadelphia is described in detail.

51. The Philadelphia Association for the Protection of Colored Women, *Report of the Fourth Year's Work, 1908* (Philadelphia: n.p., 1909), p. 1. The Historical Society of Pennsylvania has the annual reports for 1908, 1909, 1910, 1911, 1912, 1913, and 1915. It also possesses many of the flyers and bulletins of the organization.

52. *Philadelphia Tribune,* January 6, 1912, n.p.; February 10, 1912, p. 1; May 8, 1915, p. 2; Among the persons who spoke for the Philadelphia Association for the

Protection of Colored Women were Chris Perry, editor of the *Tribune* (*Philadelphia Tribune,* April 12, 1919); Ernest Tustin, Philadelphia Director of Public Welfare (April 10, 1920); John C. Asbury, Representative in the Pennsylvania General Assembly (May 14, 1921).

53. One can obtain some information on the activities of the Armstrong Association of Philadelphia from the Annual Reports, 1910–1920, which may be found at the Historical Society of Pennsylvania.

54. Armstrong Association, *Fourth Annual Report,* 1912 (Philadelphia: "In a Negro Shop," n.d.), passim; *Philadelphia Tribune,* December 7, 1912, p. 1.

55. *Philadelphia Tribune,* January 16, 1926, p. 1; March 13, 1926, p. 7; September 18, 1926, p. 9; October 2, 1926, p. 8; January 1, 1927, p. 1.

56. *Ibid.* Black and white social work trainees often served their apprenticeships with the Armstrong Association.

57. *Ibid.,* April 12, 1928, p. 1. *See also,* N. Weiss, *The National Urban League, 1910–1940* (New York: Oxford Press, 1974), pp. 176–202.

58. For information on the rallies and membership drives of the Philadelphia NAACP, *see* NAACP Branch Correspondence, Philadelphia Branch, 1913–1930, Boxes G-186 and G-187, NAACP Collection, Library of Congress; and the *Philadelphia Tribune,* February 1, 1913, n.p.; December 30, 1916, n.p.; May 3, 1919, p. 1; February 5, 1921, p. 1.

59. *Philadelphia Tribune,* March 15, 1924, p. 7; June 28, 1924, p. 1; August 23, 1924, p. 13; May 16, 1925, p. 1; February 20, 1926, p. 16; March 19, 1927, p. 7; May 31, 1928, p. 2.

60. For examples of joint lectures and activities of the NAACP and other organizations in Philadelphia, *see* the *Tribune,* November 1, 1924, p. 9; January 24, 1925, p. 4; February 7, 1925, p. 5; May 23, 1925, p. 9; March 13, 1930, p. 2.

61. *Ibid.,* January 30, 1915, p. 4; May 13, 1916, p. 1; September 18, 1920, n.p.; November 13, 1920, p. 10; for specific information on the activities of the "Colored Catholic Schools" in Philadelphia, see March 16, 1912, n.p.; June 15, 1912, p. 1; September 28, 1912, p. 1; February 8, 1913, n.p.; January 24, 1925, p. 2.

62. *Ibid.,* February 28, 1920, p. 2; March 19, 1921, p. 9; July 2, 1921, p. 1; February 2, 1924, p. 7; February 27, 1926, p. 15; February 2, 1928, p. 12. *See also,* Hardin, pp. 89–90.

63. *Philadelphia Tribune,* January 10, 1925, p. 6; February 14, 1925, p. 1; January 15, 1927, p. 9; April 23, 1927, p. 9; February 2, 1928, p. 12; January 30, 1930, p. 5.

64. On April 24, 1920, p. 5, the *Tribune* began a regular column on "School and Community News." A series on "Christianity and Modern Life" began on August 23, 1924, p. 12. A regular column on Health Problems began on October 18, 1924, p. 19; and Negro History series were initiated on that date, and on May 16, 1925, p. 9. Extensive series on Negro Education started on August 22, 1925, p. 4, and October 2, 1926, p. 16.

65. For a comprehensive history of the *Tribune* to that date, *see* the Fortieth Anniversary Issue, November 29, 1924.

66. For information on hundreds of migrants who came to Philadelphia during the period 1914–1924 and the activities of black social organizations to assist them, *see,* Migration Survey, Box 21, Philadelphia Housing Association, Temple University Urban Archives.

67. *See* Allan H. Spear, *Black Chicago: The Making of a Ghetto, 1890–1920* (Chicago: University of Chicago Press, 1967, chap. v, "The Institutional Ghetto," pp. 91–110; Gilbert Osofsky, *Harlem: The Making of a Ghetto; Negro New York, 1890– 1930* (New York: Harper and Row, 1963), pp. 81–101, 150–58; Constance M. Green, *The Secret City: A History of Race Relations in the Nation's Capital* (Princeton, New Jersey: Princeton University Press, 1967), pp. 176–83, 197–214.

68. U.S. Works Progress Administration, Illinois, *Churches and Voluntary Associations in the Chicago Negro Community* (Chicago: Works Progress Administration, 1940), p. 219. (Mimeographed.) For other discussions of race versus status conscious organizations, *see* William O. Brown, "The Nature of Race Consciousness," *Social Forces,* X (October, 1936), 90–97; Elizabeth Ferguson, "Race Consciousness Among American Negroes," *The Journal of Negro Education,* VII (January, 1938), 32–40; H. Viscount Nelson, "Race and Class Consciousness of Philadelphia Negroes with Special Emphasis on the Years between 1927 and 1940" (unpublished Ph.D. dissertation, University of Pennsylvania, 1969); James P. Pitts, "The Study of Race Consciousness: Comments on New Directions," *American Journal of Sociology,* LXXX November 1974), 665–87.

To Elevate the Race:
The Michigan Avenue YMCA and the
Advancement of Blacks in Buffalo,
New York, 1922–1940

Lillian S. Williams

The Afro-American population of Buffalo was small throughout the nineteenth and early twentieth centuries.[1] The post-Reconstruction migration of blacks to urban areas increased the black population somewhat as the city rapidly continued to industrialize. Blacks, however, were unsuccessful in gaining large scale employment in Buffalo's industries. Most blacks were employed in service occupations such as butler, pantryman, and janitor. In fact the economic condition of blacks in Buffalo seemed to deteriorate between 1855 and 1905. A trend is quite clear when one examines the changes in the percentage of skilled black workers. Whereas in 1855 the local census reported a significant percentage of black "barbers" and "sailors," then considered "skilled" positions, in 1925 the largest percentage of black males were in "crafts" and "factory labor."[2] The shift in the occupational distribution of black male workers was concurrent with other important social and economic changes for blacks in Buffalo during the period.

Throughout the nineteenth century and the first decade of the twentieth, rigid patterns of residential segregation in Buffalo were conspicuous by their absence. Blacks and whites lived in the same neighborhoods and sometimes within the same household with little, if any, discord. Whites did not establish "neighborhood protection societies" to prohibit blacks from settling in certain sections as was the case in many cities.[3] However, after 1916, when their population expanded rapidly, blacks increasingly were restricted to two areas of settlement within the city, the Ellicott and Masten Park districts, recently abandoned by the various immigrant groups.

In 1910, blacks in Buffalo numbered only 1,773, but by 1920, this figure had risen to 4,511, and in 1925 there were almost 9,000 blacks in the city.[4] The increase in population can be attributed primarily to in-migration. The black sections of Buffalo were already in a rapid state of decline and were severely taxed by the large population. As a result, blacks began moving into contiguous sections where similar housing conditions awaited them. The migrants were often compelled to pay exorbitant rents for inferior housing accommodations. Few houses available to them had adequate sanitation facilities. Recreational facilities were limited and various social ills, such as crime and disease, were becoming more apparent.

Unfortunately, as the number of blacks in Buffalo increased, white citizens often resorted to new tactics of discrimination and segregation. Previously, the sections of the city open to black residents had been restricted somewhat, but it was usually possible for an individual black to secure a "letter of recommendation" from an influential white person which would allow him access to better housing. After 1915 it was not only more difficult to secure housing in restricted sections, but blacks were also being segregated in theatres and restaurants.[5] Moreover, the popularity of the film "Birth of a Nation" and the inroads which the Ku Klux Klan made into the Buffalo white community were indicative of the rapid deterioration in race relations.[6]

The increase in the black population of Buffalo forced a reorganization of many existing "social units" and the establishment of several new ones. Black social organizations were confronted with the dual problem of improving the conditions for the black community and ameliorating the racial situation in the city at large. The Michigan Avenue YMCA was in a unique position to deal adequately with many of the more important social concerns of the black community, and an examination of the Michigan Avenue YMCA from 1922 to 1940 sheds much light on the efforts of black organizations to fulfill what was considered to be their "mission" in the community. It should be noted from the outset that the Michigan Avenue YMCA conceived of itself as a "self-help organization." The "Y's" facilities for community meetings were the best available to Afro-Americans in Buffalo. Prior to the construction of its new building, many of the Michigan Avenue YMCA public lectures were held at the local churches, especially Shiloh Baptist Church. However, the churches, because of religious antagonisms, were often not the most suitable accommodations for inter-faith meetings. The opening of the YMCA provided numerous black social and religious organizations with facilities for educational activities. Black Buffalonians took great pride in the "Y" because they collectively had worked to create it.

From the turn of the century, Alfred H. Whitford, General Secretary of the Young Men's Christian Association of Buffalo, was aware of the existence of a multiplicity of problems within the city's black community.[7] When Julius Rosenwald, president of Sears and Roebuck Company, announced in 1912 that he would offer $25,000 to any "Y" branch that would undertake the construction of a building project designed specifically for the use of the Afro-American population, Whitford was pleased. He believed that the YMCA activities could be extended to the black community with contributions from Rosenwald as well as local philanthropists. In his annual report for 1922, Whitford exhorted the Christian community to carry out its mission by working in the black community of Buffalo.

> The city churches of Buffalo are alive to the expansion program of their denomination and support missions located in the needy sections of their country and also in foreign lands and yet collectively fail to get together to help a neglected needy group who are forced to live in an undesirable, congested section between Michigan and Jefferson, and south of Broadway.[8]

In July of 1922, the Buffalo Federation of churches conducted a survey of the black sections of Buffalo.[9] Whitford included the results in his annual report because they were "of interest to all who are interested in the advancement of the colored race."[10] The report pointed out that housing conditions between Broadway and Michigan and west of Jefferson and east of Michigan were among the most deplorable for blacks in the city. It noted further that there were no public recreational facilities available for men and boys in that area. While a third of the population or 2,279 persons were members of the various Protestant dominations, these churches were indebted up to more than one third of their value, while white churches usually carried an indebtedness of less than half this amount. Such a large indebtedness virtually precluded any possibility of the black churches establishing a recreational center to meet the needs of its members. The only facilities available both day and night to the black male population were the "vicious places" that tended to demoralize even the "good citizens."

Whitford argued that if whites "who care for others would make possible a Negro Community Center for men, women and children located in the residential section near Jefferson Street, it would be a good investment for Buffalo; moreover, it would safeguard their [blacks] interests and strengthen their churches."[11] While pointing out the relatively low cost of buildings for black YMCA's throughout the country, Whitford also emphasized the extensive use to which the "Y" facilities in black communities had been put. Buffalo, he maintained, had been derelict in meeting its obligation to the growing black community. Whitford concluded with a request for funds to be designated for work specifically in the black community.

The Whitford report of December, 1922 appears to have generated little support within the Buffalo YMCA organization, for there is no indication that any arrangements were being planned to organize activities among blacks. Sometime later a group of one hundred fifty "representative" black men petitioned the Board of Directors to begin "Y" work among the men and boys of their community.[12] In direct response to their petition, the Board of Directors of the Buffalo Association announced that it had placed into its budget for the next year provisions which would allow for the organization and maintenance of a "colored" branch of the Young Men's Christian Association. This branch would serve the needs of blacks of Buffalo as well as those who resided in the nearby town of Lackawanna. Under the capable leadership of A. H. Whitford, the Buffalo Association embarked upon their plan during the summer of 1923.[13]

The Association appointed William H. Jackson of South Carolina to head the committee which would explore the prospects of establishing a branch of the "Y" to serve a population that was "needy" and "meriting" a helping hand. Jackson, a veteran YMCA man and churchman, was a good choice for this position and brought a wealth of experience to the post. After he had received his Bachelor of Arts Degree from Lincoln University in 1901, Jackson taught school in Florida and Georgia. For five years he served as Executive Secretary of the Center Avenue Branch YMCA in Springfield, Ohio, and for the next fifteen years, he was Superintendent of the Presbyterian Sunday School Mission in the Southern region. As Sunday School Mission Superintendent, he took specialized courses in religious training at Lake Geneva, Wisconsin and also spent two summers studying in the Department of Sociology at Columbia University. At the conclusion of his fifteen-year tenure as Superintendent, he returned to Orangeburg, South Carolina to continue teaching. It was from this latter post that Whitford summoned Jackson to Buffalo in 1923.[14]

By September 1 Jackson had an office in the Central Branch YMCA on Pearl Street. From there he tried to map out a viable program for black youth. With the aid of M. T. Green, T. C. Holcolm and Leonard Sears, Jackson called together the Lincoln Club of Youths of St. Luke's AME Church, and several other youngsters from the black community, to form what later became the core of the Michigan Avenue YMCA Boys Club.[15]

In trying to get the YMCA program off the ground, Jackson believed it was advantageous to surround himself with influential business and professional men from within the black community. The original members of the Board of Managers, the governing body of the Michigan Avenue Branch, were Rudolph Lane, Chairman; John E. Brent; Justice Taylor; R. W. Cohn; C. A. Sims; and Dr. I. L. Scruggs.[16] Some of these men and many of those who later joined them as managers were recent arrivals to Buffalo who had established themselves in the professional sectors of the local black community.[17]

John E. Brent came to Buffalo from his native Washington, D.C., after having attended Tuskegee Institute where he studied carpentry and architecture. He was graduated from Tuskegee in 1907. After a short teaching career in the D.C. public schools, Brent went to Philadelphia where he enrolled in the School of Architecture of Drexel Institute. He graduated from Drexel in June, 1913 and shortly thereafter, moved to Buffalo where he worked for a number of architectural firms. Brent served as a member of the "vestry" or ruling body of St. Philip's Episcopal Church, and was active in many social and benevolent organizations in the Queen City, including past president of the NAACP. His experience and knowledge would prove to be beneficial in the development of the new branch.[18]

Dr. Ivorite Scruggs, a native of Mississippi who had spent his boyhood in Memphis, Tennessee, came to Buffalo in 1921. He had received a Bachelor of Science Degree from Howard University in 1915 and a medical degree in 1919. Scruggs was an outstanding civic leader and in recognition of his services, was later appointed as a member of the Board of Directors of the Metropolitan YMCA of Buffalo, the first Afro-American in the history of the United States to be appointed to such a position.[19]

Several other men from within the black commuity shared their skills in the establishment of the Michigan Avenue YMCA.[20] The most prominent were Cornelius Ford,[21] a livestock dealer, and Dr. Jesse E. Nash,[22] pastor of the Michigan Avenue Baptist Church from 1892 until his retirement in 1953. Nash had been in Buffalo perhaps longer than any of the other founders of the "Y". He was familiar with the problems of blacks in Buffalo and had worked to alleviate their plight through participation in many community organizations, including the local branch of the NAACP and later the National Urban League.

Professionals were not the only ones who were instrumental in the establishment of the black branch of the YMCA. William Jackson related how the Michigan Avenue Branch "Y" secured its first member. Jackson was simply walking down the street when he met Welton Townsend, a machine operator, and told Townsend of his intention of organizing a chapter of the "Y" for the black community. Townsend was interested in his project and gave him $1.00 for his membership fee. Welton Townsend later became a member of the Board of Managers of the new YMCA. Other working men, both skilled and unskilled, were involved in the "Y" from an early date. Peter Lomax, a porter, and Ninde Davis, a laborer, were among the early members of the policy-making body, the Board of Managers, of the Michigan Avenue YMCA.[23]

The diverse backgrounds and experiences which the organizers brought to the planning committee were important to the initial success of the Michigan Avenue YMCA. The programs which they instituted reflected the strengths which the individuals manifested and the Michigan "Y" in turn became one of the most prestigious, respected institutions within the black commuity. Indeed it became a model for other Associations among blacks.[24]

The first major problem confronting the managers was the securing of adequate facilities. In 1923, the Metropolitan YMCA rented the former home of St. Luke's AME Church, located at 485 Michigan Avenue, as a temporary home for the new Branch because of its accessibility to the black populace. The YMCA facility designed for the black population of Buffalo and Lackawanna exclusively did not create an issue. Blacks in Buffalo had been experiencing an increase in restrictions on their personal freedom since before the War.[25] A segregated facility merely fitted into the emerging pattern. Moreover, those individuals who were making arrangements for the new facility were either ex-southerners or individuals who had spent a substantial number of their early years in the South. The influence of the late Booker T. Washington was strong among them. Brent had studied at Tuskegee, Jackson had studied and taught in the segregated school systems of the South, and Scruggs had received his medical degree from Howard University. Nash and Ford had reached maturity in the South and had studied at the missionary schools which were established for Afro-Americans during the latter half of the nineteenth century. Each of these individuals was keenly aware of the advantages that could accrue to the community through the YMCA programs they envisioned for blacks in the Buffalo area.

From the beginning, the Michigan Avenue YMCA was dedicated to the welfare of black youths in Buffalo. The program of activities continued to expand annually, attracting large numbers to the facility. The YMCA building served as a social center for Afro-Americans.

> ...these limited quarters have become a bee-hive of activity; practically the only social center for the exclusive use of colored people.[26]

By December, 1924 the Branch boasted 265 members, of whom 60 were boys.[27] The Sunday meetings had an average attendance of fifty-five. Sixty-six students were enrolled in the two Bible classes and the daily attendance at the rooms averaged forty-five. During its first year, the Michigan Avenue YMCA sponsored a two-week camping trip at the YMCA's Camp Weona for twenty-five youngsters. Shiloh Baptist Church was the seat of a mass meeting sponsored by the Michigan Avenue YMCA in conjunction with the national YMCA Conference which convened in Buffalo in 1924. Over 500 persons came to hear Major Robert R. Moton, President of Tuskegee Institute, urge the audience to "take up the sword of intelligence, industry and education in the battle for the inherent and enfranchised privileges of the Negro throughout the United States."[28]

The work of the organizers was initially very successful and "thoroughly appreciated by the colored citizens." A huge lot near the corner of Michigan and Cypress had been purchased by the Metropolitan YMCA in 1923 along with the original building to be used by blacks.[29] Also that year Julius Rosenwald, the Sears magnate, issued a challenge to the Buffalo community. He let it be known that he would donate $25,000 toward the building fund if the Buffalo community could raise $125,000 for the construction of the Michigan Avenue YMCA by December 18, 1925.[30]

A fund-raising drive for the Michigan Avenue YMCA was initiated in the Fall of 1924, and was extremely successful. The editor of a white daily newspaper, *The Courier Express,* publicized this important achievement and exhorted whites in Buffalo to follow the example of blacks in meeting their quota during the annual YMCA fund-raising drive.

> An example of such giving appears to be present in the gifts for the proposed "Y" branch for Negroes. The honor of advancing the hand of the clock at Lafayette Square yesterday fell to Rudolph S. Lane, Negro captain of the Michigan Avenue team, highest for the day. That is an honor in which the Negro citizens of Buffalo can justly take pride, for it marks their high interest in the things for which the YMCA stands and is seeking to promote in still greater degrees. Also it is a good sign that the value of the "Y" work is appreciated. Buffalo cannot afford to let slip this opportunity to make the "Y" more efficient than ever.[31]

After the Buffalo community had raised its quota of $125,000, Whitford indicated that he received Julius Rosenwald's donation on Christmas Eve, 1924.[32]

The problem of an adequate physical plant for the Michigan Avenue YMCA was still prominent when George B. Mathews, Buffalo industrialist and owner of the *Courier Express,* invited Whitford to his home in early June of the following year to discuss with him his interest in the welfare of black citizens. Whitford later informed the Board of Directors at a meeting held on June 30 that Mathews agreed to donate $100,000 to the YMCA to be used as a trust fund "to carry on and extend the educational, recreational and settlement work among the Negro population of Buffalo and vicinity."[33] The grant stipulated, however, that larger facilities than those already planned were to be provided in the projected new building. The Board accepted both the gift and the circumstances under which it was given. The trust became known as the Booker T. Washington Foundation and was the largest donation ever made for the support of "Y" work among Afro-Americans in the United States.[34] It was merely the first of many gifts that George and Jenny Mathews would contribute to the support of the Michigan Avenue YMCA. By the time of his death 20 years later, Mathews' contributions totaled over $500,000.[35]

The Metropolitan "Y" had included a new building for the black community in its five-year plan for the years 1922-1927.[36] However, the Mathews contribution, along with the Rosenwald grant and the successful fund-raising drive of the Michigan Avenue "Y" in 1924 guaranteed the construction of a new building to house the "Y" much sooner than previously planned.[37] Before the Mathews donation, foundation support for the Michigan Avenue "Y" totaled about $440,000.

After reviewing the credentials of potential architects for the new structure, Secretary General Whitford, upon the approval of the Board of Directors, commissioned John Brent, an original organizer of the Michigan Avenue YMCA, to perform the task. He was only the second black architect to receive an assignment to design a YMCA for blacks. Brent subsequently resigned from his post at Oakley and Schallmore to establish his own firm,[38] and the Michigan Avenue YMCA was his first large scale commission. Plans for the proposed four-story structure got underway immediately. They included class rooms, separate men's and boy's departments with social rooms, billiard rooms, a library, locker rooms, and a standard size gymnasium and swimming pool. The plans called for a fifty-four room dormitory and a cafeteria with a seating capacity of 80. Space for a barber shop and a tailor shop were also incorporated into the design. The building was to be constructed for $200,000, but it actually was erected at a cost of $285,000.[39]

The new Georgian colonial style branch of the Michigan Avenue YMCA was opened and dedicated amidst great pageantry and splendor on Sunday, April 15, 1928. Three thousand people visited the structure during the day, and a total of 5,000 for the week. More than 1,500 people attended the dedication ceremonies over which Rudolph S. Lane, chairman of the Michigan Avenue Board of Managers, presided. Many local as well as national dignitaries attended the ceremonies, among whom were George and Jenny Mathews and Julius Rosenwald. YMCA secretaries Thomas Taylor of New York City, A. L. Comither of Brooklyn, Charles E. Trye, Cleveland, Thomas A. Bulling from Rochester, George Arthur of Chicago, and B. W. Overton of Cincinnati were among the YMCA officials present. In his address, Julius Rosenwald congratulated John Brent on "the completeness and architectural beauty of the building both inside and out"; he summoned Brent to the platform to congratulate him personally on the "beautiful and successful building he had created for the colored group in Buffalo."[40]

People from all over the community rallied to the support of the Michigan Avenue YMCA and it became the most important social center for the black community. The "Y" became an arena in which individuals of varying political persuasions could come together in harmony. Their views ran the gamut from Garveyites to Democrats. The membership was not only made up of persons from the various Protestant denominations and social groups within the black community, but also those individuals who lacked other organizational affiliations. These participants, like the organizers, perceived of the YMCA as a self-help project — a means of ameliorating the race's condition and of displaying the achievements of Afro-Americans in science, sports, education, the arts, and other areas.[41] But more importantly, black Buffalonians believed that it provided a forum in which black youths could receive recognition for their accomplishments in fields which were not readily accessible to them, and a means by which young men and women could build character.

The Michigan Avenue YMCA was certainly the finest structure and the best equipped social center available to the black community when it opened in 1928. To make certain that the "Y" was accessible to most members of the black community, fees were kept at a reasonable level. Men paid an annual fee of $2.00 for a basic or "social" membership which entitled them to use the reading room and the game rooms, to rent rooms in the dormitory, and to participate in religious activities; a $5.00 membership included all of the aforementioned plus the right to use the physical educational facilities; a full senior membership for $7.00 permitted them to have complete use of the YMCA and to be assigned a locker on the premises.[42]

Membership for boys varied according to age. Children from age nine to twelve paid an annual membership fee of $2.00; those aged thirteen to sixteen paid $3.00. High school students and working young men were charged a $4.00 membeship fee. Those who were enrolled in the Young Men's Division paid an annual fee of $5.00. These charges and fees were less than those at other YMCA branches in Buffalo.[43] At the same time, a number of subsidized memberships were offered to youths who could not afford membership fees. These memberships were made available from individual contributions or through donations from various black and white civic groups or from foundation monies set aside for this purpose.[44] During the economic crisis of the 1930's, the number of free memberships increased substantially.

In the new building the Board of Management continued the policies which it had instituted previously. The building was staffed by experienced professional, clerical, and service personnel who often served as role models for the youth.[45] Each YMCA program was designed to fulfill the goals of building character, educating, and assuring the physical development of black youths. In essence, its programs were intended for physical and mental improvement.[46] The "Y's" mission was carried out by the various committees which operated within the larger structure. There were six major subdivisions within the organization: the Physical Education Department, the Religious Work Committee, the Boys Work Committee, the Girls Work Committee, the Education Committee, and the Health Week Committee.

A traditional concern of the YMCA for developing the physical prowess of youth meant that the Michigan Avenue YMCA was also concerned about the "physical" development of black youth. During the first year in the new building, the Physical Education program was the most well attended of all the programs offered at the "Y". Activities scheduled for every day of the week (except Sunday) included regular gym classes, volleyball, basketball, tumbling, and wrestling. The department's offerings were designed specifically for "mass appeal." This policy fitted into the scheme of the Founders and Managers of the "Y". The Physical Education Committee described its program in the annual reports.

> The Physical Department is a laboratory where a practical demonstration of moral development as well as physical development is conducted. In the Gym the boys and young men are taught to play the game of life squarely and manly, through play. There is no better way to train characters than through well supervised play.[47]

In addition, the program of the Physical Education Department provided an excellent "public relations forum," for it displayed well disciplined youths, who not only enjoyed using the facilities, but who also exhibited the various skills which they had acquired at the "Y" at conferences and celebrations.[48]

For example, basketball was an extremely popular sport and in 1927 the Michigan Avenue "Y" teams were victorious in 41 out of 45 games. These and other group activities were used as a vehicle for maintaining and improving relationships among various sectors of the community and throughout Erie County. Seventeen Inter-Church Basketball League games were played at the "Y".[49]

Herman Daves and his assistant in the Physical Department, Leon Hall, organized and supervised activities which included "leadership training" for the youth of the black community. Each of eight clubs which met regularly at the "Y" had its own set of officers who were responsible for arranging and directing the club's annual program. The Boys Department program usually included features which were both entertaining and educational. Bible instruction, literary programs, social and business meetings, and movies of a "socially redeeming character," were a part of the regular calendar of events. A number of youth groups held conferences at the "Y", among them were the Hi-Y Clubs and the Older Boys Clubs. The conferences pursued such themes as "Employment and Youth," "Health and Hygiene,"and "Black Youth in Higher Education." From the very beginning these conferences focused upon issues of significance to youth in Buffalo and from the surrounding area.[50] Indeed, the Michigan Avenue YMCA was intended to be the funnel through which black youth could filter into the mainstream of Buffalo's black community.[51]

The organizers of the Michigan Avenue YMCA were quite aware of the social background of the youngsters they served. They firmly believed that the family was the "center of Christian living" and that their ultimate success in promoting youth, "the hope of tomorrow" for the community was, to a great extent, contingent upon the entire family's participation or at least support of the "Y's" overall program. Thus, the committees regularly planned activities which involved parents as much as possible.[52] There were annual Father and Son, and Mother and Son Banquets. Tickets for the banquets were available for a nominal fee of $.75 for both parent and son. Subsidized tickets were also available to assure that those parents who wanted to attend could accompany their sons. There was also a special "Parents Night" when parents were given the opportunity to observe the physical skills which their children had learned during the year at the "Y". The swimming exhibition and ping pong and billiards tournaments, which were sponsored by the Boys Department, provided family entertainment and attracted large numbers to the YMCA. Moreover, these projects did much to enhance the self-concepts and self-images of the youths. Two thousand seven-hundred and nine boys attended some 187 meetings in 1927, the most popular of which were the Sunday afternoon religious and social activities.[53]

Although religion pervaded all of the activities of the Michigan Avenue "Y", there were specific programs designed to meet the religious needs of the members. Charles Sims, Peter Lomax and Justice Taylor of the Religious Work Committee scheduled Bible study sessions every Sunday morning. These sessions were planned primarily for the men who lived in the dormitory. The Sunday afternoon meetings, however, were open to the public and consisted of a lecture followed by a general discussion. The topics usually dealt with contemporary concerns such as the problem of young people and the church or themes selected from the Bible.[54] Through these programs youth had a forum in which to discuss some of their problems in a wide variety of areas. Once a month high school girls were even invited to these discussions. The Religious Work Committee also scheduled movies on Tuesday, Friday and Saturday evenings, with the intention of keeping the youngsters off the street and away from the "vicious places" of the city.

The task of creating and implementing a program which would affect not only the social conditions of Afro-Americans in Buffalo, but would also have significant ramifications for their economic situation was assigned to the Education Committee. Secretary Jackson, Ninde Davis, Attorney C. M. Maloney, and J. Herman Daves comprised the Education Committee of Michigan Avenue in 1928. The "Y" scheduled several classes during the 1928–1929 fiscal year and students could enroll by paying the $2.00 registration fee.[55] The curriculum of the Educational Department also reflected the philosophy of the Managers and Founders. These men were generally pragmatists and thus the courses were designed to meet the immediate and long term needs of the black community. While at first glance the course offerings appear to be somewhat conservative, the chief goal of the Michigan Avenue YMCA was to elevate the black community, thus the Managers usually sought the most efficacious methods for solving the immediate contemporary problems. Music appreciation was the only "academic" subject offered. Students who enrolled in this course underwent a rigorous six-month training program which intended "to prepare persons for successful singing for positions in church choirs and through them to advance the cause of *artistic* singing" (emphasis added).[56] Students in the music institute frequently performed in public concerts. These musical performances and concerts guaranteed that the Michigan Avenue "Y" would continue to attract the attention of potential benefactors, both black and white.

The Metropolitan YMCA in Buffalo had established vocational courses including auto mechanics, accounting and plumbing in the branches in 1900.[57] Yet those which required greater skills and commanded higher wages were absent from the Michigan Avenue "Y" program. Only two vocational courses were offered at the black branch of the "Y" in 1928, furnace operation and household management. It is likely that these courses were offered because individuals who completed them were generally able to secure immediate employment. Males enrolled in the "Essentials of Furnace Operation," a four-month course designed to promote safety and economy for those persons interested in operating steam boilers. Topics for discussion included: how to start a good fire, dampers, fire doors, coal, how or when to put on or take off the draft, fluctuations of furnace temperatures, and steam pressure.[58] The four-month course in household management, or "domestic science," included topics on household values, house management-arithmetical problems, housewifery and renovation, menu planning, preparation of food, table service, child care, budgets and home life, and hospitality.[59] The course was justified by the Education Committee because of the marketability of the skills which were taught.

> Positions requiring special skill in the household industries are multiplying. The skilled household assistant who is capable of assuming responsibility for the wise administration of the household activities, as well as for their performance, is demanded in the modern home, and training in home economics is imperative for one who would fill such a position.
> There is an increasing demand for the intelligent young woman trained in child care to act as children's nurse. Homemaking training offers an opportunity for development of special talents and for active participation in the *progress* of the race (emphasis added).[60]

The Michigan "Y" also served as an employment agency for black workers and William Jackson was successful in placing many individuals in positions requiring those skills which they had acquired from courses taught at the "Y".[61]

In the 1920s, the Metropolitan Branch YMCA of Buffalo had expanded but when the Great Depression hit the city, the "Y's" emphasis shifted to that of conserving financial resources and in some instances guaranteeing the survival of the branches. The staffs of the branches were reduced and salaries decreased, and the YMCA was able to continue its programs in most of the branches mainly because they were well organized and utilized volunteer assistance.[62]

By the 1931-1932 fiscal year the course offerings of the Michigan Avenue YMCA had been expanded greatly. The Music Appreciation course saw the greatest revision. The title of the course was changed to the YMCA Institute of Music and included sight reading, vocal training, organ, and a capella choir for women. The "Y" sponsored its own Quintette which was composed of members of the Institute of Music.[63] Although no YWCA was established for blacks in Buffalo, classes were set up for women and girls at the black YMCA. A sewing course designed primarily for female heads of households taught the making of garments and remodeling and repairing older clothes.

> We feel certain with every housewife having knowledge of how to do those things, she and her children will have more clothes, better clothes, and a larger bank account.[64]

The Needle Art Club, which had been organized for girls ranging from age nine to fifteen during the 1929-1930 fiscal year, was quite popular. This course was concerned with teaching girls to appreciate "the beauty of art" and to give them the advantage of "making a home beautiful as they grow into womanhood.''⁶⁵ A Public Speaking course, taught by J. Edward Nash, and English grammar, with Otis Davenport Jackson as the primary instructor, were also added to the academic program.

While the program of the Education Committee provided opportunities for blacks to advance, it did not provide courses in the skilled trades from which blacks had virtually been excluded. This policy prevailed throughout the 1930s and the 1940s because of the basic utilitarian outlook of the Board of Management of the Michigan Avenue YMCA. However, during the 1936–1937 fiscal year, the Education Committee set up a college catalogue library and counseling service for those individuals who wished to pursue a college education. By 1939 there was concern among the Committee members about the lack of guidance programs for the hundreds of black youths who were graduating from high school with little knowledge of what the future held for them. The Committee believed that a guidance program would help black youth ''steer clear of the pitfalls of the passing generation'' of high school graduates.⁶⁶ Moreover, in October, 1937, Secretary Jackson announced that because of the increasing opportunities in business for black women that courses in shorthand and typing would be formed. It was necessary that these courses become a part of the YMCA curriculum, for business schools in Buffalo refused to admit and place black women in positions.⁶⁷ Students who enrolled in these courses were required to pay only a small fee for the rental of the typewriters.⁶⁸

One of the most popular and elaborate educational programs which the Education Committee implemented was a series of public forums beginning in the 1929–1930 fiscal year. Although the forums ostensibly were directed at the adult members of the ''Y'', they were open to the public. One could purchase an admission ticket for the season for $1.25 or pay $.50 for each session. Prominent national Afro-American figures were invited to participate in the forums. The list of those who accepted speaking engagements reads like a ''Who's Who in Black America.'' Between 1930 and 1936, among the individuals who participated in the Annual Forums were: Dr. Mordecai Johnson, President of Howard University; Dr. W. E. B. DuBois, Editor of *The Crisis;* Congressman Oscar Depriest; Mary McCleod Bethune, President of Bethune-Cookman College; Nannie Burroughs, President of the National Training School for Women and Girls; Walter White, Executive Secretary of the NAACP; and Mary Church Terrell, first President of the National Association of Colored Women.⁶⁹

These lecturers, like the Founders and Managers of the Michigan Avenue YMCA, were overwhelmingly associated with the South, particularly through their educational backgrounds. Most of them depended upon the black community for their livelihood, and either worked within the community or performed services which were organized explicitly to serve that community. They, too, were imbued with the philosophy of self-help. C. C. Spaulding, President of the North Carolina Mutual Insurance Company of Durham, lectured on ''Negro Achievement in Business.'' During one of his visits to Buffalo, in 1936, W. E.B. DuBois addressed himself to the topic "Italy and Ethiopia." The Italian attack on Ethiopia was a major concern of Afro-Americans and blacks throughout the country rallied to aid the Ethiopian cause.[70] Their support represented both self-help and racial pride.

The lecturers often presented goals toward which the youth of the black community could strive. President Johnson of Howard University in his address, "Religion and Poverty," at the 10th anniversary celebration of the Michigan Avenue YMCA, exhorted the community:

> The message that religion gives to the poor man is the message God gave to Ezekiel; "Son of man, stand upon your own feet..." God makes no promise to take care of you unless you stand up on your own feet.[71]

Johnson also asked Orthodox Christians to consider "dispassionately and constructively all adverse criticisms against religion, admit its shortcomings, and seek improvements in the light of present-day needs." The public forums were a means for providing increased self-awareness within the black community. Patrons of the YMCA were well represented at the forums, along with hundreds of people from within the community at large. Newspaper commentators continuously referred to the well-attended performances and lectures, as well as the interracial composition of the audiences.[72]

The Michigan Avenue YMCA was involved in numerous other programs which were designed to advance the social, economic and intellectual conditions of blacks in Buffalo. Oftentimes professionals and organizations from the larger Buffalo community joined with black individuals and groups to present social programs. In the 1930s, the Association established the "Negro Health Week" lectures. Dr. I. L. Scruggs presided over the Negro Health Week program, and was joined by Dr. Marvin Israel and Dr. Nat Kutzman from the larger Buffalo community, Dr. Yerby Jones, and Dr. Theodore Kakaza, former president of the local branch (or "unit") of the Universal Negro Improvement Association, in presenting a series of lectures dealing with such topics as "Health Problems in Your Family," "Dental Hygiene," "Communicable Diseases," "Heart Disease," and "Personal Hygiene."[73] Twenty other organizations coalesced with the "Y" in sponsoring the health series, including the Prince Hall Masons, the Adult Education Center, the Buffalo Department of Health, Public School 32, the Memorial Center and Urban League, Inc., the City Federation of Women's Clubs, and the Book Lovers Club.[74] Sessions were held at the Michigan Avenue YMCA and other social and community centers throughout the city.[75]

The Michigan Avenue YMCA addressed many of the social needs of its black constituents through its guidance program, its health program, its course offerings, its physical education department, its living accommodations, and most importantly, its educational programs. Under the capable leadership of

William Jackson, it was considered quite successful by local residents. Jackson's dedication to the "Y" led one contemporary to remark:

> W. H. Jackson, Executive Secretary of the "Y" Branch, has done more for the Negro race in Buffalo than any other colored man....[76]

The leadership ability demonstrated by Secretary Jackson and his aides was recognized by individuals inside and outside of Buffalo. William Pickens contacted Jackson in an attempt to gain his assistance in reorganizing the floundering local chapter of the NAACP during the early years of the Great Depression.[77]

The men and women who were instrumental in the establishment and direction of the Michigan Avenue YMCA had a vision for the black people of Buffalo. They conceived of the "Y" as a force in elevating or improving the social, cultural, intellectual, and educational conditions of that community. They moved with what, at times, appeared to be a "messianic fervor" in planning and promoting activities which would improve the social environment within the community and, at the same time, ameliorate race relations within the city. Indeed, in an environment plagued by discrimination and segregation, with limited opportunities to climb the social or occupational ladder, the "Y" provided an opportunity for some black youths, such as Russell Service and Arthur Griffa to achieve professional status within the "Y".[78] Leroy Coles, the Executive Secretary of the Buffalo Urban League, and Daniel Acker, a recent president of the NAACP, grew up as members of the Michigan Avenue YMCA.[79] Many youths were placed in jobs in industry and private homes as a result of the recommendations which they received from the "Y". Still others were encouraged to attend college through the career guidance program offered at the Michigan Avenue YMCA.

The Michigan Avenue "Y" was generally at the forefront of social activities in the black community. Its tournaments, forums, and later the newspaper which it published portrayed favorable images of Afro-Americans to the populace of Buffalo. The expansion of its programs and facilities, the increase in attendance at its functions, and the long list of successful persons today who grew up as members of the Michigan Avenue "Y" all attest to its achievements.[80] The self-help emphasis of the "Y" and the efficiency ethic of the 1920s led to the creation of an educational program that became an important source of "racial pride" for black Buffalonians. The success of the Michigan Avenue YMCA in meeting its challenges can be attributed primarily to the men and women who provided shrewd leadership in mobilizing and bringing into the "Y" diverse groups from within the Buffalo community. Moreover, the programs which they established attracted a large endowment fund which guaranteed that the Michigan Avenue YMCA's programs would continue to serve the Buffalo black community.[81]

NOTES

1.

Year	Population*
1855	704
1875	707
1892	1,118
1905	1,199

*New York State Manuscript Census

2. Selected Occupations of blacks in Buffalo, N.Y., 1855–1925*

Occupation	1855.N:133 % Negro		1875.N:188 % Negro		1892.N:346 % Negro		1905.N:425 % Negro		1925.N:211[c] % Negro	
	N	Males 1855	N	Males 1875	N	Males 1892	N	Males 1905	N	Males 1925
Barbers	21	16.0	16	8.5	9	2.6	6	1.4	3	1.4
Sailors	11	8.0	7	3.7	3	0.9	0	0.0	0	0.0
Musicians	1	0.8	3	1.5	10	3.0	18	4.2	0	0.0
Bldg. Trds.	6	6.0	8	4.3	7	2.0	7	1.6	10	4.7
Masons	1	0.8	0	0.0	2	0.6	14	3.3	2	1.0
"Crafts"[a]	6	4.5	5	2.7	6	1.7	10	2.4	25[b]	11.8
Factory Lbr.	0	0.0	0	0.0	0	0.0	2	0.5	47	22.0
Clk., Msngr.	0	0.0	0	0.0	13	3.7	7	1.6	1	0.5
Storekeeper	0	0.0	0	0.0	0	0.0	0	0.0	1	0.5
Professional	6	4.5	3	1.5	5	1.4	4	0.9	3	1.4

a Some of those listed under particular crafts must have labored in factories or workshops, but the census did not make such distinctions.

b Does not include railroad firemen and brakemen.

c The 1925 data are a sample that drew all Negro males older than 15 residing in every twentieth Negro-headed household in wards 6, 7, and 8.

*I wish to thank Laurence Glasco, professor of history at the University of Pittsburgh, for giving me permission to quote from "The Negro Family, Household Structure and Occupational Structure, 1855–1925," which he and Herbert Gutman of William and Mary wrote for the Yale Conference on 19th Century Cities, November, 1968 (unpublished manuscript in possession of author).

3. Evans, William, "Fear and Housing," National Urban League, (New York, 1946), p. 9. Charles Johnson makes similar observations in "The Negro in Buffalo, A Survey," National Urban League, (New York, 1923), unpublished manuscript, State University of New York at Buffalo Archives.

4. *Buffalo American,* June 21, 1923. United States Population Schedule, 1910, 1920; New York State Manuscript Census, 1925.

5. Interview, B. Lee, long time resident of Buffalo and son of prominent Buffalo black family, Chevy Chase, Maryland, April, 1970. *Crisis,* XVI (March, 1918), 249.

6. Jackson, Kenneth, *The Ku Klux Klan in the City* (New York, 1967), p. 173.

7. Hausauer, Kenneth C., *The Second Fifty Years* (Buffalo, 1970), p. 48.

8. *Men of Buffalo,* XXI (December, 1922), 13.

9. *Ibid.,* p. 13. *See also* Buffalo Federation of Churches, *Foreign Speaking and Negro Sections of Buffalo* (Buffalo, 1923).

10. *Ibid.,* p. 13.

11. *Ibid.,* p. 13.

12. *Men of Buffalo,* XXII (May 1, 1922 – May 1, 1923), 5.

13. Records of the Michigan Avenue YMCA, *Handbook,* 1928. These records are located in the Archives of the Afro-American Historical Society of the Niagara Frontier, North Jefferson Branch Library, Buffalo and Erie County Library, Buffalo, New York. Hereafter referred to as Records, MAYMCA. The official history of the Buffalo YMCA lists the founding of the Michigan Avenue "Y" in the fall of 1922. *See* Hausauer, *op. cit.,* p. 51. Also see *Men of Buffalo,* XXII, 5. The discrepancy can be attributed to the fact that the historian of the Michigan Avenue "Y" wrote about it only after William Jackson had been appointed Executive Director.

14. Records, MAYMCA. "Recognition Week Programs," April 21–27, 1947.

15. *Ibid.,* Abbreviated History.

16. *Ibid.*

17. *See* biographical sketches below.

18. Records, MAYMCA, "Memorabilia, 1926–1936."

19. *Ibid., Buffalo Courier Express,* March 17, 1955.

20. Rudolph Lane, a member of the Bethel AME Church, former president of the local chapter of the NAACP and the first chairman of the Board of Managers of the Michigan Avenue YMCA, worked as a bookkeeper for the Buffalo Optical Company (Buffalo City Directory, 1923). Justice Taylor was a contractor. The 1923 City Directory listed Ray W. Cohn as an agent. It is impossible to determine the nature of his business. Charles E. Sims operated a furniture store with Edward Towne on Michigan Avenue, across the street from the future site of the "Y". With the exception of Taylor, these men reresided in the heart of the black community.

21. In 1906, Ford moved to Buffalo from Addison, Michigan. He was a native of Jonesboro, Tennessee. Ford worked his way through Warner Institute, an American Missionary school in Jonesboro. One of Ford's instructors was impressed favorably with his performance and he secured a job for him on his father's farm in Addison. After working for Fred H. Smith for only three years, Smith entered into a partnership dealing in livestock with him. Business demands necessitated that Ford travel to Buffalo frequently. He soon decided to remain there and to set up a livestock brokerage firm in 1906. Ford was active in the NAACP and served as treasurer of the *Buffalo American,* a black newspaper which was affilliated with the National Negro Press Association (*Buffalo Courier Express,* April 20, 1951).

22. Dr. Jesse E. Nash was born in Occoquam, Virginia in 1868. His parents had been slaves and Nash was compelled to secure positions as farm laborer, dockhand, teamster, mason and blacksmith while acquiring an elementary education. He was able to save money and at the age that most American youths who enroll in institutions of higher learning do, Nash entered Whalen Seminary, today known as Virginia Union University, where he completed the requirements for a Bachelor of Divinity Degree. Nash had been in Buffalo perhaps longer than any of the other founders of the "Y". He was familiar with the problems of blacks in Buffalo and had worked to alleviate their plight through participation in other community organizations. (*Buffalo Evening News,* January 26, 1957).

23. *Buffalo City Directory,* 1923.

24. Interviews, Bessie Williams, Garveyite and member of Women's Committee, Michigan Avenue YMCA, Buffalo, New York, February 26, 1976; Arthur Giffa, Associate General Executive, East Side Branch YMCA, Buffalo, New York, February 27, 1976; Raymond Jackson, former member, Board of Management, Michigan Avenue YMCA, June 20, 1977. *Men of Buffalo,* XXVI (December, 1927), 2.

25. Letter, Amelia G. Anderson to Robert Bagnall, June 7, 1922; letter, Walter White to Amelia G. Anderson, November 12, 1922; letter, Amelia G. Anderson to Walter White, November 9, 1922, NAACP Branch Files, G-130, Administrative Files, Box C300, Manuscript Room, Library of Congress.

26. *Men of Buffalo,* XXIV (July, 1925), 3.
27. *Ibid.,* p. 4. Afro-American YMCAs in larger cities had been constructed before World War I. *See* Spear, *Black Chicago,* (Chicago, 1967); Osofsky, *Harlem: The Making of a Ghetto* (New York, 1966); Katzman, *Before the Ghetto* (Urbana, 1973); Franklin, "In Pursuit of Freedom" above. The black population of Buffalo before the War was too small to warrant the establishment of a separate branch of the YMCA. While there is no evidence that local Afro-Americans were in contact with other black YMCA directors, William Jackson, Secretary of the Michigan Avenue Branch, and himself a newcomer to Buffalo, was a veteran YMCA man who had served as Secretary of the Center Avenue Branch YMCA in Springfield, Ohio. Undoubtedly he had contacts among other black YMCA secretaries across the nation. Apparently, interest in YMCA work among blacks was renewed in the 1920s. A conference was held in Washington, D.C. in 1925 to discuss the purpose of the "Colored" YMCA, its present field, what new fields it should enter and how these plans could best be implemented. *Crisis,* 31 (November, 1925), 14.
28. *Buffalo American,* December 4, 1924.
29. *Men of Buffalo,* July, 1925, p. 3.
30. *Ibid.,* p. 4.
31. Records, MAYMCA, Memorabilia.
32. Hausauer, *op. cit.,* p. 63.
33. Hausauer, *op. cit.,* p. 64; *Men of Buffalo,* XXV (November, 1926), 5; Records, MAYMCA, Memorabilia 1926–1936.
34. William Jackson was notified of the terms of the donation in the letter; a copy of the Deed of Trust which was to remain undisclosed was included also. Whitford to Jackson, November 6, 1926, Records, MAYMCA.
35. Records, MAYMCA, Memorabilia.
36. Hausauer, *op. cit.,* pp. 50–56, *Men of Buffalo,* December, 1922, p. 13.
37. *Ibid.,* Michigan Avenue Branch YMCA, *Twenty Years in the Service of Youth,* 1943.
38. *Buffalo American,* March 4, 1926.
39. *Op. cit., Twenty Years,* p. 7. The plans for the Michigan Branch were enlarged to comply with the request of George Mathews (Records, MAYMCA, Memorabilia, 1926–1936).
40. Records, MAYMCA, Memorabilia.
41. Interview, Mrs. Bessie Williams, *op. cit., Twenty Years,* pp. 10, 12, and 21.
42. Interview, Mr. Arthur Griffa, Buffalo, New York, February 27, 1976.
43. Hausauer, *op. cit.,* p. 84.
44. Griffa, *op. cit.*
45. Herman Daves was added to the staff as Boys Work Secretary in 1927. Leon J. Hall assumed the position of Physical Department Director and Boys Work Secretary. Records, MAYMCA.
46. *Buffalo American,* May 3, 1923 and December 4, 1924, *The "Y's Messenger,* November, 1938.
47. Records, MAYMCA, *Handbook for 1928–1929.*
48. Each club was scheduled to use the gymnasium twice a week with the exception of the younger boys clubs which were assigned three weekly sessions. Physical Director Leon Hall's report for the fiscal year May 1, 1928 through April 1, 1929 indicated that 537 senior members, 755 young men, and 1,869 boys used the gymnasium; 4,751 men and boys used the swimming pool. During that same period, 60 persons participated in individual work programs and 52 visitors availed themselves of the services offered by the YMCA (Records, MAYMCA).
49. Records, MAYMCA.

50. *Ibid.,* Memorabilia.

51. The Michigan Avenue YMCA received the National Program Award at the New York World's Fair for its Second Western New York Assembly of black youths and for its work with young people.

52. *Ibid., The Y's Messenger,* Vol. 1, January, 1937.

53. *Op. cit., Handbook,* 1928–1929.

54. Records, MAYMCA, "Program Y Activities, Fall and Winter, 1931–1932," "Studies for the Fall of 1931. The following topics were scheduled:

October	2	What and Who is a Christian?
	9	How May One Get Acquainted With God?
	16	Is the Spiritual Life Real or Just Say-So?
	23	Why is the Gate Narrow Which Leads to Life?
November	6	Does a Christian Need to Join a Church?
	13	Is the Bible a Book to Live by Today?
	20	What is Sin?
	27	What has the Death of Jesus to Do with Me?
December	4	Does Prayer Get Us Anything or Anywhere?
	11	Is the Golden Rule Workable?
	18	Are Any of Us Wholly Bad or Wholly Good?
	25	Is There Life After Death?

55. *Op. cit., Handbook,* 1928–1929.

56. *Ibid.* "Artistic" seemed to refer to classical music, i.e., European music.

57. Hausauer, *op. cit.,* pp. 16–17. Hausauer indicated that the YMCA had established a Plumbing Trade School, an Automobile School, and an Accountancy School. Moreover, it had established the Lackawanna Institute in 1912 which was an extension program designed primarily to teach English and to "extend a helping hand to the foreigner seeking Americanization (*ibid.,* pp. 17–18)."

58. *Op. cit., Handbook,* 1928–1929.

59. *Ibid.*

60. *Ibid.*

61. Michigan Avenue YMCA, *The Y's Messenger,* November, 1937. Although there was no formal employment agency at the "Y", Secretary Jackson was able to place individuals in jobs because of his numerous contacts within the city and because of the respect which he had earned.

62. Hausauer, *op. cit.,* pp. 72–76.

63. The Sunday afternoon tea provided the setting for a music appreciation hour which allowed young people an opportunity to display their unique musical talents. Special courses on piano and the violin were also offered.

64. Michigan Avenue YMCA, Program 1931–1932.

65. *Ibid.*

66. *Op. cit., The Y's Messenger,* April, 1939.

67. *Buffalo American,* July 8, 1920.

68. *Op. cit., The Y's Messenger,* October, 1937.

69. *Op. cit., Scrapbook,* Memorabilia, 1926–1936. Dr. R.S. Wilkinson, President of State College at Orangeburg, South Carolina; Dr. Channing H. Tobias, National Council, YMCA; Dr. R.R. Moton, President, Tuskegee Institute; Dr. George Washington Carver; Dr. A.L. McCrory, President, Johnson Smith University; Bishop L.W. Kyles, AME Zion Church; Dr. Charles H. Garvin, President, National Negro medical Association; Congressman Arthur Mitchell, also participated in the annual forums.

70. *Ibid.,* Charles H. Houston to Walter White, 23 May 1923; 31 July 1935, NAACP Papers, Administrative File, Container C-64; folder Charles H. Houston. Also see Franklin, J. H., *From Slavery to Freedom* (Chicago, 1974).

71. *Ibid., Scrapbook,* Michigan Avenue YMCA.

72. *Ibid.;* Interviews, Mrs. Bessie Williams, *op. cit.*

73. Records, MAYMCA, Memorabilia.

74. In 1927, the Urban League was incorporated as part of the Memorial Center, a settlement house within the black community, because it was felt that the two organizations performed the same kinds of functions (Urban League Papers, Series V, William Evans to Eugene Jones, February 5, 1929, Container 13, Manuscript Room, Library of Congress).

75. *Op. cit.,* Memorabilia, newspaper clippings, July 24, 1932.

76. *Ibid.*

77. Antoinette Ford to Robert Bagnall, May 13, 1932; Bagnall to Anderson, October 11, 1932; Pickens to Anderson, June 20, 1933; Pickens to Jackson, October 18, 1933, NAACP Branch Files, Container G131, Manuscript Collection, Library of Congress.

78. Interview, Griffa. Records, MAYMCA, "Recognition Week Program," April 21-27, 1947. *The Y's Messenger* (January, 1937), 1.

79. Interview, Griffa.

80. By 1934, additional property on Cypress Street was purchased so that the "Y" could provide accommodations for transient couples who were visiting Buffalo. Wales Hollow, a forty acre camp site, was purchased and equipped by the Michigan Avenue "Y". Both of these purchases were gifts of The Mathews (*op. cit.,* "Program Recognition Week," April 21-27, 1947).

81. Interview, Griffa, *op. cit.*

To Meet the Group Needs:
The Transformation of Howard University
School of Law, 1920–1935

Genna Rae McNeil

The historical examination of black legal education recently has been advanced by the work of several scholars who have insisted upon characterizing the phenomenon as something more than the usual success stories of unusual black Americans. These studies have surveyed black legal education on a national scale and provided answers to a number of pertinent questions relative to how blacks gained entry into the legal profession historically, the socio-economic status of black lawyers and their impact upon the life of the nation, legal educational opportunities for blacks, and the role of predominantly black schools in the United States.[1] This essay takes as its basic assumption the general belief that if the past is to be usable in designing blueprints and providing guidelines for a progressive educational future in the field of law, then historical studies of black legal education must begin to focus upon specific policies and programs of predominantly black law schools not only within the more general framework of American legal education, but also with regard to the evolving position and power of black Americans in the overall social structure of American society. Howard University Law School launched "the first effort to attract blacks to the legal profession," and by 1910 had trained over 500 of the estimated 779 black lawyers in the United States.[2] During the period 1920–1935, however, the school underwent a radical transformation in the face of the emerging elite consensus in the American legal profession and the need to train more lawyers to protect the basic civil rights of black Americans.

The United States does not have an overly long history of formal legal education and training. Apprenticing oneself to a jurist and reading law to gain admission to the bar was quite common until the first decade of the twentieth century when formal law school education became the preferable vehicle for entry into the profession.[3] The emergence of university law schools and the

149

professionalization of law teaching had just become settled phenomena when the idea of a greatly improved legal education entered the consciousness of some members and organizations within the American bar. The rise of industrial urban America at the turn of the century spawned governmental bureaucracies, business corporations, special private and public interest groups, and greater ethnic heterogeneity in the society at large. As a consequence, the American legal profession was experiencing shifting priorities, ethnic stratification, and some racial diversification. Between 1900 and 1920 the number of American lawyers foreign-born and of foreign-born parentage increased rapidly and added to the growing ethnic diversity within the profession. In this same period black Americans began entering the ranks of the legal profession in greater numbers and among them were some who achieved national distinction. George H. White, a former Congressman, William H. Lewis, appointed in 1911 an Assistant Attorney General of the United States, and William Henry H. Hart, successful petitioner and counsel in one of the first segregation cases, *Hart v. State (of Maryland)* were already respected members of the American bar when this latest phase of professional legal reform began. However, as early as 1912, three black lawyers, interested in a "unitary bar" in the United States, applied for membership in the expanding American Bar Association (ABA). The Association admitted them without knowledge of their race, but subsequently excluded the three and resolved that it would abide by its long-established tradition of accepting white lawyers only. Although the bar was undergoing an unmistakable change in its identity, some white members viewed change as undesirable and objectionable, while others believed that the new minority demand for admission should be subjected to formal study. In these changing circumstances, some lawyers contemplated taking positive action if the situation warranted it.[4]

In January, 1913, the Carnegie Foundation for the Advancement of Teaching, at the request of the American Bar Association, undertook an investigation of legal education in the United States. A scholar who was not a member of the legal profession, Alfred Z. Reed, was selected by the Foundation to prepare an objective, detailed study of American legal education. Reed committed himself for eight years to the Carnegie sponsored project, and produced a book-length study, *Training for the Public Profession of the Law.* His report, "rich in information which [was] gathered with exceptional industry and meticulous care" dealt with the historical development of legal education in the United States, problems of training for the legal profession, the characteristics of the bar in the United States, and qualifications for admission. Many of the conclusions were both novel and controversial, evoking positive and negative responses from legal scholars and practitioners associated with the American Bar Association and the Association of American Law Schools (AALS).[5]

On one issue the Carnegie Foundation report had a particularly explosive impact. In *Training for the Public Profession of the Law,* Reed recommended that afternoon or evening part-time law schools neither be condemned nor abolished.

> [T]o confine the right to practice law to one economic group would be to deny to other economic groups their just participation in the making and declaring of law. Such a restriction would properly be resented by the public.
>
> It follows that opportunities must be given to those who are obliged to support themselves during their legal studies. If a man has completed two years, or better still, four years of a college course, he will do best if he attends a law school which commands substantially all of working time. But if he has come to the point where he finds it necessary to support himself, and perhaps his family, he should not be denied admission to the public profession of law. For such a man the afternoon or evening school is the only resource.
>
> [I]n recognizing the necessity for afternoon and evening schools we do not recognize the propriety of permitting such schools to operate with low educational standards. We should not license a badly educated man to practice law simply because he has been too poor to get a good education. On the contrary, the democratic necessity for afternoon and evening schools compels a lifting of these schools to the highest standards which they can be expected to reach.[6]

Thus, after accepting the "democratic necessity" of part-time legal education, Reed then proceeded to outline the primary activities of lawyers graduating from these part-time schools and to suggest the legal training which would be "adequate for the type of work in which its graduates engage."Reed contended that serious thought should be given to a qualitative and a functional division of responsibilities among lawyers and the assignment of training for certain types of professional work to afternoon/evening part-time schools which could offer relatively superficial courses as compared with those offered at university law schools.[7] Reed made no response to the generally held proposition that, indeed, once being admitted to the bar an individual lawyer might handle any case which a client would entrust to him or her. Reed did suggest, however, that "conveyancing, probate practices, criminal law and trial work are examples of topics that seem particularly appropriate for the relatively superficial schools,"[8] and insisted that the community of legal scholars and practitioners confront the increasing reality of a differentiated, not a "unitary," bar and accept this transformation with a greater democratic spirit.[9]

Alfred Reed's conclusions and suggestions went to the very core of several contemporary controversies surrounding American legal training, bar qualifications, and the relative position of power and prominence to be occupied by members of the legal profession within the United States. Between 1890 and 1910 the number of day schools increased from 51 to 79, or 60 percent while the number of night schools soared from 10 to 45 or 350 percent. This latter figure represented the increased access to the American legal profession, and therefore positions of influence and power within the United States, by persons of different classes, ethnic backgrounds, races, and levels of preparation in law. For those who favored part-time schools an expanded profession meant not only greater access for minorities but also greater diversity within the profession. In many ways these changes would lead to the strengthening of social control mechanisms used to placate racial and cultural minorities and poor citizens in general in the United States.[10]

Overt opposition to the afternoon/evening or part-time law schools was often considered a questioning of the propriety of legal education for substantial numbers of persons already enrolled in law schools. But these opponents did not consider themselves undemocratic; they objected to the existence of schools which accepted all students who could afford tuition and then not only offered a less than thorough treatment of legal subjects taught by part-time professors who generally used the lecture — as distinguished from the case — method, but rarely provided their students with adequate library facilities. Moreover, these lawyers believed that increasing the number of years of study at part-time schools would not meet the basic objection to the training of students regardless of the level of aptitude, energy and alertness for the legal profession.[11] However, not simply the desire for a highly competent American bar of limited size and high standards of excellence induced these law professors and practitioners to move against the part-time evening school; "Self-conscious professionalism," wrote Jerold Auerbach in *Unequal Justice,* "spurred teachers whose self-esteem was bolstered by more exacting standards of admission to their institution.... Successful practitioners, fearful of thrusts from below within the profession, wielded higher standards as a weapon in defense of the elitism that enhances their own stature...."[12]

Expressions of support of high standards and democratic principles, however, were crucial to the anti-part-time school position as articulated by two of its best known spokesmen, Harlan Fiske Stone, Dean of Columbia University's Law School and Felix Frankfurter, during the twenties, a professor of Law at Harvard. Harlan Stone, naively believed that "the man of good health, who is worth educating, can today [1921] give himself a college and professional education..," and insisted that " [T]he preservation of the democratic principle in law making and in law administration does not require that it should be made easy for all members of the community to enter the legal profession.... The bar in America ... [has been] recruited very largely from the young men of slender financial resources, and the observation of the writer is that all classes of society would be well represented at the bar today and the democratic principle adequately preserved if the membership of the bar were drawn exclusively from the full-time law schools requiring three years of college training for entrance.... For us weakly to surrender to a policy of perpetuating an admittedly superficial system of training for the bar ... is to give up the fight for democracy itself."[13] With regard to the dispute over part-time evening schools, Felix Frankfurter adjudged that Reed threw his "weight on the side of incompetence and inevitable degrading standards because [he] support[ed] the necessity of night-schools." Frankfurter made it very clear to Reed; "I am not unaware of the problem presented by a political democracy, but my conclusion from those difficulties is not to yield to the pressure for low standards but educate the whole level of democracy up to the recognition of the fact that no form of society needs stiffer standards than does a democracy." The positive approach to the problem according to Frankfurter was to "[M]ake democracy realize the function of the law and the equipment necessary to exercise it, and then make it possible for the poor man's son to obtain the necessary training."[14]

The ideological strife among members of the legal profession continued as professors and practitioners in light of the Carnegie Report debated the ABA Root Committee report and the official requirements for membership in the AALS. The former recommended two years of college for admission to accredited law schools, three years of full-time law study, and a special examination in order to qualify for the bar in the United States. The AALS specified between 1919 and 1923 first, that no law schools should be admitted which offered an evening law course for students desiring to enter the profession, and second, that "night schools" of law be excluded from AALS membership. However, by 1928, the AALS permitted institutions which had "mixed" curricula (i.e. day and evening) to apply for membership providing they could meet for two consecutive years the Association's criteria which included two years of college work as a pre-legal studies requirement, employment of full-time instructors, maintenance of a library with adequate national and state reporter systems, volumes of statutes, legal periodicals, and related legal materials.[15]

Given this turbulence within the profession, the administrators and professors of Howard University School of Law deemed it both necessary and important to re-evaluate its mission and its work *qua* a predominantly black institution. Howard was still the primary institution offering formal legal education to blacks. By 1920 it had trained over three-quarters of the black lawyers in the United States.[16] Moreover, by the early 1920s it had become apparent to many black members of the legal profession that this clamoring for higher standards, stiffer law school admission requirements, condemnation and/or disdain for the evening, part-time schools would also have a negative impact upon the Law School of Howard University and its future graduates. Further it was clear that the emerging elite consensus within the profession held sway in both the ABA and the AALS, and through determinations of accreditation and membership, these bodies controlled the professional destiny of all private and public law schools whether part- or full-time, black or white.

Howard University's Law School was "an unaccredited and little known — though undoubtedly useful — institution" which had operated as a part-time school of law in the late afternoon and evenings since its inception as a law department in 1869. From that time as a part-time evening school it had created a rare opportunity for over seven-hundred persons aspiring to a career in law.[17] Yet quite apart from its service to black America through the *numbers* of black lawyers it graduated, it was a useful institution because of the notable scholars, practicing attorneys, and judges associated with it. Over the years, among the most prominent jurists associated with the School were John Mercer Langston, the first Dean of the Law Department, a former slave, Congressman and Minister-resident to Haiti; Charlotte E. Ray, daughter of the famed abolitionist, Charles B. Ray, and, it is reported, the first woman to be trained at an American law school and the first woman admitted to practice in the District of Columbia; James A. Cobb, one-time Special Assistant in the United States Attorney's office, Municipal Court Judge for the District of Columbia and professor of law at Howard Law School; D. A. Straker, professor of law and Dean of Allen University's School of Law; Henry Baker, highest ranked black in the United States Patent office before 1920; James C. Napier, former Register of the Treasury for the United States and Trustee of Howard University; Robert H. Terrell, Howard Law Department professor and judge of the District of Columbia Municipal Court; and George W. Atkinson, after graduation a member of Congress from the state of West Virginia, former governor of West Virginia, and judge on the United States Court of Claims. Among early twentieth-century graduates of eminence were Robert A. Pelham, editor of the *Plain-dealer* and later the *Washington Tribune;* Robert Brockenburr, former Deputy Prosecuting Attorney for Marion County in Indiana and subsequently judge *pro tem,* Marion County Circuit Court, Criminal Court and Municipal Court; A. Mercer Daniel, professor of law and law librarian at Howard University; Garnet C. Wilkinson, one-time Assistant Superintendent of the District of Columbia Public Schools; Jesse H. Mitchell, President of the Industrial Bank of Washington (D.C.); and George E. C. Hayes, practitioner in the District of Columbia and faculty member of Howard's Law School with special expertise in Constitutional Law.[18]

Nevertheless, despite the eminence of its faculty, as early as 1920 the Law School was compelled to recognize the growing significance and, perhaps, necessity of accreditation by national organizations, such as the ABA and the AALS. The point was driven home when one of its students was required to repeat legal studies at Fordham because his prior work had been done at Howard University's unaccredited Law School. The repetition of courses taken at Howard meant that courses in a non-accredited part-time law school could not be viewed as equivalent to those offered at an accredited school. The success of many Howard law graduates seemed to challenge the underlying assumption. Nevertheless there were weaknesses in the legal training offered at Howard before the academic year, 1920–21. Breadth and adequate coverage in the individual courses were still problems though Howard's course offerings were not atypical of part-time law schools. Even in the standard curriculum of Howard's Law School there were conspicuous omissions when compared with course offerings at many full-time university law schools of the era. For example, Labor Law, Taxation, Remedies and Public Utilities were excluded. At the June, 1920 meeting the Trustees voted that "steps be taken to so advance the School of Law that it may become eligible for membership in the American Association of Law Schools."[19]

Between 1921 and 1926 under the new Law School Dean, Fenton W. Booth, judge in the District of Columbia Municipal Court, adjustments were made in entrance requirements, holdings of the library, salaries of faculty members, and a number of persons were appointed to full-time teaching positions. In 1924, Charles Hamilton Houston, the son of a Howard Law graduate and professor, William LePre Houston, became a faculty member. Graduating Phi Beta Kappa from Amherst College, Houston went on to earn an LL.B. (1922) and S.J.D. (1923) at Harvard Law School. While a student under the tutelage of Roscoe Pound and Felix Frankfurter, he looked forward to a law teaching career and hoped to combine his legal scholarship with private practice. Having particular interest in legal education, Houston spent an additional year of studies in Madrid, Spain, observing and participating in the University of Madrid's program of legal education. Interestingly, two years thereafter, at the suggestion of Felix Frankfurter and others, Julius Rosenwald contributed in excess of two thousand dollars to Howard University Law School for the purchase of law books to improve the School's library. The Howard faculty and Board of Trustees also decided that the post-graduate (i.e. LL.M.) program should be discontinued and that efforts of the faculty and administration should be concentrated on teaching for the LL.B. course of study and meeting the AALS membership criteria. Feeling some pressure, the Trustees approved these limited recommendations for the up-grading of the Law School.[20]

These slow steps toward accreditation and AALS membership were unacceptable to Mordecai Johnson, the first black President of Howard University. The direction of the professional discussions of standards and part-time schools was generally toward the position that admission to the bar would be closely correlated with formal law training and that greater respect in the future would be accorded the accredited institutions and their graduates. In the late 1920s President Mordecai Johnson sought advice and counsel about the situation at the University's professional school. One influential informal advisor was Supreme Court Justice Louis Dembitz Brandeis. On several occasions the two spoke frankly on the subject of black civil rights and the law. Brandeis' often expressed his belief in the over-riding importance of well-trained black advocates to argue Constitutional principles before the United States Supreme Court. Johnson was also impressed with many of the new and somewhat compelling ideas of the young professor, Charles Hamilton Houston, who believed that if Howard were to continue to be a useful and important school for black Americans it had to gain national accreditation and begin to provide for its students a legal education program which was competitive in relation to the highest quality full-time university law schools in the country. In addition, Houston also believed that the new legal program should be designed to take into account the historical conditions and contemporary legal and social struggles of black Americans.[21]

The elevation of the Dean of Howard University Law School, Fenton W. Booth, to the position of Chief Justice of the United States Court of Claims in 1928 brought an administrative change at a crucial period in the Law School's development. The Law School Commitee of the Board of Trustees had previously concerned itself with bringing the law school up to the standards of the American Bar Association (ABA) and the Association of American Law Schools (AALS). At this juncture the Trustees attempted to continue this thrust, but also began searching for a dean to perform the administrative duties and guide the Law School to full accreditation. The Board of Trustees, concurring with the Law School Committee's earlier report, requested that Dean Booth remain as Acting Dean for one year (1928-1929) to allow a smooth transition in the administration of the Law School. The Trustees also authorized the hiring of two additional full-time instructors for Fall, 1928 and to initiate a three-year day school curriculum to replace the three year part-time evening curriculum; but kept the four-year part-time evening program.[22]

Although still recovering from a bout with tuberculosis, Charles Houston was anxious to involve himself in the reorganization of the Law School.[23] During his leave of abence, the law library was enlarged as a result of a grant of twenty thousand dollars from the Laura Spelman Rockefeller Memorial Fund. This brought the Law School's library holdings up to and above the AALS requirements. The Law School of Howard University was very close to full compliance with the AALS criteria for accreditation in 1929 and Houston, the other faculty members, administrators, and Trustees, earnestly sought full accreditation.[24]

This also meant that if Howard University School of Law was to become not merely an accredited, full-time, day school, but also a politically and socially significant first-class law school, some clarification or re-statement of the school's historic mission and educational objectives was needed. Since 1869 the law department had had as its goal the best possible professional training for all persons — black and white, male and female — seeking instruction in the law. Moreover, according to the first dean, John Mercer Langston, it was the obligation of the Howard student — as indeed, it was for all Americans — to support "the claim of the Colored Americans to complete equality of rights and privileges and abolish slavery, establish freedom and free institutions upon the entire American Continent."[25] With great attention to detail, Charles Houston elucidated the general position he had earlier presented to President Mordecai Johnson. The "indispensable social function" of Howard University Law School has been the production of competent black lawyers "to care for the needs of the Negro population." Yet despite the many graduates, "the Negro needs more lawyers.... There are not enough capable and socially alert Negro lawyers to meet the group needs...," Houston asserted.[26] The immediate objective of the Howard Law School "should be to make itself a more efficient training school." The aims of Howard Law School, *qua* professional training school, were clearly stated.

> The aims ... should be to equip its students with the direct professional skills most useful to them, and to give them as deep and as broad a societal background as possible.... From the standpoint of public function the Negro lawyer (ought to) be trained as a *social engineer* and group interpreter ... prepared to anticipate, guide, and interpret his group advancement.... To qualify such group leaders, the law school must give its students a thorough understanding of the administration of law with its inherent limitations, superimposed upon a broad societal background.[27] (Emphasis mine)

Houston elaborated on the concept of "social engineering" in this and other documents. Growing out of tenets of Roscoe Pound's sociological jurisprudence, "social engineering" entailed a duty to "guide ... antagonistic and group forces into channels where they will not clash." A social engineer is "the mouthpiece of the weak and a sentinel guarding against wrong." In the face of social and economic changes, such a lawyer is required to insure that "the course of change is ... orderly with a minimum of human loss and suffering" and this is to be done skillfully and conscientiously. The black social engineer, is under an obligation to not only "use ... the law as an instrument available to [the] minority unable to adopt direct action to achieve its place in the community and nation", but also consistently and competently interpret black "rights and aspirations."[28]

For Houston the second major objective for the Law School was more inclusive. "Howard ... School of Law should gradually move into a larger sphere of usefulness as its resources and abilities increase." As Houston perceived this task part of the Law School's "usefulness would certainly be research on and interpretation of the legal aspects of Negro economic, social, and political life...." Moreover, at the start of the program all of the research carried out, he believed, should bear directly upon Howard Law School's training work. For example, faculty members might direct or engage in studies of "the administration of ... criminal law as affecting the Negro, ... representative Negro business developments, and other group activities."[29]

Charles Houston's provocative ideas, serious interest in the Law School, and zeal and commitment were immediately recognized by responsible persons within the University hierarchy. He was soon given the opportunity to put some of his theories into action, and was appointed Resident Vice Dean in charge of Howard Law School's day course of study, as of July 1, 1929. The growth of the day enrollment and the decline of the evening school prompted Johnson, Houston, concerned law faculty members, and the Trustees to consider the possibility of concentrating their energies and resources on the day School and accreditation of Howard as solely a full-time day Law School. The relevant factors were discussed and on February 4, 1930, the Trustees voted to abolish the Law School's evening course as of June 6, 1930. Students enrolled in the evening program protested, however, and the Trustees voted on June 9, 1929 to continue the evening course until all part-time students had been graduated or had transferred into the day school program. Houston, at the same meeting, was appointed Vice Dean to lead the School in its drive to become an accredited full-time law school offering the best possible professional training with a special emphasis on the legal conditions of black Americans.[30]

From the day after the meeting, President Johnson, Houston and the other proponents of the day school came under attack. The *Washington Tribune* editorialized about the suggested thrust of the Law School.

> The decision of the trustees of Howard University to eliminate the night law classes is one that seems to be against the needs of the people. Ever since the law department was established in Howard University there has [sic] been night classes. It is only recently that the day classes were established.
> Many of the country's best lawyers among our people, secured their training by being able to work in the day and attend evening classes. Our economic condition is of such that few of our young men have the means to attend college in the day time.[31]

The *Tribune* continued to focus on the Howard Law School in a feature article captioned, "Alumni Protest Abolition of Night Classes." It reported that several members of the Alumni Association were emphatic in their "collective disapproval of the proposed discontinuance of the evening classes of the University School of Law." The *Tribune* article included a chief reason for discontinuance, namely, "that each year the enrollment in the first year class of the evening school becomes smaller and smaller. [A]t the present there are only six second year men in the evening school, and only one first year student." The bulk of the article, however, was devoted to the arguments of students and others opposing the proposed change. These individuals believed first, that "there are among the race's most capable barristers those who graduated from an evening class"; and second that "among the two groups, those who pursue their law study in the day and those who take advantage of the evening possibility, the latter are in most cases more conscientious ... because the men ... realize better the advantage to be gained." The *Tribune* also asserted that "with the abolition of the evening classes, the Law School faculty will suffer the loss of such sterling professors as Dean Fenton W. Booth, George E. C. Hayes, Judge J. A. Cobb, (and) W. L. Houston." These speculations apparently were not informed by personal interviews with any of the three black professors, for Cobb, Hayes and Houston continued to teach courses well into the 1930s.[32]

The *Washington World* brought this smouldering controversy to the attention of the entire District in August, 1930. In a statement to the *World*, one of the white faculty members of the Law School, Charles Imlay, announced that all the white members of the faculty of Howard Law School had tendered their resignations. "The exact reasons for ... resignation [were] set forth in full in communications to the Trustees of the University,'' Imlay told a *World* reporter. Although Imlay would volunteer no specific information either about his resignation or those of the other white professors — Justice and Acting Dean Fenton Booth, Dion Birny, Edward Stafford, Dale Drain, and Gilbert Lewis — the *World* insisted that its reporter's information pointed to ''dissatisfaction with the present administration of the law school.'' Alleged grievances included exclusion of Booth from school policy-making, unfair changes in rank and employment status of older white professors, and insufficient office space for Booth. In an interview, President Mordecai Johnson stated that the white members of the law faculty were resigning because ''most of the professors were on part-time and they advised that it would not be advisable for them to discontinue their regular practice and devote more time to teaching . . . . that the university regretted losing all of the men, but the pressure of outside business forced them to resign. . . .'' The *World* article concluded by allying itself with the white professors who had resigned, and claimed that President Mordecai Johnson had ''tried to conceal the real reason for the resignation of the white members'' and that his action had caused widespread dissatisfaction. The newspaper further alleged that the extent of dissatisfaction ''could not be verified as everybody connected with the University are [sic] reticent about talking on any subject.''[33]

Race had become an important issue. It had been an issue since Mordecai Johnson was named the first black president, but it was becoming more sharply defined as the white temporary dean assumed less importance and power and a young black vice dean with considerable power seemed to be ushering in a new order. It should, however, be noted that race was not the only issue involved and it certainly was not the key to the controversy. Many responsible men — black and white — believed the abolition of the evening school was part of a conscious attempt to model Howard after Harvard Law School with respect to admissions requirements, curriculum, and classroom performance expectations. Significant opposition grew up around the belief that ''Harvardizing'' the Howard University School of Law would ultimately be detrimental. Opponents argued that this would eliminate the greatest opportunity to ''render the service for which [Howard Law School] was organized and is now maintained by public appropriation. . . .''[34] Few close observers of the situation underestimated the enormity of the predicament. Howard Law School's white professors (including a former dean and Chief Justice in the District of Columbia judiciary) were resigning as a result of actions approved by the University's first black president who appeared to the resigning professors, protesting alumni, and other supporters of the evening law school to be a man ''that . . . has been led up a blind alley . . .'' by a ''fortunate,'' but ''insensitive'' Harvard graduate.[35]

Vice Dean Charles Houston was affected by the dissatisfaction and unrest, but he was still persuaded that to discontinue the evening curriculum for a time was the best alternative. Given the dual issues of accreditation and increasing funds, Houston believed that in the final analysis, it was in the interest of the University to try and provide the best possible education during the day until funds could be obtained for a new and better evening course of law study. The school's financial resources would not permit both curricula to be carried on concurrently as long as Howard sought to offer a consistently high standard of legal training. Meanwhile, although the controversy raged, Houston went about his daily administrative chores and continued his close supervision of the accreditation drive.

With respect to accreditation, Houston focused primarily on the up-coming inspection of the Law School by the American Bar Association's Will Shafroth, advisor to the section on legal education and admission to the bar. This would be the first time that the ABA had made such an inspection of a predominantly black law school. Moreover, at that time only seventy-one Law schools in the United States were approved by the ABA. Nevertheless, Howard School of Law anticipated the inspection with some confidence because its drive to become accredited by the AALS had simultaneously become an effort to meet the standards of the ABA. If the more stringent standards of the AALS were met, then the ABA standards had been surpassed. The American Bar Association required that entering students have at least two years of college, that there be a minimum of 7,500 approved volumes in the law library, that three full-time instructors be employed, that there be adequate housing of the school, that any day program be conducted for three years and any evening program must be conducted for four.[36]

To become a member of the Association of American Law Schools, institutions were similarly required to have students with two years of college from institutions rated "Class A" in the entering class and adequate facilities and housing for the school. In addition, the requirements included a minimum of ten thousand volumes in the library with a portion of these volumes being a complete National Reporter System, Supreme Court Reporters, Federal Statutes and Digest, State Reporters, published records of decisions of courts of last resort in one-half of the states and at least six legal periodicals, by September,1932. Moreover, AALS was requiring that a minimum of ten thousand dollars be spent within five years for additional acquisitions for the library. A minimum of four full-time instructors and, over and above that, one full-time instructor per one hundred students had to be retained for approval by the AALS, and membership could be awarded only after the school had complied with the AALS standards for two consecutive years.[37]

The first test of the success of the accreditation drive came in October, 1930. Will Shafroth inspected Howard Law School for the American Bar Association. By the month of inspection Howard boasted a full-time three year law school program, four full-time professors, a full-time librarian, a library of ten thousand volumes, several part-time instructors, and a reasonable separate facility at 420 Fifth Street in Northwest Washington. The summary of the Annual Report of President Johnson to the Secretary of Interior, who oversaw the running of federally funded institutions, stated that "work of the school of law was examined by the council of legal education and admittance to the bar of the American Bar Association, [and] was found to maintain standards acceptable to that body, and was accredited by them." Howard's Law School was also registered as "satisfactorily meeting the requirements of the State of New York."[38] Approval by the ABA having been achieved, it remained the task of the Law School and University administration to secure membership in the AALS. Approximately fourteen months after the ABA inspection, accreditation by the AALS was achieved and Howard Law School was elected a member of that Association "without qualification."[39]

Still concerned, however, about what he had described earlier as an "essentially formless" curriculum, Vice Dean Houston, the chief administrator of the Law School, undertook the evaluation and improvement of the entire curriculum between 1931 and 1935.[40] This caused some dissension among faculty, students, and alumni/ae. One local black newspaper editor assessed the situation in the following terms:

> Washington, D.C. must have its annual eruption in the colored colony. Either in the public schools, Freedman's hospital, or Howard University must have had a shock, and this year the Washington statemen are charging Vesuvius to blow up Howard University. It is now being charged that President Johnson is too autocratic and that Vice Dean Charles Hamilton Houston is trying to Harvardize the Law School; and that will never do for Johnson and Houston to raise the standard of Howard University to the class of Harvard University ... (i.e.) Harvardizing the school. Of course the inference is that the Negro is not ready for a Harvard University of his own and Howard must be kept within the reach of the Negro's mental ability....[41]

This statement, however, was a somewhat superficial view of the situation for there was a significant conflict of principles involved in the accreditation-improvement drive which had resulted in the abolition of the evening school and the lengthening of school terms. It involved principles which were related to the general controversy between Alfred Z. Reed and his opponents, i.e. democratic principles versus professional elitism. But, it was not precisely the same conflict.[42] For black American jurists these questions almost out of necessity had to be framed with special cognizance of the on-going struggle for black civil rights. Would the group needs be better served by Howard's continuing to provide more opportunities for greater numbers of Afro-Americans desirous of becoming lawyers or by limiting the opportunities available at Howard by raising the quality of the education and designing the curriculum to serve the purpose of training more highly-skilled lawyers who would be prepared to argue more competently and effectively for the civil rights of black Americans in the courts of the nation? Should black educators determine educational priorities and policies with reference to principles of individualism or maximization of collective benefits? Should the primary considerations be the requirements of "democracy" or liberation from racist oppression? And more importantly, to what extent should considerations relative to external factors, such as white control, "the exercise of 'power' ... from a position of 'authority,' " limited Afro-American influence or ability to "sway, persuade, or otherwise have an effect upon those who control from a position of authority," and generally racist attitudes define the perimeters of black educators' conduct?[43]

The changes within the Howard Law School subsequent to the decision to seek accreditation by the ABA and membership in the AALS reflected a complex response to these and related questions. By 1930, the chief administrator, Charles Houston, had begun to implement programs that he believed appropriately took into account "the particular needs of Negro students" being trained for the profession of law and the struggle for equal rights.[44]

One thorny problem was inescapable as he sought to meet the needs of the black students. Membership in the AALS necessitated a smaller enrollment and a different composition of the student body. The economic depression of the 1930s and the AALS rating of colleges directly affected the number of students which Howard Law School could accept. Moreover, because several years beyond the initial two were required for entering students if they had not attended "Class A" institutions, black students of modest means who had matriculated at "Class B" white colleges or predominantly black institutions were often denied admission. In 1934, fifty percent of the colleges from which Howard Law School students might be accepted were no longer acceptable. While Mordecai Johnson noted this in reports to the Secretary of Interior between 1931 and 1935, he simultaneously emphasized that there was a marked improvement in the caliber of the student body. By 1935 "the most significant thing about the student body" was, in President Johnson's view, that "the law school [was] approaching a purely graduate basis. Every member of the senior class ... had his college degree; 31 of the [total] 46 students had Bachelor degrees, and of the remainder 9 had at least three years of college work."[45]

Curriculum revision was also central to the Vice Dean Houston's plans for up-grading the Law School and clarifying its modern mission. In 1929 he had noted that the curriculum was "essentially formless." Houston sought to arrange and synthesize courses in order "to give the curriculum a more functional aspect." It was the duty of the Howard Law School, Houston submitted, to "equip its students with the direct professional skills most useful to them" and to train them to become "social engineers."[46] The curriculum with regard to the content and placement of courses within particular years had been the product of "a compromise imposed by the limitations of time and energy of a part-time faculty."[47]

Association of American Law Schools membership and American Bar Association accreditation had also changed the composition of Howard's faculty. With the evening school phased out after 1930, the number of full-time faculty increased. Four full-time faculty members joined an average of six part-time instructors between 1931 and 1935. Also in this period Harvard University's Law School established graduate fellowships for a cooperative program with Howard Law School and as a result several faculty members from Howard earned graduate degrees in Cambridge. A heavily weighted Howard-Harvard faculty which included for a time George E. C. Hayes and James A. Cobb, and the young legal scholars, who were quickly distinguishing themselves, William H. Hastie, Leon A. Ransom, Bernard Jefferson, and William E. Taylor, implemented the Howard University program of black legal education.[48]

By the beginning of the 1931-1932 academic year the transformation of the Law School was readily apparent. Entering students could take courses only during the day (8:30 a.m.–12:30 p.m.), Monday through Saturday, and the Law School was opened on September nineteenth instead of the first week in October so that students might attend thirty-three weeks. The announcement of courses and requirements reflected a further revision in the curriculum and objectives. The standard courses, such as Contracts, Constitutional Law, Criminal Law, Domestic Relations, Evidence, Federal Jurisdiction, Moot Court, Negotiable Instruments, Property and Torts remained, but fewer textbooks and more case-books were required by professors who were moving away from the lecture-method of instruction. More sophisticated courses in public utilities, surety, trusts, and wills were added. Students were specifically advised that they would be expected to draw and file pleadings, perfect and argue appeals, and write three appellate briefs. By 1934-1935 the case-method was utilized by most professors and case-books were *dominant* among the required course materials. Students were offered new courses such as the History of Law, Office Management and Ethics, and a greater amount of time was allotted for courses which involved the "mechanics of law" such as pleading, trial work, and preparation of documents. These "mechanics" were stressed because of the commitment to a functional curriculum and also because of the fact that racial prejudice still constituted a serious barrier to the employment of blacks as law clerks. Familiar traditional law courses such as Insurance, Equity Pleading and Practice, Evidence, Criminal Law and Constitutional Law were taught with particular attention to the black experience in regard to business practices and administration of justice in the United States. Activist professors such as Taylor, Hayes, Ransom, Hastie and Houston regularly included examples of encounters with federal, state, and municipal agencies and courts. Students of the first day school classes were involved in field trips to prisons, courts and the Federal Bureau of Investigation as part of their course work. Oliver Hill of Virginia, Edward Lovett of Washington, D.C., Thurgood Marshall of Maryland, and other students selected Howard Law School in part because of the practical-functional focus of the curriculum and the commitment to civil rights.[49]

The breadth and the emphasis of the curriculum were reflected in the courses offered by Vice Dean Houston, the chief proponent of "social engineering." He taught, between 1930 and 1935, Criminal Law Laboratory, History of Law, Legal Bibliography and Argumentation, Evidence, Common Law Pleading, Municipal Corporations, and Conflict of Laws. He insisted upon "unqualified excellence" from not only his faculty, but also students, as Howard Law School sought "to provide a fertile 'educational field for the working out of special problems of [black] lawyers' and to produce black lawyers who were both capable and socially perceptive enough 'to meet the groups needs.' "[50] Houston regularly alarmed students by his frequent recitation of the sobering tenet "no tea for the feeble, no crepe for the dead."[51] He was "so tough" that some students called him "Iron Shoes." Yet he was generally considered an excellent teacher, "absolutely fair, and the door to his office was always open," because he believed that accessibility to students with questions was crucial to the learning process and the goals of the Law School.[52] Most importantly, as one student recalled, Houston was a professor who "tried to teach the pupils ... that there was a greater job than just training to become lawyers in the commercial sense, and that they should attempt — while they acquired their legal training — to understand the problem of racial discrimination and prepare themselves to go out in the community and become to some extent social engineers."[53]

Under Vice Dean Houston's leadership, according to James Nabrit, later a President of Howard University, "the Law School ... was reorganized and made into a three year accredited law school and ... under this guidance the first great faculty of [black] lawyers highly trained was assembled." This faculty and its immediate successor included Houston (before 1935 when he accepted the position of NAACP Special Counsel), William H. Hastie, Jr., W. Robert Ming, Jr., George Marion Johnson, Leon A. Ransom, George E. C. Hayes and James N. Nabrit, Jr. These men embraced the newly-defined mission of the Howard University School of Law and devoted their best energies to the education of Howard students for the struggle for equality of Afro-Americans. Further, as members of the Howard faculty, they worked with students to "formulate ... theories for basic attacks upon civil disabilities affecting minorities" in general and black Americans in particular. Beyond theorizing, they went on to "develop ... the struggle in the court."[54] Howard's School of Law became virtually a laboratory for civil rights and many Howard graduates became distinguished advocates for the race.[55]

Within the narrow confines of American academia, it has been customary for scholars, educational theorists, and administrators to formulate policies based upon assumptions about who could learn, who ought to be educated, and who ought to be afforded the privileges of higher and professional education. Historically, many individuals in positions to determine policy and programs have embraced noble goals in word, but not in deed. Black Americans frequently have found themselves compelled to debate their actions and aspirations in a context circumscribed by cultural and racial attitudes of the white majority and black perceptions of life chances and personal risks involved.

Thus, adversarial race relations and institutional racism have been central to the black American experience and had a disabling effect on blacks who sought to rise above rejection, exclusion, limited opportunity, and poverty in the United States.[56] For Charles Houston, the crux of the issue was understanding the oppression of black Americans, *qua* a racial minority, and moving against the restrictions by the most viable and effective means.[57]

The examination of the process by which Howard University School of Law altered its image and transformed its educational program raises as many questions as it answers about the educational aspirations of minorities, skills acquisition, the political ramifications of curriculum development, the power of elitist professions, the distribution of rights and power in a democracy, and the role of educational institutions in a climate of oppression. Although these questions in the main will linger, the Howard Law School experience between 1920 and 1935 provides some insights into the historical resolution of many of these issues. The institution responded directly to racism and professional elitism which threatened to exclude blacks from the enjoyment of rights and good standing within the legal profession. In so doing the administrators and policy-makers at Howard University, led by Charles Hamilton Houston, focused upon the plight of the Law School and assessed the educational realities to determine what the exigencies of the time dictated. The mission and the work of the School of Law were then re-evaluated. Houston proposed a legal education program with aims which presupposed the necessity of establishing priorities based upon the race's collective needs. The underlying assumption was simply that the struggle against oppression and for fundamental rights was to be both protracted and pre-eminent in the concerns of Howard-trained lawyers. The implementation of the program for the Law School involved the limiting of opportunities for some individuals to obtain legal training in order that broader opportunities might be won for black Americans as a group. And finally, the educational program reflected a basic commitment to the proposition that the legal scholars and practitioners trained by Howard were obligated by virtue of the opportunity afforded them and their membership in an oppressed racial group to be activists in the on-going struggle for equality.[58] In sum, the Howard University School of Law experience from 1920 to 1935 profoundly demonstrates the manner in which educational policy and ideology are inextricably bound together, and underscores the importance of openly confronting ideology. If basically, "To have ideology is to know what you want in your own condition"[59] then, the transformation of Howard Law School reveals that ideological clarity should be a primary duty of teachers and administrators functioning within educational institutions serving the needs of oppressed minority populations.

NOTES

1. Kenneth S. Tollett, "Black Lawyers, Their Education and Their Community," *Howard Law Journal,* 17 (1972): 326-357 Kellis E. Parker and Betty J. Stebman, "Legal Education for Blacks," *Annals of the American Academy of Political and Social Science,* 407 (1973): 144-155 and Harold R. Washington, "The History and Role of Black Law Schools," *Howard Law Journal,* 18 (1974): 385-422.

2. Kellis E. Parker & Betty J. Stebman, "Legal Education for Blacks," *Annals,* 407: 145; Kenneth S. Tollett, "Black Lawyers...," *Howard Law Journal,* 17: 332-333; Rayford W. Logan, *Howard University: The First Hundred Years, 1867-1967* (New York, 1969), pp. 49-50, 94, 133, 159.

3. For discussions of the American bar before 1920 *see* U.S. Department of Interior, "Recent Progress in Legal Education" (Bulletin No. 3, 1926) prepared for the Bureau of Education by Alfred Z. Reed (Washington, D.C., 1926) pp. 1-4; Lawrence M. Friedman, *A History of American Law* (New York, 1973) and William Miller, "American Lawyers in Business and Politics," *Yale Law Journal,* 60 (January, 1951): 66-76. Legal education in the United States is examined by Alfred Z. Reed, *Training for the Public Profession of the Law,* Bulletin No. 15, Carnegie Foundation for the Advancement of Teaching (New York, 1921); Elizabeth Brown, *Legal Education at Michigan, 1859-1959* (Ann Arbor, 1959), Robert Stevens, "Two Cheers for 1870 The American Law School," in *Law in American History* edited by Donald Fleming and Bernard Bailyn (Boston, 1971); Arthur Sutherland, *The Law at Harvard* (Cambridge, 1967; and *The Centennial History of the Harvard Law School, 1817-1917* (Cambridge, Mass., 1918).

4. On stratification and diversification of the bar, historical analysis of the profession in the United States and critical examination of the impact of the profession on the United States *see* Jerold Auerbach, *Unequal Justice: Lawyers and Social Change in Modern America* (New York, 1976); *see also* J. Auerbach, "The Xenophobic Bar," *Nation,* 214 (June, 1972): 784-86; Walter J. Leonard, "The Development of the Black Bar," *Annals of the American Academy of Political and Social Science,* 407: 134-143; J. Clay Smith, Jr. "Black Lawyers in the United States, 1840-1900," (unpublished address, 1975) which discuss ethnic and racial diversification. William H. H. Hart's case is reported in the *Atlantic* Reporter 60: 457. Regarding the American Bar Association and Black lawyers the reader should consult Raymond P. Alexander, "The National Bar Association," *National Bar Journal,* 1 (1941): 1-15; and S. Joe Brown, "Our Origin," *National Bar Journal,* 2: 161-163.

5. Harlan Fiske Stone, "Legal Education and Democratic Principle," in *American Bar Association Journal* (December, 1921), pp. 639-646, passim, copy among the Papers of Felix Frankfurter, Manuscript Division, Law Library, Harvard Law School, Cambridge, Massachusetts; J. Auerbach, *Unequal Justice* (New York, 1976), pp. 74-157, passim; and correspondence between Felix Frankfurter and Alfred Z. Reed, January, 1922–March, 1922, Papers of Felix Frankfurter, Manuscript Division, Law Library, Harvard Law School, Cambridge, Massachusetts.

6. Alfred Z. Reed, excerpt from *Training for the Public Profession of the Laws,* quoted in A. Z. Reed, "Recent Progress in Legal Education," (Washington, D.C., 1926), p. 23, Papers of Felix Frankfurter, Manuscript Division, Law Library, Harvard Law School, Cambridge, Massachusetts.

7. Letter from Alfred Z. Reed to Felix Frankfurter, March 7, 1922, Papers of Felix Frankfurter, Manuscript Division, Law Library, Harvard Law School, Cambridge, Massachusetts.

8. Reed quoted in Harlan F. Stone, "Legal Education and Democratic Principle," in *ibid.,* p. 643, Papers of Felix Frankfurter, Manuscript Division, Law Library, Harvard Law School, Cambridge, Massachusetts.

9. Letter from Alfred Z. Reed to Felix Frankfurter, March 7, 1922, Papers of Felix Frankfurter, Manuscript Division, Law Library, Harvard Law School, Cambridge, Massachusetts. *See* Reed, *Training for the Public Profession of the Law.*

10. J. Auerbach, *Unequal Justice,* p. 95, 98-99; Letters from Alfred Reed to Felix Frankfurter, January 27, 1922 and February 24, 1922, Papers of Felix Frankfurter, Manuscript Division, Law Library, Harvard Law School, Cambridge, Massachusetts; U.S. Department of Interior, "Legal Education, 1925-1928," (Bulletin No. 31, 1929) prepared for the Office of Education by Alfred Z. Reed (Washington, D.C., 1930), pp. 6-18, passim (This Bulletin includes a summary of the period 1909-10), Papers of Felix Frankfurter, Manuscript Division, Law Library, Harvard Law School, Cambridge, Massachusetts.

11. Letters from Felix Frankfurter to Alfred Reed, February 23, 1922 & March 8, 1922, Papers of Felix Frankfurter, Manuscript Division, Law Library, Harvard Law School, Cambridge, Massachusetts; Harlan F. Stone, "Legal Education and Democratic Principle," pp. 639-646, passim, copy among papers of Felix Frankfurter, Manuscript Division, Law Library, Harvard Law School, Cambridge, Massachusetts; and J. Auerbach, *Unequal Justice,* pp. 93-100, passim. *See* Alfred Z. Reed, "Legal Education, 1925-1928," pp. 8-15, passim. It is noteworthy that Felix Frankfurter believed himself an authority because he wrote from the perspective of one who had attempted evening law school training: "Night schools necessarily will have superficial standards and, in the bulk, turn out superficial practitioners because there are only twenty-four hours in a day and a man's powers are very limited." (Frankfurter to Reed, March 8, 1922) "It gets down to a question of judgement [sic] as to whether the run of men who spend their day in work can get the needed equipment for the exercise of the legal function by a few hours of listening with their tired minds and bodies, at night.... I am clear the answer is 'No'! I attended night schools." (Frankfurter to Reed, February 23, 1922) "The year after graduating from college I worked during the day and attended a night law school in the evening.... I know, so far as any man can know anything, that the exactions of doing work during the day and studying in the late afternoon or night, necessarily make for superficial training." (Frankfurter to Reed, March 8, 1922) Papers of Felix Frankfurter, Manuscript Division, Law Library, Harvard Law School, Cambridge, Massachusetts.

12. J. Auerbach, *Unequal Justice,* pp. 98-99.

13. H. F. Stone, "Legal Education and Democratic Principle," pp. 640, 642, Papers of Felix Frankfurter, Manuscript Division, Law Library, Harvard Law School, Cambridge, Massachusetts.

14. Letters from Felix Frankfurter to Alfred Reed, March 8, 1922, February 18, 1922, Papers of Felix Frankfurter, Manuscript Division, Law Library, Harvard Law School, Cambridge, Massachusetts.

15. *See* the correspondence between Frankfurter and Reed, January, 1922–March, 1922, Papers of Felix Frankfurter and H. F. Stone, "Legal Education and Democratic Principle," Papers of Felix Frankfurter, Manuscript Division, Law Library, Harvard Law School, Cambridge, Massachusetts; J. Auerbach, *Unequal Justice,* pp. 93-129, passim. *See also* the *Handbook of the Association of American Law Schools* (Washington, D.C., 1931). The ABA Root Committee resolutions were approved at the 1921 Washington Conference on Legal Education, but as late as 1926 no state had adopted the resolution requiring two years of college for pre-legal studies insofar as the matter was incorporated into the statutes of any state designating who might practice law before its bar. (J. Auerbach, *Unequal Justice,* pp. 117-118). Regarding AALS members and law schools in the United States *see,* in addition, "Minutes of the 26th Annual Meeting...," Association of American Law Schools, Washington, D.C., AALS, *Directory of Law Teachers* (St. Paul, Minn., 1976) and U.S. Department of Interior, *Bulletin No. 31* (1929) which indicate that there were in excess of 150 law schools in

1920 but only 52 were AALS members that year and in 1928, with the new regulations, only 70 were members.

16. *See* Walter Dyson, *Howard University, The Capstone of Negro Education* (Washington, D.C., 1941), the chapter entitled "Law"; Rayford W. Logan, *Howard University*, pp. 94, 133 & 159; Walter Leonard, "The Development of the Black Bar," *Annals*, 407: 134-139; K. Parker and B. Stebman, "Legal Education for Blacks," *Annals*, 407: 145-146. Interview with Mordecai Johnson, Washington, D.C., January 16, 1975 and interview with Belford Lawson, Jr., Washington, D.C., December 23, 1972.

17. William H. Hastie, Jr., "Charles Hamilton Houston, 1895-1950," *Negro History Bulletin*, 13 (June, 1950): 207; Rayford Logan, *Howard University*, pp. 94, 119-121, 133, 151-159, 225-227; Walter Leonard, *ibid.*

18. J. Clay Smith, Jr., "Black Lawyers in the United States;" Walter Leonard, *ibid.*, p. 145; Sadie T. M. Alexander, "Women As Practitioners of Law," *National Bar Journal*, 1: 56-58; [Genna Rae McNeil] "James A. Cobb, 1876-1958" (Washington, D.C., 1976); Harold R. Washington, "The History and Role of Black Law Schools" in *ibid.*, pp. 385-397, passim; Letters and papers of A. Mercer Daniel (including an unpublished manuscript on the history of Howard Law School) Howard University School of Law, Washington, D.C. *See also* the official files of the Howard Law School, Washington, D.C. and Rayford Logan, *Howard University*, pp. 49-272, passim.

19. Rayford W. Logan, *Howard University*, p. 225; Transcript of student who attended Howard Law School before 1920 enclosed in letter to Dean of Columbia University Law School, February 16, 1921 (Official files, Howard University School of Law) indicated the usual course of study for three years: first or Junior Year — Contracts, Personal Property, Domestic Relations, Criminal Law, Real Estate, Torts, Negotiable Instruments; second or Middle year — Common Law Pleading, Contracts II, Criminal Procedure, Equity, Real Estate, Moot Court; and third or Senior year — Partnership and Sales, Corporations, Executors (Administrative and Insurance), Evidence, Constitutional Law and Moot Court. Additionally, *Howard University Catalogues* (volumes 8 & 9) report a substantially similar list of courses offered in the three years and emphasize text-books as distinguished from case-books. Also compare with the transcript of Houston, Charles H., 1919-1922, Harvard University School of Law, Cambridge, Massachusetts.

20. Rayford W. Logan, *ibid.*, pp. 226-227; Walter Dyson, *Howard University, The Capstone*, pp. 219-239, passim; Genna Rae McNeil, *Charles Hamilton Houston* (forthcoming), chapter 3, "Howard University Law School." *See also* Chapters 1 & 2 in McNeil, *Charles Hamilton Houston* (forthcoming) which discuss William L. Houston's education and practice in addition to Charles Houston's college and law school years.

21. Interview with Mordecai Johnson, January 16, 1975; McNeil, *Charles Hamilton Houston* (forthcoming), Chapter 3.

22. U.S. Department of Interior, Annual Report, 1928, "...Howard University," pp. 1-13, passim; *ibid.*, 1929, "...Howard University," p. 86; Rayford Logan, *Howard University*, p. 266.

23. Letter from Charles H. Houston to Senior Class, Howard University Law School, January 18, 1929, "Houston, Chas. H., Misc. notices, school," Papers of A. Mercer Daniel and Memorandum from J. C. Waters to the Faculty of Law, March 15, 1929, "Houston, Chas. H., Misc., notices, school," Papers of A. Mercer Daniel, Moorland-Spingarn Research Center, Howard University.

24. U.S. Department of Interior, Annual Report, 1929, "...Howard University," p. 86.

25. John Mercer Langston, *Freedom and Citizenship* (Washington, 1883), p. 152, 189 (excerpts from the May, 1874 address, "Equality Before the Law"); Rayford W. Logan, *Howard University,* pp. 48, 62, 64, 74, 81; Letters and papers of A. Mercer Daniel, Howard University School of Law (including unpublished manuscript on the History of Howard Law School). *See also* Langston's autobiography, *From Virginia Plantation to the National Capital* and William Cheek's "John Mercer Langston: Black Protest Leader and Abolitionist," *Civil War History,* 16 (1970): 101-20.

26. Charles H. Houston, "Personal Observations On The Summary of Studies In Legal Education As Applied To The Howard University School Of Law" (typescript, May, 1929), pp. 1-2 (hereinafter, "Personal Observations..."), Files of Charles Hamilton Houston, Houston & Houston Law Firm (presently Houston & Garner), Washington, D.C. (hereinafter CHH, firm files).

27. C. H. Houston, "Personal Observations...," pp. 6, 8, 9.

28. C. H. Houston, "Law As A Career" (typescript, July 1932), pp. 1, 5, CHH–Howard University, firm files; Houston, "Outline of Lecture, New School [for Social Research]," December 12, 1946, p. 1, CHH, firm files; Houston, "Personal Observations...", p. 8, CHH–Howard University, firm files; Houston, "The Need for Negro Lawyers," *Journal of Negro Education,* 4(1935): 49. Charles Houston's concept of social engineering is to be distinguished from the earlier Progressive era notion of independent derivation. *See* for example, Ross and Cooley essays in Clarence Karier, Paul Violas, editors, *Roots of Crisis: Essays in Twentieth Century Education* (Chicago: Rand McNally, 1973).

29. C. H. Houston, "Personal Observations...," pp. 2, 9.

30. Rayford Logan, *Howard University,* p. 267, 285 and U.S. Department of Interior, *Annual Report,* 1929, "...Howard University," p. 86; *ibid.,* pp. 118-119; "Alumni Protest Abolition of the Night Classes," *Washington Tribune,* June 6, 1930, clipping, A. Mercer Daniel Collection, Moorland-Spingarn Research Center, Howard University. With the graduation of the 1932 class, the evening school ceased to exist. (Howard University Catalogue, 1930-31, p. 303 and *ibid.,* 1931-32, p. 332, 342.)

31. "Night Law Classes," *Washington Tribune,* June 6, 1930, clipping, A. Mercer Daniel Collection, Moorland-Spingarn Research Center, Howard University.

32. "Alumni Protest Abolition of Night Classes," *Washington Tribune,* June 6, 1930, clipping, A. Mercer Daniel Collection, Moorland-Spingarn Research Center, Howard University. *See Howard University Catalogues,* 1928-29 through 1931-32 wherein Cobb, Hayes and Houston continue to be listed as instructors.

33. "Dissatisfaction Disrupts Law School Faculty," *Washington World,* August 8, 1930, clipping, A. Mercer Daniel Collection, Moorland-Spingarn Research Center, Howard University.

34. "Howard Law School," *Washington Tribune,* August 15, 1930, clipping, A. Mercer Daniel Collection; Interview with Belford Lawson, Jr., Washington, D.C., December 23, 1972.

35. "Day Classes to Cut Attendance at Law School," and "Dr. Johnson's Predicament," *Washington World,* August 15, 1930, clippings, A. Mercer Daniel Collection.

36. "Law School Quizzed By Bar Association," *Afro-American* (Capital edition), October 18, 1930, clipping, A. Mercer Daniel Collection; U.S. Department of Interior, *Annual Report,* 1931, "...Howard University," p. 149.

37. *Handbook of the Association of American Law Schools and Proceedings of the Twenty-ninth Annual Meeting,* pp. 197-205, passim, (December, 1931), Association of American Law Schools, Washington, D.C.

38. "Law School Quizzed...," *Afro-American,* October 18, 1930, clipping, A. Mercer Daniel Collection. According to the minutes of the Council of May, 1931:

"voted, that the School of Law of Howard University be approved except as to those students who commenced their law school study prior to April 14, 1931," (ABA Staff Assistant, J. Kirkendall to author, December 9, 1974).

39. U.S. Department of Interior, *Annual Report,* 1931, "...Howard University," p. 149; *ibid.,* 1932, p. 150; Rayford W. Logan, *Howard University,* pp. 267, 314; AALS, *Handbook...,* pp. 197-205, passim; "Law Schools in the United States and Canada," in *Directory of Law Teachers* (1973), p. 865.

40. Charles H. Houston, "Personal Observations...," p. 15; Memorandum from Charles Houston to faculty, February 5, 1931, Charles H. Houston, firm files; "Howard Academic Year Is Increased Bulletin Reveals," *Washington Post,* March 31, 1931, clipping, A. Mercer Daniel Collection.

41. *The Independent* (Atlanta, Georgia), April 16, 1931, clipping, A. Mercer Daniel Collection.

42. Compare arguments expressed by Reed, Stone and Frankfurter, pp. 152-53, with press accounts of anti-Johnson, anti-Houston, anti-evening school abolition forces, pp. 158-60, *supra.*

43. G. William Domhoff, *Who Rules America* (Englewood Cliffs, New Jersey, 1967).

44. Charles Houston, "Personal Observations...," pp. 15, 2-8.

45. U.S. Department of Interior, *Annual Report,* 1931, "..]Howard University," p. 149; *ibid.,* 1932, p. 150; *ibid.,* 1933, pp. 304-06, 317-318; *ibid.,* 1934, pp. 382, 384, 397-398; *ibid.,* 1935, pp. 406, 408, 420-21; Student Information Bulletin, June 30, 1934, CHH-Howard University, firm files.

46. Charles Houston, Personal Observations...," pp. 2-9, 15-17, passim.

47. Ibid., pp. 5-15, passim. *See* Houston's Appendix to this document entitled "Curriculum."

48. U.S. Department of Interior, *Annual Reports,* 1931-1935 (*See* note 45 above); Student Information Bulletin, June 30, 1934, CHH, firm files; "Standing Law Committees," William L. Houston-Law School, firm files; *Howard University Catalogues* and *Law School Bulletins,* 1930-31 through 1934-35. In 1934 James A. Cobb was serving his final year as a Municipal Court Judge. George E. C. Hayes, in private practice, was the chairman of the Legal Committee of the Washington, D.C. NAACP branch. William Hastie, Harvard graduate, was appointed Assistant Solicitor in the Department of Interior, November, 1933 and was a member of the legal staff of the New Negro Alliance. Leon A. Ransom assisted Houston with the NAACP's George Crawford murder case in Virginia and received, in 1934, a fellowship from Harvard Law School to work on a graduate degree. Bernard Jefferson was a recent Harvard Law School graduate (1934) and while there was the first black appointed to the Board of Student Advisors. William E. Taylor was an active campaigner for jobs for blacks in white-collar divisions of several emergency programs connected with the government and a member of the District branch NAACP. (Student Bulletin, June 10, 1934 and McNeil, "James A. Cobb.")

49. Memorandum to Faculty, February 5, 1931, CHH-Howard University, firm files; *Howard University Catalogues,* 1930-31, pp. 309 & ff; *ibid.,* 1931-32, pp. 332 & ff; *Law School Bulletin,* 1934-35; McNeil, *Charles Hamilton Houston* (forthcoming), chapter 3. Compare Houston, "Personal Observations...," pp. 2-9, 15-17, passim and his Appendix. Interview with Oliver W. Hill, Richmond, Virginia, December 8, 1972.

50. Genna Rae McNeil, "Charles Hamilton Houston," *Black Law Journal,* 3 (1974): 123-131 at 124; *Howard University Catalogues,* 1930-31 through 1932-33; *Law School Bulletins,* 1933-34 & 1934-35. *See* Class Record Books of Charles H. Houston, 1931-32 & 1932-33, A. Mercer Daniel Collection; Papers of William Hastie, Leon Ransom and William Taylor, Official files, Howard University School of Law.

51. William H. Hastie, Jr. "Charles Hamilton Houston," *Negro History Bulletin,* 13: 208; Interview with Edward P. Lovett, Washington, D.C., January 18, 1973; Interview with William H. Hastie, Jr., Philadelphia, Pennsylvania, September 19, 1972. *See* Spotswood Robinson III, "No Tea For The Feeble: Two Perspectives on Charles Hamilton Houston," *Howard Law Journal,* 20: 1-9.

52. Thurgood Marshall as quoted in Richard Kluger, *Simple Justice* (New York, 1977), pp. 127-128; "Faculty Bulletin," October 9, 1931, CHH–Howard University, firm files, *See also* Papers of Charles H. Houston, Official files, Howard University School of Law and S. Robinson, "No Tea For The Feeble...," in *ibid.*

53. Interview with Edward P. Lovett, Washington, D.C., January 18, 1973.

54. James M. Nabrit, Jr., "Atty. Charles Houston Inspired Many Lawyers," *Pittsburgh Courier,* May 6, 1950, p. 10.

55. Interview with William Hastie, Jr., September 19, 1972; W. Hastie, Jr., "Towards An Equalitarian Legal Order," *Annals,* 407: 21-23. *See also* Loren Miller, *The Petitioners* (New York, 1966) and Richard Kluger, *Simple Justice* (New York, 1977) and Papers of William Hastie, Charles Houston, Leon Ransom, George Marion Johnson, Official files, Howard University School of Law.

56. *See* Colin Greer, "Public Schools: Myth of the Melting Pot," *Saturday Review,* 52: 84-86 (November 5, 1969); Colin Greer, *The Great School Legend* (New York, 1972); Jacob W. Getzels, et al., *Educational Administration As A Social Process;* Horace Mann Bond, *The Education of the Negro in the American Social Order* (New York, 1934). *See also* John Hope Franklin, *From Slavery To Freedom* (Revised edition; New York, 1974), a survey of the black American experience.

57. *See* McNeil, "Charles Hamilton Houston," *Black Law Journal,* 3: 123-131.

58. In an important sense the role of the "social engineer" as propounded by Houston is similar to that of Fanon's colonized writer or scholar who deals with the matter of liberation: "You may speak about everything under the sun; but when you decide to speak of that unique thing in man's life that is represented by the fact of opening up horizons ... and by raising yourself and your people to their feet, then you must collaborate on the physical plane ... work and fight with the same rhythm as the people to construct the future and to prepare the ground where vigorous shoots are already springing up." Frantz Fanon, The *Wretched of the Earth* (New York, 1968).

59. Africa Information Service, editor, *Return To The Source: Selected Speeches by Amilcar Cabral* (New York, 1973), p. 88.

The Pursuit of Professional Equality: Meharry Medical College, 1921–1938, A Case Study

Darlene Clark Hine

This essay is a case study of Meharry Medical College in Nashville, Tennessee and is part of a larger study of blacks in the learned professions: law, science, medicine, education and theology. In the last half of the 19th century black medical colleges arose because blacks desiring a medical education were generally excluded from white ones. In spite of the almost insuperable difficulties of attracting competent faculty and acquiring adequate financial resources, black medical schools did accomplish one significant thing. They provided blacks the opportunity to become physicians and to enter the professional class. The institutional development of Meharry Medical College between 1921 and 1938 provides many insights into the larger problems and conditions affecting the emergence of a black professional class in the United States.

Many long overdue improvements occurred in the quality of medical education for white Americans during the opening decades of the twentieth century. A number of inferior white medical schools ceased operation; admission requirements and standards were upgraded; modern libraries, laboratories and clinical facilities became integral components of the medical schools; medical specialization was encouraged, and faculties were enlarged.[1] However, the medical education available to blacks, at the privately controlled Meharry Medical College from 1921 to 1938 was generally considered substandard. Laboratory facilities were grossly inadequate; instructors were overworked, poorly paid, and undertrained; library resources were virtually non-existent; and students were indiscriminately admitted with little attention paid to their prior records or other indices of competency. Meharry admitted students who had failed at other schools and consequently acquired a reputation of being a haven for "flunkies." The clinical component of the medical training provided in association with the neighboring George W. Hubbard Hospital for blacks was, at best, insufficient. Hubbard Hospital suffered from such acute shortages of funds that it annually ceased operation in April and did not re-open until October. But perhaps its limited operating period was a blessing in disguise; such a cloud of incompetence, suspicion, and lack of confidence hung over Meharry and Hubbard that blacks in Nashville suffered the indignities accompanying requests for medical treatment at the segregated white hospitals rather than risk their own and the lives of loved ones at Hubbard "for the colored."

Meharry's white president in 1920, "the belligerent and autocratic" John J. Mullowney did not help matters at the institution, indeed, conditions stagnated during his tenure. After serving approximately ten years, Mullowney had so alienated and intimidated the black faculty, staff, and student body that a group of alumni, enraged to the point of hysteria, sent a letter to the General Education Board of the Rockefeller Foundation (the major financial benefactor of the school) demanding Mullowney's removal. The letter described the Meharry president as "an untrained, uneducated, uncouth, and unethical vulture.... A man who thinks no more of the feelings of those working with him than a bandit would of pressing a gun to your side.... A dog who is absolutely satisfied to bite the hands that are feeding him." This description preceded a catalogue of offenses and indiscretions Mullowney allegedly had committed.[2] Essentially unmoved by these attacks, Mullowney, who seriously questioned the professional competence and intellectual ability of blacks in the first place, observed, "knowing Negro psychology to be what it is ... there is apparently a racial trait of reluctance against authority..., and there is always a tendency to pit 'the big white house' against the lesser house."[3]

The officers of the General Education Board (GEB), not unaware of Mullowney's "faults," issued polite and somewhat apologetic responses to the criticisms and denied that it possessed power to fire him. The GEB leaders argued that it was extremely difficult to obtain a first rate white man from the North to head up an institution for blacks who would "accept the social ostracism that the position carried." They reminded the disgruntled alumni of the lack of "qualified" blacks who could handle such a position and informed them that the GEB was not the appropriate body to express their grievances against the Meharry president. The power to remove Mullowney, they staunchly maintained, resided in the hands of the "removed and disinterested" Meharry Board of Trustees.[4]

In the private inter-office correspondence, the leaders of the GEB were not so polite. They often patronizingly referred to Mullowney as "well meaning but ignorant." One GEB field agent conceded that "There is more than a germ of truth in the charges" against Mullowney. The Associate Director of Medical Sciences at the GEB, Robert Lambert, lamented, "The disturbing factor in the situation at Meharry is the incompetency of the present leadership.... A glance through the Meharry catalogue is quite sufficient to convince one that M[ullowney] is out of touch with modern medical school organization." Lambert concluded, "The administration at Meharry is a paternalism without an able dictator."[5]

Meharry's transition from a third rate medical college into a high ranking institution dedicated to the training of black physicians occurred in essentially three phases. The first stage encompasses the formative years, 1876 to 1915; the second phase, briefly alluded to above, was the period of paternalistic white control, 1920-1938; and the third era of black and white cooperation spanned the years between the late 1940s and the present. This essay focuses primarily on the second phase and addresses some of the important questions and critical issues affecting the professional development of black physicians. During the 1920s and 1930s how did black medical education develop? Who sustained it and by what mechanism? What role did the white-controlled licensing and ranking organizations, such as the American Medical Association's Council on Medical Education, play in Meharry's development? How did black physicians, political leaders, and the masses respond to Meharry's inadequacies and how effective were they in changing conditions? What was the nature of the relationship between black doctors and the black community, between white administrators and black faculty and staff, between philanthropic foundations and black medical students, faculty, and staff at Meharry? And finally what were some of the major obstacles blocking the professional development of black physicians, medical educators, and students at Meharry Medical College between 1921 and 1938?

A frequently repeated and perhaps embellished story asserts that Meharry Medical College originated in Adams County, Ohio. According to the story, Samuel Meharry, one of seven children of Ohio pioneers, was hauling grist from a mill in Kentucky to his farm in Ohio when his wagon slipped over the edge of the road and became stuck in the mud. While he struggled to release the wagon, an old black man came along and assisted him and later invited the young Meharry to share his cabin. Meharry was unable to repay the man but is purported to have vowed that if he were ever in a position to do so he would do something worthwhile to help black people. Eventually Samuel Meharry acquired what was then considered to be "considerable property." Years later, the story goes, Reverend John Braden, president of Central Tennessee College which was supported by the Freedmen's Aid Society of the Methodist Episcopal Church, came into contact with Meharry who by then had moved to Shawnee Mound, Indiana. Braden asked Meharry to contribute to the establishment of a medical school for blacks. Meharry donated the first $500 towards the creation of the black medical college. His brothers, Alexander, Hugh, David, and Jesse joined him and collectively the Meharry family contributed over $30,000.

In 1876 Dr. R. S. Rust, secretary of the Freedman's Aid Society, authorized Braden to employ George W. Hubbard to organize this rudimentary medical school as a department of Central Tennessee College. Hubbard had migrated to the South after the Civil War and eventually graduated from Vanderbilt

University Medical School in Nashville, Tennessee.He became the first dean of the medical college which began its first year of operation with nine students. Under his supervision a Department of Dentistry was added in 1885, a Department of Pharmacy in 1889, and the Nurse Training Department in 1902. In 1900 the name was changed to Meharry Medical College of Walden University (the new name of Central Tennessee College). Fifteen years later, the state of Tennessee granted Meharry a separate charter. After the school was incorporated Hubbard became its president. The George W. Hubbard Hospital was added in 1912 to provide practical clinical training for the medical students.

During the first thirty-eight years of its existence Meharry graduated 1,287 physicians, 263 dentists, 206 pharmacists, 47 nurses. This output constituted approximately one half of the regularly educated black medical professionals in the southern states. The largest number of black medical students originated from two states, Texas and Tennessee.[6]

In 1910 the entire American medical profession received a severe jolt with the publication of Abraham Flexner's *Medical Education In the United States and Canada*. This Carnegie Foundation financed study criticized and evaluated the entire medical establishment and found much room for improvement. Flexner devoted an entire chapter to black medical schools, the training of black physicians, and the health care needs of black Americans.

At the time there were seven medical schools for blacks in the United States: Howard University in Washington, D.C.; Flint Medical College, New Orleans; Leonard Medical School in Raleigh; Knoxville Medical College in Knoxville; The Medical Department of the University of West Tennessee in Memphis; National Medical College in Louisville, and Meharry Medical College. Flexner proclaimed that except for Meharry and Howard the black medical schools were "...in no position to make any contribution of value" and were "wasting small sums annually sending out undisciplined men, whose lack of real training is covered up by the imposing M.D. degree." He contended that the future of Howard was assured because of support allocated by the Federal Government. He advised that potential benefactors concentrate upon upgrading and supporting Meharry which would "profit the nation much more than the inadequate maintenance of a larger number of schools."[7] In subsequent comments Flexner elaborated upon his reasons for insisting that Meharry should be saved; "It is in management, location and other essential factors considered — the most important school for the training of Negro physicians in the country."[8] The Flexner Report sounded the death knell not only for the black medical schools but for the vast majority of white medical colleges as well.

The Flexner Report is of pivotal importance in the history of black medical education. In addition to passing judgement on black medical schools the Report recommended the way that the larger medical profession should view black physicians and outlined the roles and responsibilities of black doctors. "The practice of the Negro doctor," Flexner declared, "will be limited to his own race." "The pioneer work in educating the race to know and to practice fundamental hygienic principles must be done largely by the Negro doctor and the Negro nurse." Flexner proclaimed, "The Negro needs good schools rather than many schools — schools to which the more promising of the race can be sent to receive a substantial education in which hygiene rather than surgery, for example, is strongly accentuated." The Report pointed out the importance of imbuing black medical men "with the missionary spirit so that they will look upon the diploma as a commission to serve their people humbly and devotedly...." Flexner went so far as to define "the place" of the black physician; "their duty calls them away from large cities to the village and the plantation." In sum, the Flexner blueprint for the black doctor dictated that he be humble, devoted to cleanliness, and treat the medical needs of blacks in small villages and plantations. Indeed, Flexner questioned the intellectual or rational capabilities of blacks and asserted that "the Negro is perhaps more easily 'taken in' than the white" and it was "cruel to abuse his ignorance." Consequently he argued, "a well-taught Negro sanitarian will be immensely useful" while "an essentially untrained Negro wearing an M.D. degree is dangerous."

Flexner's concern for the proper medical education of Negroes, in part, grew out of his interest in protecting white Americans. He oberved that "the physical well-being of the Negro is not only of moment to the Negro himself. Ten million of them live in close contact with sixty million whites. Not only does the Negro himself suffer from hookworms and tuberculosis; he communicates them to white neighbors ... he has, besides the tremendous importance that belongs to a potential source of infection and contagion." Flexner explained, "The Negro must be educated not only for his sake, but for ours" and concluded "self-interest seconds philanthropy ... self protection not less than humanity offers weighty counsel in this matter."[9]

The Council of Medical Education of the American Medical Association intensified its efforts to eliminate inferior medical colleges after the appearance of the Flexner Report. In 1913 the Council and Association of American Medical Colleges inspected and rated every school in the country. Schools ranked in the *A* class provided the highest caliber of medical training. Schools with a *B* classification were acceptable but needed improving. Class *C* schools were considered inferior, provided inadequate medical education, and needed to be completely reorganized.

Beginning in 1914 the Council on Medical Education and the Association of American Medical Colleges supported by various state medical examining boards successfully encouraged many schools to upgrade admission requirements. Approximately 85 per cent of the medical colleges made admission contingent upon the completion of one year of college work.[10] In spite of Flexner's plea that Meharry be saved the movement to upgrade standards in the medical profession had an adverse effect and threatened the survival of the institution.

Meharry reluctantly adopted and instituted the new admission requirements. Entering students had to have completed one year of a pre-medical course which included college physics, chemistry, biology and one modern language. Dean Hubbard quietly shared with Flexner his "fear that this will diminish the enrollment of the freshman class...." He anticipated continuous decline for at least three years. Hubbard's fears were justified. When the 1915 school year opened 18 of the 31 new freshmen possessed college credits. In January, 1916, Hubbard informed Flexner that "owing to the enforcement of the requirement for the pre-medical year, the present Freshman class had been reduced 54% from that of the preceding year and 77% from the year 1913-1914."[11]

Flexner, recently appointed General Secretary of the General Education Board of the Rockefeller Foundation, shared Hubbard's anxiety; "I fear very much that Meharry will be choked." While he applauded the work of the Council on Medical Education he questioned their overzealousness and deemed its policy "calculated to do more harm than good." Flexner added that it was "the duty of those who know the facts to protest against the undue speed with which the Council is trying to obtain results." Ironically, just four years after the publication of the Flexner Report, which called for universal upgrading of medical institutions, Flexner indicated his willingness to lower standards for blacks. He asserted that "it would be better if the one year of college work was not required of these colored schools."[12]

As the number of students seeking admission to Meharry steadily declined the school's financial situation deteriorated and Hubbard was compelled to seek additional funds from foundations and wealthy individuals. He confided to Flexner, "the future success and even the life of Meharry seems to depend upon our obtaining aid from your Board and the Carnegie Foundation." Hubbard also appealed to Julius Rosenwald for additional funds. Flexner used his considerable influence to support Hubbard's fund raising efforts. He wrote the Rosenwald foundation, "something of a crisis in the history of the institution had been precipitated by the elevation of the entrance requirements which had cut down the number of students and therefore the income and by the necessity simultaneously of improving the educational facilities needed to train a more highly competent student body. Thus the institution needs more money precisely at the moment when less is coming in."[13] America's entry into World War I further exacerbated Meharry's financial difficulties. The increased manpower requirement of the war effort plus the heightened admission requirements led to a 16 per cent reduction in students seeking admission in the 1917-18 school year.[14]

By 1919 complete financial collapse seemed imminent. The disaster, however, was averted by a timely donation of $300,000. The GEB and the Carnegie Foundation each contributed $150,000 to the college. The gifts came with several stipulations. Meharry had to successfully take over the property of the now defunct Walden College and raise on its own another $200,000. The GEB required that Meharry Medical College be completely reorganized "along modern educational lines," and that upon Hubbard's retirement in 1920, "a man of sound scientific training in medicine should take his place." The Board insisted that "the qualifications of this man ... be communicated to it before the appointment is made...."[15] Thus by 1920 the philanthropic foundations had essentially acquired a medical college and would through the man selected to be the president, exercise tremendous power over the lives and destinies of black doctors, students, faculty and by extension the black masses. With this Meharry entered into the second phase of its development.

Several factors complicated the selection of a new president for Meharry. P. J. Maveety, secretary of the Freedmen's Aid Society, summarized the situation; "the men whom we regard as eligible do not want to take the place, and those who are willing hardly come up to the standards which you [the GEB] and we have set for ourselves." Later Bishop Thomas Nicholson of the Methodist Episcopal Church which made substantial contributions to Meharry, reported that "two men who might have done the work declined to consider the presidency of a school for negroes." Flexner was not surprised by the difficulty encountered in the search. He indicated that "under the most favorable circumstances positions of this kind are not readily filled. There are factors that make it more than usually difficult in this instance." One of the hindrances which made the presidency of Meharry unattractive, according to Flexner, was the quality of training provided by the institution. To illustrate, Flexner recounted a recent experience involving one of Meharry's graduates. He told Maveety that the outstanding honor student in the Class of 1919 had received a Rosenwald fellowship for advanced study at Harvard. After a short time, however, it was apparent that the student's "training had been so unsatisfactory that instead of advanced opportunities it had been necessary to place him in the ordinary undergraduate classes."[16]

In October, 1920 the search committee jubilantly announced the selection of Dr. John J. Mullowney as their choice. Maveety sent Flexner, in compliance with the earlier stipulation, a biographical profile of Mullowney. The president elect was born in Seacomb, England in 1878. He attended Phillips Exeter Academy for three years and studied one year at Lawrence Scientific School, Harvard University. He graduated from the University of Pennsylvania Medical School in 1908. He spent the next four years working in Peking, China where he served at the Methodist Hospital and taught at the Union Medical College. While in China, he helped to organize a corps of workers who went with him into North China in 1911 "to combat the epidemic of pneumonic type of Bubonic Plague." Upon returning to the United States, Mullowney worked in a variety of public health positions in Philadelphia and with the Pennsylvania State Department of Health. In 1918 he became Head of the Department of Science and Professor of Hygiene and Chemistry at Girard College in Philadelphia.[17]

Various letters supporting Mullowney's candidacy provided additional insights into his personality and abilities. One unsigned note praised Mullowney's fund raising talents and added that Mullowney's "acquaintance with other races has led him to *feel* differently towards the negro than most of us

feel no matter how much we may be disposed to do him justice." The anony-
mous informant speculated "his daily association with negro would therefore,
not present those difficult personal problems which they might present to one
not having had his experience."[18] Flexner was completely sold on Mullowney
whom he thought to be made "of stern and excellent stuff." In December
1920, the Meharry Board of Trustees unanimously voted to hire Mullowney at
a salary of $6,000 per year.[19]

Mullowney's greatest challenge as new president was the improvement of
Meharry's standing in the medical profession. The Council on Medical Education ranked Meharry as a class B institution which indicated the need for continued improvement. This classification seriously handicapped Meharry's
graduates and negatively affected enrollments which, in turn, created more
financial problems for the college.

Graduates from class B colleges were prohibited from taking examinations
for licenses to practice medicine in at least thirteen states. Consequently
Meharry graduates were barred from acquiring licenses to practice medicine in
Arkansas, Alabama, Florida, Kentucky, North Carolina, South Carolina, Virginia, Delaware, Montana, New Hampshire, North Dakota, Rhode Island, and
Illinois. Over half of these states were precisely where most of the Meharry
graduates hoped to locate, southern or border states. In 1922 three members of
the senior medical class transferred to Howard because they were from and
hoped to return to one of the thirteen states that did not allow graduates from
a class B medical college to take the licensing examinations.[20]

Meharry graduates also suffered in competition for internships. For example, the Commissioner of Hospitals in St. Louis, Missouri issued a statement
declaring that after 1923 "no graduates from a Class B medical college will be
allowed to enter any hospital under the supervision of the City of St. Louis."
City Hospital #2 in St. Louis had long been one of the few hospitals in the
country where Meharry graduates could take internships. Competition for the
few available internships was so intense that approximately one-half of all the
black medical graduates from Meharry and Howard went without "the very
valuable training which they should acquire by serving their internships in a
well regulated hospital."[21]

Flexner, intensely aware of these handicaps, attempted to persuade Henry S.
Pritchett, President of the Carnegie Foundation, and Maveety to join him in
efforts to convince the Council of Medical Education to grant Meharry an A
classification. The Council, however, was reluctant to cave in to this pressure.
Copies of the numerous investigative reports sent to the GEB headquarters
illuminate conditions as they existed at Meharry during the early 1920s.

On November 29, 1921, N. P. Colwell, secretary of the Council on Medical
Education and Hospitals, ruled that an alteration in Meharry's class B classification was unwarranted. Before Meharry could receive a higher ranking,
Colwell maintained, it was imperative that the school acquire additional funds
to operate Hubbard Hospital and its dispensaries in order that the hospital

operate on a continuous basis instead of closing in April and reopening in October. The College was also expected to exhibit greater use of the clinical facilities in the instruction of medical students, develop a working library, and employ more full-time teachers in the medical, dentistry, and pharmacy departments.[22]

A second visit in the following year (1922) resulted in Meharry's retention of the same classification. Colwell again cited the lack of funds as the major obstacle. His inspection report focused on the woefully inadequate library facilities. He observed that a small number of old books were scattered in several rooms and students were limited to a very few hours in which to use them because there was no librarian. He recommended that the Library purchase or acquire a larger number of medical texts and reference books, bound periodicals, and the essential indices.[23] Another more thorough inspection occurred later in the same year. At this time Colwell cited "the greatest weakness" as being "the clinical end of the school." He conceded that it was "difficult to find negro clinicians who are also competent teachers." He noted that "the students are now attending section clinics at the bedside and are also doing clinical clerk work," however, he added with dismay, "unless the histories are supervised by the already overburdened superintendent, I fear they are not reviewed or corrected at all."[24]

At the beginning of each inspection report, Colwell painstakingly acknowledged the many advances and achievements made at Meharry. In 1921 he commented, "More improvements have been made in this institution during the last few months than in all the years since 1906." He singled out for particular commendation, "The remarkable development of Hubbard Hospital" where "an efficient white superintendent had been employed." He pointed out that pay and free cases were admitted to the hospital on the same basis and attending staff physicians were no longer permitted to receive fees. Instead the Hospital collected donations and fees directly which helped to "do away with considerable friction between members of the attending staff." A major change which "brought order and efficiency in place of more or less wrangling and confusion," Colwell asserted, was the assignment of patients to the appropriate staff physician on the basis of that individual's specialty. Previously "each member of the attending staff cared for any and all classes of patients...." Colwell further observed that "better control of students is everywhere in evidence.... Nowhere were groups of idle students seen as had been commonly noted on previous inspections."[25]

Flexner, somewhat impatient with the Council's reluctance to grant Meharry a higher classification, argued that "the American Medical Association grants the 'A' rating to the best white schools of the South regardless of whether they come up or do not come up to a real Class A standard." He asked rhetorically "should they not in all wisdom and mercy apply the same principle to Meharry making it an 'A' school, not because it is entirely satisfactory ... but because it is the best possible under the circumstance?" He insisted that should the AMA change Meharry's status "it would be regardful of the public interest and not the reverse." To Pritchett he contended "Meharry is as good as an *A* school for the Negro race as half a dozen institutions or more rated *A* for whites." Moreover he elaborated, "*A* schools are ... simply the best schools in their respective sections. On no other basis could many of the schools classed as *A* be called *A*." He adamantly urged that "the Council do the same thing with the blacks" and added that "under constant prodding and reminding [Meharry] would go ahead and do better."[26]

In late 1922 Colwell informed Flexner that the Library and Clinic were the only things standing in the way of the Council's granting the class *A* rating to Meharry. He admitted that the Council was only considering this step "because of Meharry's being a college for negroes...." and he hoped that the granting of a higher rating at this time would "really be a great help to them whereby further advances would be made." On one point Colwell remained firm. He insisted that coupled with the improvements in the Hospital and the Library, Meharry must acquire an annual income "over and above student fees" of not less than $50,000.[27]

To meet this latter stipulation Maveety established an Endowment Committee and initiated a massive campaign to increase Meharry's endowment to at least one million dollars. He urged the Board of Education for Negroes of the Methodist Episcopal Church to appropriate $10,000 per year towards the $50,000 required for annual operating expenses.[28] The General Education Board quickly awarded Meharry an annual appropriation of $15,000 until the college acquired a permanent endowment of $1,000,000. The GEB stipulated that its $15,000 be used to provide a new operating room, hospital supplies, and laboratory equipment. The GEB also provided substantial funds to increase the Hospital's capacity to 150 beds and an emergency capacity of 175 beds.[29] The Carnegie Foundation likewise contributed significant funds.

These monies proved sufficient. In January, 1923, Mullowney confidentially informed Flexner that Colwell had received "the affirmative vote from the majority of the members of the Council" to raise the rating of the College from "B" to "A" classification. Mullowney pleaded that this news not be released for several months, however, because he was convinced that the alumni would cease sending in contributions and "lay back in the harness if they knew that the college was already in the classification for which they were all eager and anxious." The College of American Surgeons similarly impressed by the new developments gave Hubbard Hospital a class one grade.[30]

It is clearly evident that Meharry received a Class *A* rating as a result of Flexner's behind the scene machinations and massive infusions of Rockefeller money, and not because of merit. Operating under no illusions, eight years and hundreds of thousands of dollars later, Robert Lambert poignantly concluded that "Meharry is far from being on par with the better U.S. schools. The institution must still be ranked as one of the low grade schools of the country, scarcely worthy of the Class A rating benevolently given it'' by the American Medical Association.[31]

In the late 1920s different administrators assumed control of the GEB. Their perceptions of the purpose and future direction of black medical education differed from those of Abraham Flexner. It was not long before they discovered that their opinions, expectations, and plans for Meharry also conflicted with those of President Mullowney. Accordingly, discussions of Mullowney's competence as president became a more frequent topic of discussion in the GEB board rooms. By 1936 Robert Lambert wrote that he had ''come to the conclusion ... that no further improvement [at Meharry] can be expected so long as Mullowney is there.''[32] Both Mullowney's handling of the school's finances and his outdated approach to medical school organization distressed the new GEB leaders.

During the early years of his administration Mullowney acquired ''apparently unchecked responsibility'' of the institution's funds yet was unable to provide the GEB with a clear and complete financial statement. Furthermore, Mullowney failed to provide satisfactory explanations for the existence of ''double salaries.'' He received a separate salary as Professor of Public Health and another salary for his presidential duties. The Professors of Gynecology and Roentgenology both received second salaries from the Hospital. Lambert criticized Meharry's total salary structure. He discovered that there was no definite salary schedule and Mullowney arbitrarily dispensed increases. Those whom he favored received larger salaries. Lambert learned that part time clinical teachers were paid rather well ''whereas the ablest full-time teacher in the medical school [Dr. W. S. Quinland], an exceptionally well-trained man, receives after ten years' service only $3,600.'' An exasperated Lambert noted ''Mullowney in his arbitrariness seems to have shown a poor sense of values.'' He elaborated, ''While paying some of his office workers more than similar employers get at Vanderbilt and giving graduate nurses more than they would get elsewhere, the laboratory departments have been inadequately supplied with technicians and helpers, and the library has been starved.''[33]

Mullowney's inability or refusal to adopt new modes of medical organization was perhaps the greatest frustration. Mullowney insisted that Meharry was a small ''independent'' medical school and should avoid research and concentrate simply on teaching medicine. To Lambert's and Richard M. Pearce's (Director, Division of Medical Education) annoyance, he managed to become fiercely defensive of this position and frequently postulated that this was exactly the kind of medical education most appropriate for blacks.[34] The official GEB position, however, stressed that while Meharry's task was to produce medical practitioners, yet if it was to become a ''high grade institution'' more emphasis had to be placed on research and ''the general advance of medical knowledge in the negro population.'' Pearce like Lambert expressed doubt as to whether Mullowney's ''views would tend to encourage this development.''

They thought not. Another GEB investigator stated more bluntly, Meharry "is conducted more like a high school" than anything else.[35]

Once the GEB leaders agreed that Mullowney actually impeded further development and growth of Meharry they explored ways to rectify the situation, or simply put, looked for means to get rid of Mullowney. During the discussions they recalled that the GEB on Flexner's recommendations had "backed Mullowney's administration for nearly ten years through annual appropriations for maintenance, aid in training teachers through fellowships, and finally through capital grants for land and buildings." Lambert added that the issue was further complicated by Mullowney's relationship with the Meharry Board of Trustees. Mullowney's "prejudiced attitude toward the Negro," his "lack of sympathy with notions of social equality," and his "preference for practical as opposed to cultural education" it was pointed out, "made him so acceptable to his Board" of Trustees that it was completely supportive of him.[36] They agreed that before any steps were taken, a thorough understanding of conditions at Meharry was necessary. The GEB deployed Dr. Franklin C. McLean (a Chicago based white physician) to Meharry to write a comprehensive evaluation and survey of the school. McLean spent the week of October 3, 1933 at Meharry. He critically scrutinized and inspected every component of its physical plant, instruction, and overall faculty and staff personnel. McLean's comprehensive report found little to praise. He declared the Library's collection of recent (within the last 5 years) books adequate but found neither foreign periodicals nor a complete back file of any periodical. He noted, "when it is realized that the faculty and students of Meharry have practically no access to any other source of medical literature, it therefore becomes quite clear that they are completely cut off from original sources."

While the hospital and out-patient facilities were judged acceptable, McLean complained that both were operated at only part, "perhaps fifty per cent," of their capacity. McLean rejected the explanation advanced most often that attributed low utilization of the hospital by blacks in Nashville to "lack of confidence of Negroes in physicians of their own race." He suggested that a more accurate reason was "lack of confidence in Meharry as it is now operated." McLean devoted a great deal of attention to the teaching and clinical staff. He concluded that only two men were outstanding; Dr. M. J. Bent, Professor of Bacteriology and Dr. W. S. Quinland, Professor of Pathology. Both were West Indians who had received some advanced training with the aid of Rosenwald fellowships, at Harvard and Columbia University Medical Schools. The teaching and clinical personnel was predominantly black. "Without a single exception" all were Meharry graduates. But, as McLean interjected, they unfortunately "graduated before Meharry had the advantages of its new physical plant." On the basis of performance and ability, McLean divided the Meharry faculty into three groups. The first group consisted of older men of limited background and attainments who nevertheless possessed considerable native ability. In the second group were "the younger men of ability, but limited training and experience," who often were "assuming responsibilities beyond the present stage of their development." The third group were both "older and younger men," who lacked ability and background. Drs. Bent and Quinland were the exceptions and as such did not fit into any of the three categories. Most teaching emphasized "textbook knowledge and learning the answers to questions." Overall, McLean concluded, "teaching may be considered as distinguished in bacteriology and pathology, and as adequate or less than adequate in other fields."

The clinical departments functioned under severe limitations. They were seriously understaffed and as McLean pointed out "the men with native ability are lacking in maturity and experience." Only two men on the faculty were allowed to perform major surgical operations. McLean commented that "exclusion of certain others of professorial rank from the privilege of operating appears to be the result of experience, and in the interest of the patient." McLean described some of the other professors in the medical department. Dr. D. R. Neil (white) was "an older man without a local reputation for clinical ability." The Professor of Obstetrics, Dr. E. F. Alleyne, "while having a large collection of certificates covering post-graduate study," was "not permitted to do obstetrical operations," because he showed "no evidence either of intellectual or practical ability."

McLean's remarks concerning research and advanced instruction at Meharry were of particular interest to the GEB. He discovered that "neither research nor any work more advanced than the teaching of undergraduate students and the routine care of patients" existed. While there were no administrative orders prohibiting research, McLean found that "independent work was discouraged by the failure to provide funds, by a full schedule of teaching and clinical work, and by a regulation that everyone must be out of the laboratories by five p.m." That no provision was made for advanced instruction, McLean concluded, was "clearly the result of a definite policy limiting the function of the college to undergraduate instruction." In a follow-up note, McLean elaborated on the lack of research at Meharry. "Mullowney stated in reply to a direct question that the reason for this is wholly financial." McLean was unconvinced and explained that "His [Mullowney's] attitude towards research in general and research by Negroes in particular, as expressed in various ways leads me to doubt whether the restriction is entirely due to economics."

McLean ended his report with an evaluation of Meharry needs. Uppermost, he insisted, was the need for reorientation, "both with respect to the attitude toward the Negro and with respect to medical education. This involves first and foremost new leadership." He recommended that medical education at Meharry be thoroughly reorganized as "neither the present faculty, nor any faculty recruited at present exclusively from Negroes could reach a satisfactory standard." He speculated that what he needed was "a group of young Negroes growing up, being trained and weeded out, against a first-rate background."

In other words, Meharry should grow her own "qualified Negroes." He toyed with but ultimately rejected the idea of importing "qualified" blacks from the North because of prohibitive high costs and also, he reasoned, such action "would lead to difficulties of elimination as the younger men grow up and are ready to assume responsibilities." For the short run then, McLean strongly urged the GEB to consider cooperative arrangements with individual white members of the Vanderbilt University Medical School faculty. If white faculty members from Vanderbilt could be interested in teaching part-time or acting in a supervisory capacity, McLean maintained that Meharry "within a few years," would "attain a wholly satisfactory standing in American Medical education."[37]

McLean's Report strengthened the GEB officers' resolve to apply pressure on the inactive and for the most part disinterested Meharry Board of Trustees. The GEB now demanded that the Trustees assume broader responsibility in the control of Meharry's finances. Lambert suggested that "Mullowney should not be permitted to give preference in use of funds as budget shows he is inclined to administration and clinical techniques," as opposed to supporting research laboratories. The Board of Trustees learned definitively "of the doubts which the officers of the [General Education] Board have about the effectiveness of the leadership of the Medical School." Lambert ominously insinuated that if all else failed and improvements were not immediately forthcoming the alternative was cessation of "further contributions towards maintenance" and the withholding of an "ultimate capital grant for endowment."[38]

Alarmed, Charles Nelson, chairman of the Board of Trustees, quickly secured the services of a younger more competent "understudy." The understudy, Dr. Edward L. Turner, agreed to study the school in detail for two years and seriously consider succeeding Mullowney to the presidency. The GEB officers were absolutely delighted with the selection of the thirty-six year old Turner. Turner joined the faculty officially as Professor of Medicine on September 1, 1936. One GEB officer wrote, "We know Turner and are satisfied that few men are his equal in capacities and experience for such a post.... Excellent successor to President Mullowney!"[39]

Turner completed his premedical and clinical work at the University of Chicago where he received BS and MS degrees. He earned his medical degree from the University of Pennsylvania and spent twelve years at the American University in Beirut, first as a teacher of physiology and later as Acting-Dean and Professor of Medicine. His experience with Arab students and peoples was considered valuable preparatory training for the new position.[40]

After a few weeks on campus, Turner provided the GEB officers with detailed, informative, and lengthy reports on every conceivable facet of the Meharry operation. Many of his observations echoed McLean's earlier evaluation. Six months later Turner possessed, what he thought to be, a clear understanding of Meharry's strength and deficiencies. He painstakingly developed reorganization plans for the whole institution but concentrated first on the Medical Department and the Hospital. A brief visit and examination of Hubbard Hospital evoked this response: "It is going to be a very long pull to build up confidence in the Negro public as well as in the Negro practitioner here." He admitted, however, that he "was not surprised that Negroes prefer the white hospitals when I watch some of our clinical staff."[41]

Turner's efforts to reorganize the clinical department proceeded smoothly primarily because he gained the support of Dr. Hale. The fifty-five year old, tall and imposing, part-time Professor of Surgery possessed a "most forceful personality" and was regarded as "the outstanding Negro surgeon in Nashville" who commanded the respect of both white and black colleagues. Most of his co-workers were quite intimidated by him and did not question what he had asked of them. Turner, uncomfortably at first, observed that most black doctors on the staff were "afraid of disputing diagnoses with him," because "he can talk well, freely and glibly, even though he may be absolutely wrong while doing it." Turner quickly developed a deep appreciation and respect for Hale. Within two months he wrote Lambert, "I have gained more and more respect for Doctor Hale and am beginning to appreciate a little better why he has so dominated the picture here. Without reservation Doctor Hale is a good surgeon." Turner conceded that Hale's domination was "certainly justified in the mere fact that he has been heads and shoulders above the rest of them...." In spite of the fact that he did not have "a very brilliant scientific background," Turner implored the GEB to grant additional money to obtain Hale's full time service and insisted that, "Hale is a man whom we should not do away with."[42]

Turner introduced a number of reforms to foster faculty development. He organized a series of weekly departmental seminars to encourage faculty members to discuss their research or problematic hospital/clinical cases. He pressured some of the faculty to return to school for advanced training and arranged for fellowship grants to finance this retooling. He likewise encouraged the faculty to adopt more innovative teaching techniques.[43]

Turner was acutely conscious of the shortcomings of his faculty and staff personnel. He provided incentives to those who showed promise and patiently waited for the opportunity to weed out the weaker, more incompetent professors and physicians. One professor, the head of the Department of Anatomy, was fired not because of incompetence, however, but because of, as Turner phrased it, "irregular ... morals." Dr. V. G. Tolbert, "an unquestionably good anatomist" was an alcoholic and tended to take liberties with women students. Turner justified his dismissal after one incident involving Tolbert and four freshmen women from neighboring Fisk University on the basis that Tolbert "in spite of his knowledge of anatomy, was an exceedingly bad influence for freshman medical students." Dr. Numa P. G. Adams, the black Dean of Howard Medical School when appraised of the Tolbert affair was not surprised and dismissed Tolbert as "an ordinary crap shooting vagabond."[44]

Shortly after the Tolbert incident Turner found it necessary to fire Dr. Adamson of the Obstetrical Department. Adamson received his training at Provident Hospital in Chicago and joined the Meharry faculty and hospital staff in 1935. He instantly alienated not only his colleagues and other physicians in the city, but also the local black community. Turner indicated to Lambert that Adamson was a loner who "carried himself aloof and ... managed to make enemies of practically all who would like to have been friendly." He shunned Dr. Hale's offers to assist in surgical operations and refused to cooperate with anyone. Turner pointed out that "If anyone offered a suggestion his attitude was always 'that's my business and you keep out.'" His operative work in gynecology left much to be desired and was often so disastrous that the junior staff nicknamed him "Blood." Adamson was extremely fair skinned and as Turner explained it, he had "One of these interesting and very trying complexes that makes him refuse to have dark skinned Negro nurses on his service. If the nurse is a light complexioned Negro he gets along well with her even though she may be one of our poorest rather than one of our best."

Because of his disagreeable personality and character, Turner resolved to terminate Adamson's contract at the end of the 1938–39 school term. A serious incident occurred in late October while Turner was out of town, which forced him to take more immediate action. The registrar's daughter who was married to one of the surgical instructors entered Hubbard Hospital to give birth to their first child. The husband demanded that three other physicians, particularly Dr. Hale, be asked for consultation. Adamson grudgingly consented and then proceeded to make the consultants "feel that they were unnecessary." The case was a breech presentation and the consultants advised Adamson to wait until labor was more progressed. Adamson ignored their suggestions and continued with the delivery. Both the patient and the child died.

Turner called a meeting of the hospital committee to discuss the incident. The members of the committee unanimously agreed that Adamson should resign. Prompt action was mandatory as Turner later reported to Lambert because, "The reaction in the community was about as bad as it could be...." Lambert reflected upon the details of the case, agreed with Turner's handling of it, and noted in his diary, "The advancement of Negro medical education is not the easiest of undertaking — the human material available being what it is."[45]

Turner's efforts to improve the faculty paralleled his work to strengthen the student body. In April, 1937, William D. Cutter of the Council on Medical Education and Hospitals delivered a davastating critique of Meharry's faculty: "At Meharry, the faculty is about the poorest that we have found anywhere in the United States or Canada." His comments, regarding the student body, however, were even more critical; "Medical students at Meharry have, in general, poor academic records indicating inadequate preparation or lack of ability. It may be questioned whether such material can be trained so as to be capable of assuming the responsibilities of medical practice." A stunned and annoyed Lambert responded to Cutter's remarks on Meharry; they "should be taken with considerable reserve in view of the attitude he reveals in the first paragraph where he frankly questions the capacity of the Negro to be trained for medicine."[46]

Unfortunately Cutter could not be so easily dismissed. The Council voted to place Meharry on probation until it improved its student body. Failure to do so would result in the loss of its class *A* rank. Turner investigated the situation and found, to his dismay, that some of Cutter's criticism were justified. In direct conflict with "the generally understood policy of a Class 'A' medical college" Meharry annually admitted a large number of freshmen who had flunked out elsewhere. The executive secretary of the Association of American Medical Colleges, Fred Zapffe, confided to Turner that the practice of accepting Howard "repeaters" had "hurt Meharry terribly" in the eyes of the medical educational bodies.[47]

Mullowney was the person responsible for this violation of Council policy. For years he with the registrar's assistance had assumed the entire responsibility of student admissions. When Turner confronted Mullowney with the probationary problem, Mullowney defended his actions with "these men should be given another chance." An enraged Turner vehemently exclaimed, "I am 100 per cent opposed to a policy of giving 'flunkies' from another institution another chance when it reflects on the general rating and status of our entire institution." Shortly after this and other clashes, which increased the antagonism and hostility between the two men, Mullowney as anticipated resigned. On July 1, 1938, two years after his arrival Turner became the third white president of Meharry.[48]

Lambert strongly supported Turner's view of the "flunkies issue" and encouraged him to take the steps necessary to get Meharry off probation. Turner created an admissions committee composed of faculty members from the three schools of dentistry, nursing, and medicine.[49] After considerable discussion and friendly persuasion Turner convinced the Committee and the premedical deans to revamp the whole medical school application process. He urged the establishment of an admissions application deadline. All applications would be required to be in by July 1st of each year. Some of his colleagues balked at the setting of a deadline because Meharry had always admitted students "all through the summer up until the day the college opened." Turner persisted in spite of these reservations. He jubilantly reported to Lambert that "on June 30th we had already selected 58 freshmen for next year out of a deluge of applications."[50]

On December 4, 1938 the Council on Medical Education and Hospitals agreed to remove from its publications indications that Meharry was on probation.[51]

The major difficulties Meharry confronted during the critical period under consideration were the upgrading of the faculty and staff, selecting better prepared students, maintaining its class "A" status, improving the library and physical plant, winning the confidence of the black community, overcoming the overtly racist attitudes of the larger society and the negative beliefs and actions of those who occupied managerial and administrative positions, acquiring capable and committed leadership, and finally, securing adequate financial resources. While significant strides had been made by 1938, it would take Meharry approximately fourteen years to become a truly respectable medical school.

This account of Meharry from 1921 to 1938 provides another view into the racial reality of the times. Very few blacks were admitted to white colleges. Because of the difficulties discussed above, Meharry could only provide substandard medical education. The problems were compounded because Meharry could only draw upon a pool of applicants who had received inferior preliminary education. To fill the seats and to add to the income of the college, they admitted all they could find and in the process perpetrated the myth that blacks were inferior to whites in practicing medicine. This undoubtedly had repercussions for the entire black population. It is unlikely that any of the black medical students expected to practice medicine with whites as patients. In future investigations of black medical education, researchers must examine not only the adequacy of the medical training available, but also the relationship of black medical professionals to the overall social and economic advancement of blacks in America.

NOTES

1. For a good overview of the history of medical education in America *see* Martin Kaufman, *American Medical Education: The Formative Years, 1765-1910* (Westport, Conn.; Greenwood Press, 1976).

2. The communication was signed Unanimously Yours, Nashville Public and Alumni to the General Education Board, July 17, 1933; General Education Board Papers (hereafter GEB Papers), Rockefeller Archive Center, Tarrytown, New York. Box 134.

3. John J. Mullowney, Confidential Memorandum: Points For Serious Consideration, copy sent to GEB on April 4, 1934; GEB Papers, Box 134.

4. Trevor Arnett, President of the General Education Board to A. W. Armour, July 26, 1933; Armour to Arnett, July 24, 1933; Leo M. Favrot, General Field Agent to Armour, July 27, 1933; GEB Papers, Box 134; Summary of Conference on Meharry Medical School, October 8, 1928, GEB Papers, Box 133.

5. Robert A. Lambert, Memorandum: "Meharry Medical College," March 1, 1931; GEB Papers, Box 134.

6. Description of Walden College by President, T. R. Davis, November 4, 1925; Sketch of Meharry Medical College by G. W. Hubbard, June 30, 1915; G. W. Hubbard to Abraham Flexner, December 12, 1914; GEB Papers, Box 133; John J. Mullowney, "Meharry: Her Past, Her Future," Speech, November 9, 1930; GEB Paper, Box 134.

7. Abraham Flexner, *Medical Education in the United States and Canada* (New York: Carnegie Foundation, 1910), chapter 14. Copy in GEB Papers, Box 133.

8. Flexner to William C. Graves of the Rosenwald Fund, March 19, 1917, GEB Papers, Box 133.

9. Flexner, *Medical Education,* Chapter 14.

10. Kaufman, *American Medical Education,* pp. 176–177.

11. Hubbard to Flexner, December 12, 1914, December 6, 1915, January 18, 1916, GEB Papers, Box 133.

12. Flexner to Hubbard, December 16, 1914; Flexner to Arthur D. Bevan, Chairman of the Council on Medical Education of the American Medical Association, February 8, 1915; GEB Papers, Box 133.

13. Hubbard to Flexner, December 2, 1916; Flexner to Graves, March 19, 1917; GEB Papers, Box 133.

14. Hubbard to E. C. Sage, November 20, 1917, GEB Papers, Box 133.

15. Henry S. Pritchett, President of the Carnegie Foundation for the Advancement of Teaching to Bishop Thomas Nicholson of the Methodist Episcopal Church, February 24, 1919; Wallace Buttrick to Nicholson, March 3, 1919; GEB Papers, Box 133.

16. Reverend P. J. Maveety to Buttrick, December 24, 1919; Nicholson to Buttrick, January 22, 1920; Flexner to Maveety, December 27, 1919; December 31, 1919; GEB Papers, Box 133.

17. Maveety to Flexner, October 28, 1920, GEB Papers, Box 133.

18. Copy. National Association of Dental Faculties to Bruce R. Payne of Peabody College for Teachers, April 24, 1919, GEB Papers, Box 133.

19. Flexner to Maveety, November 29, 1920; Robert Ewing of the Meharry Board of Trustees to Mullowney, December 23, 1920, GEB Papers, Box 133.

20. Mullowney to Buttrick, December 14, 1921; Nicholson to Arnett, January 27, 1922; Mullowney to Anson Phelps Stokes, February 21, 1922; GEB Papers, Box 133.

21. Mullowney to Flexner, October 11, 1922; Copy of Mullowney, "The Weakest Link" a speech, November 11, 1928; GEB Papers, Box 133.

22. Nathan P. Colwell to Flexner, December 16, 1921; GEB Papers, Box 133.

23. Copy of inspection report. Colwell, Meharry Medical School Nashville, Tennessee, October 27–28, 1922; GEB Papers, Box 133.

24. Colwell to Flexner, December 20, 1922; GEB Papers, Box 133.

25. Colwell to Flexner, December 16, 1921; Copy of Inspection Report, Colwell, Meharry Medical College, November 29, 1921; GEB Papers, Box 133.

26. Flexner to Pritchett, April 27, 1921, April 25, 1921; GEB Papers, Box 133.

27. Colwell to Flexner, December 20, 30, 1922; GEB Papers, Box 133.

28. Maveety to Flexner, December 22, 1922; GEB Papers, Box 133.

29. Flexner to Mullowney, February 24, 1923; GEB Papers, Box 133. Also see: Agreement, General Education Board and Meharry Medical College, June 28, 1923, Box 133.

30. Mullowney to Flexner, January 17, 1923; Mullowney to Buttrick, October 30, 1923; GEB Papers, Box 133.

31. Lambert, Memorandum, "Meharry Medical College," March 1, 1931, GEB Papers, Box 134; Mullowney to Flexner, September 6, 1923, Box 133.

32. Lambert to Allan Gregg, April 28, 1936, GEB Papers, Box 134.

33. Lambert, Diary entry, February 14, 1931; Memorandum, "Meharry Medical College," March 1, 1931; "Further Notes on Meharry," March 28, 1931; GEB Papers, Box 134.

34. Mullowney to Richard M. Pearce, Director, Division of Medical Education, November 16, 1926; Box 133; Lambert to Mullowney, September 30, 1930, GEB Papers, Box 134.

35. Pearce to Mullowney, November 19, 1928; Pearce, Memorandum: Meharry Medical College, November 19, 1928, GEB Papers, Box 133.

36. Lambert, Memorandum, "Meharry Medical College," March 1, 1931; Franklin McLean of the Julius Rosenwald Fund to Lambert, June 18, 1934; Lambert, "Special Memo: President Mullowney and Dr. E. L. Turner, Meharry Medical College," December 28, 1937, GEB Papers, Box 134.

37. "Comments of Meharry Medical College Embodied in a Report by Doctor Franklin C. McLean to the General Education Board, Following a Visit to Meharry at the Boards Request during the Week of October 3, 1933; McLean to Gregg, December 19, 1933; GEB Papers, Box 134.

38. Lambert to Gregg, May 7, 1934; Lambert, "Memorandum, Meharry Medical College," March 1, 1931, GEB Papers, Box 134.

39. Charles Nelson, Chairman, Meharry Board of Trustees to W. W. Brierley, Secretary of the GEB, August 22, 1936; Gregg, "Memorandum," August 11, 1936; GEB Papers, Box 134.

40. "Annual Report of Meharry Medical College, 1936–1937," by J. Mullowney, June 4, 1937, GEB Papers, Box 134.

41. Turner to Lambert, January 29, 1937; GEB Papers, Box 134.

42. Turner to Lambert, October 4, November 22, 1936, March 15, 1938; GEB Papers, Box 134.

43. Turner to Lambert, October 4, 1936, November 22, 1936; GEB Papers, Box 134.

44. Turner to Lambert, May 25, 1938; Lambert interview with Numa P. G. Adams, November 18, 1938; GEB Papers, Box 134.

45. Turner to Lambert, November 6, 1938; Lambert, Reflections, November 18, 1938; GEB Papers, Box 134.

46. William D. Cutter to Ray Lyman Wilbur, April 5, 1937; Lambert, "Dr. Cutter's Comments on the Meharry Medical College," April 8, 1937; GEB Papers, Box 134.

47. Turner to Lambert, February 22, 1938; March 7, 1938; Turner, "Summary of Suggested Future Meharry Readjustments," March 18, 1938, GEB Papers, Box 134.

48. Turner to Lambert, May 23, 1938; GEB Papers, Box 134.

49. Turner to Lambert, February 10, 1938; Turner "Suggested Future Meharry," March 18, 1938; GEB Papers, Box 134.

50. Turner to Lambert, March 23, 1938, July 12, 1939; GEB Papers, Box 134.

51. Turner to Lambert, December 1, 1938; Cutter to Turner, December 7, 1938; GEB Papers, Box 134.

American Values, Social Goals, and the Desegregated School: A Historical Perspective

Vincent P. Franklin

The increasing efforts to bring about the desegregation of American public education have generated a voluminous literature which focuses on many aspects of this important educational policy. There have been analyses of the politics of the desegregated process; the effects of the desegregation upon race relations, academic achievement, and self concepts of black and white children in desegregated schools; the plight of the black teacher in the desegregated system; and many other aspects of the process.[1] Moreover, several essays and books have recently appeared which attempted to address the broader issues raised by public school desegregation, by asking, "Is School Desegregation Still a Good Idea?" In answering this question, the writers examined a number of issues including the role of social science research in determining the positive and negative effects of desegregation, their personal involvements in the process, and most importantly, the actions of school boards, administrators, and public officials to try and thwart the implementation of desegregation plans. Despite widespread opposition and minor setbacks, these writers ultimately conclude that "Yes, school desegregation is indeed a good idea," and it should continue to be supported by the society at large.[2]

The basic reason given for the need to pursue public school desegregation was the fact that it had really not been given a viable chance to work. It was argued that if the process was allowed to continue, the desegregation of the public schools has great potential for improving interracial and majority-minority group relations in this country. Stiff opposition to school desegrega-

I would like to acknowledge the financial assistance of a Summer Faculty Fellowship from the University of Illinois, and a Spencer Fellowship from the National Academy of Education in the completion of this essay.

tion in general, and busing in particular, however, have slowed and sometimes blocked the implementation of desegregation orders. In addition, school officials and educators who openly opposed forced or court-ordered desegregation were supported by many sophisticated and unsophisticated anti-busing tracts.[3] But the lack of significant negative effects upon the self-concepts and achievement levels of black and white children in desegregated schools led these writers to conclude that there is no good reason to abandon desegregation as a national educational policy.

This line of argument in support of public school desegregation, however, did not really address the more important social issues this policy raised. Is school desegregation a viable and important social and educational policy? Is school desegregation an end in itself, or a means to an end? Is this educational policy related to other social goals, or is school desegregation contrary to certain basic American values and beliefs? In this essay the relationship between American values and social goals, and the historical development of American public education will be discussed. The social goals to be achieved by "segregated" public schooling will be examined in order to make clear the historical background of the contemporary opposition to public school "desegregation." The adequacy of the social goal of "equality of educational opportunity" will be evaluated in light of the recent suggestion that "equality of condition" between majority and minority groups should be the new social goal for American society.

Values, Goals, and American Public Education

The basic values and social goals of the American people as articulated by its leaders were mirrored in the overall social purposes of American public education. During the Revolutionary era, Thomas Jefferson argued for the extension of educational opportunity for both humanitarian and societal objectives. In his famous "Bill for the More General Diffusion of Knowledge," Jefferson posited the need for an "enlightened citizenry" in order to allow democracy to flourish. Educated and able leadership is chosen only by a knowledgeable citizenry informed about its own best interests.[4] With Noah Webster and Jedidiah Morse the goal of creating a genuine "American nationalism" was paramount, and in 1788 Webster admonished Americans for their dependence on "foreign books and education," and sounded the challenge: "Americans, unshackle your minds.... You have now an interest of your own to augment and defend — you have an empire to raise and support by your exertions — and a national character to establish by your wisdom and virtues. To effect these great objects, it is necessary to frame a liberal plan of policy, and to build it on a broad system of education."[5] Jedidiah Morse in publishing his famous *American Geography* (1791) hoped to instill in the American an awareness of himself as well as a knowledge of his country. Nationalistic values underpinned

Morse's belief that the new United States of America ought to present to the rest of the world "authentic information" about its physical boundaries.[6]

Early state constitutions often acknowledged the need for education, if for no other reason than to stem "vice and immorality." The Pennsylvania Constitution of 1800 went beyond many others by calling for the establishment of a system of public schools for the education of the poor. But public charity schools only served to whet the appetites of those who hungered for free, universal, common schools.[7] The Common School campaign of the 1830s and 1840s produced many statements and arguments which juxtaposed American values and social goals, and the need for public schools. Horace Mann, for example, argued for the support of the schools for the economic development of the entire community. The common schools would allow all to contribute to the "general" prosperity and guarantee the dissemination of democratic and egalitarian values. "Education, then, beyond all other devices of human origin, is the greater equalizer of the conditions of men," wrote Mann in 1848, "the balance wheel of the social machinery."

> I do not here mean that it so elevates the moral nature as to make men disdain and abhor the oppression of their fellow-men. This idea pertains to another of its attributes. But I mean that it gives each man the independence and the means by which he can resist the selfishness of other men. It does better than to disarm the poor of their hostility towards the rich; it prevents being poor.[8]

During the same years that Mann, the Superintendent of Public Schools in Massachusetts, was arguing that the common schools should be the "great equalizer"; the State Supreme Court, reflecting other "American values" was placing limitations upon how much "equality" would be legally allowed in the new public schools. In the famous case of *Roberts v. City of Boston* (1849), the father of a black child who was being forced to attend a badly run-down segregated school sued the School Committee of Boston. Charles Sumner, the lawyer for the plaintiff, argued that the exclusion of black children from public schools open to whites, in effect, meant that "the black and white are not equal before the law.... The separation of children in the Public Schools of Boston, on account of color or race, is in the nature of Caste, and is a violation of equality...."[9]

Chief Justice of the Massachusetts Supreme Court, Lemuel Shaw, in ruling against the plaintiff, however, pointed out that "the broad, general principle of equality before the law" is perfectly sound in the abstract.

> But, when this great principle comes to be applied to the actual and various conditions of persons in society, it will not warrant the assertion, that men and women are legally clothed with the same civil and political powers, and that children and adults are legally to have the same functions and be subject to the same treatment; but only that the rights of all, as they are settled and regulated by law, are equally entitled to the pater-

nal consideration and protection of the law for their maintenance and security. What those rights are, to which individuals, in the infinite variety of circumstances by which they are surrounded in society, are entitled, must depend on laws adapted to their respective relations and conditions.

With regard to the segregated schools, Shaw acknowledged the plaintiff's argument that they were the result of "a deep-rooted prejudice in public opinion," but concluded that "this prejudice, if it exists, is not created by law, and probably cannot be changed by law." Shaw believed that the opening of separate schools for black children "is a fair and proper question for the [school] committee to consider and decide upon...."[10]

The *Roberts* decision served as an important legal precedent for many subsequent cases involving legal segregation. But it was even more significant because it demonstrated that from this early era the establishment of the universal, free, public school system would not be used to challenge the more basic value of white supremacy in American society in general. And black Americans were alerted that the public schools would not be the means through which they would attain full social, economic, and political equality in this country.

In the South in the post-Civil War era the common school ideal gradually came to be accepted by the white population. Whereas the newly-emancipated blacks actively sought schooling and supported the establishment of the public schools, the upper and lower class whites were reluctant to introduce the "northern institution" into their region. When public schools were established, however, the various southern states also adopted the northern practice of separating blacks and whites. The small black populations in most northern cities and states in the last quarter of the nineteenth century required merely the opening of a few "colored schools." The large black population in the South, however, making up half of the citizens in some states, led the southern legislatures to establish two separate public school systems in each state.[11]

"Jim Crow" or the legal segregation of blacks and whites was spreading throughout the South after the Civil War and Reconstruction and blacks continually challenged the practice in the courts. This legislation, in effect, codified the white supremacist values of the dominant white majority. The Fourteenth Amendment to the Constitution guaranteed all citizens "equal protection of the law," and in a series of court cases in the 1870s and 1880s blacks tried to get the state and federal courts to uphold their civil rights. The Louisiana legislature in 1890 passed a law which called for the segregation of blacks and whites on railway coaches within the state. On June 7, 1892 Homer A. Plessy was arrested for refusing to vacate a New Orleans railway coach which was designated "for whites only." Judge John Ferguson of the Criminal District Court ruled against Plessy's argument that the segregation law violated the Fourteenth Amendment guarantee of equality before the law. The ruling by Ferguson was appealed to the Louisiana Supreme Court which granted Plessy's petition to take his case to the Supreme Court of the United States.[12]

The majority and dissenting opinions of the Supreme Court in the case of *Plessy v. Ferguson* (1896) are replete with statements about American values and social goals. In the majority opinion, for example, the limitations on the Fourteenth Amendment were spelled out.

> The object of the amendment was undoubtedly to enforce the absolute equality of the two races before the law, but in the nature of things it could not have been intended to abolish distinctions based upon color, or to enforce social, as distinguished from political equality, or a commingling of the two races upon terms unsatisfactory to either.[13]

The beliefs and values which inspired court decisions and legislation for the establishment of separate black public schools were discussed and found acceptable for sanctioning the correctness of Jim Crow legislation. Justice Henry Billings Brown who authored the majority opinion believed that the only real point at issue was the "reasonableness" of the Louisiana regulation.

> In determining the question of reasonableness it [the Supreme Court] is at liberty to act with reference to the established usages, customs and traditions of the people, and with a view to the promotion of their comfort, and the preservation of the public peace and good order. Gauged by this standard, we cannot say that a law which authorizes or even requires the separation of the two races in public conveyances is unreasonable, or more obnoxious to the fourteenth amendment than the acts of congress requiring separate schools for colored children in the District of Columbia, the constitutionality of which does not seem to have been questioned, or the corresponding acts of state legislatures.

In the last few paragraphs of the opinion, however, Justice Brown added a few words about the black interpretation of segregation laws.

> We consider the underlying fallacy of the plaintiff's argument to consist in the assumption that the enforced separation of the two races stamps the colored race with a badge of inferiority. If this be so, it is not by reason of anything found in the act, but solely because the colored race chooses to put that construction upon it. The argument necessarily assumes that if, as has more than once been the case, and not unlikely to be so again, the colored race should become the dominant power in the state legislature, and should enact a law in precisely similar terms, it would relegate the white race to an inferior position.

Brown was alluding to the movements in the contemporary political struggle between blacks and whites in some southern states. The violence and terrorism of southern whites was ultimately successful in pushing most blacks from the political arena by the end of the 1890s, so that Brown could confidently add that "we imagine that the white race, at least, would not acquiesce to this assumption" of black political power.

Justice Brown also wrote of the "natural antipathy" between the black and white races which could not be eliminated by laws.

> Legislation is powerless to eradicate racial instincts, or abolish distinctions based upon physical differences, and the attempt to do so can only result in accentuating the difficulties of the present situation. If the civil and political rights of both races be equal, one cannot be inferior to the other civilly or politically. If one race be inferior to the other socially, the constitution of the United States cannot put them on the same plane.[14]

Thus the often-enunciated social goal of "equality" was construed to be trinitarian, with political, civil, and social components. The Constitution and laws of the country views citizens as either "political" or "civil" individuals. Whereas the law can adjudicate instances of political or civil inequalities between and among individuals, the natural social or physical inequality of the races could not be changed. Separation of blacks and whites was in accord with certain "instincts," and as long as civil and political equality obtains, according to Justice Brown, the courts really have no jurisdiction.

In his dissent from the majority opinion, however, Justice John Harlan made very clear the real values and goals in question in the *Plessy* case. "Every one knows that the statute in question had its origin in the purpose, not so much to exclude white persons from railroad cars occupied by blacks, as to exclude colored people from coaches occupied or assigned to white persons...."

> The thing to accomplish this was, under the guise of giving equal accommodation for whites and blacks, to compel the latter to keep to themselves while traveling in railroad passenger coaches. No one would be so wanting in candor as to assert the contrary....
> The white race deems itself to be the dominant race in this country. And so it is, in prestige, in achievements, in education, in wealth, and in power. So, I doubt not, it will continue to be for all time, if it remains true to its great heritage; and holds fast to the principles of constitutional liberty. But in the view of the constitution, in the eye of the law, there is in this country no superior, dominant, ruling class of citizens. There is no caste here. Our constitution is color-blind, and neither knows nor tolerates classes among citizens. In respect of civil rights, all citizens are equal before the law.

Harlan also agreed with the black viewpiont on the purposes of the segregation laws. "The arbitrary separation of citizens, on the basis of race, while they are on a public highway," wrote Harlan, "is a badge of servitude wholly inconsistent with the civil freedom and the equality before the law established by the constitution. It cannot be justified upon legal grounds." The dissent by Harlan would not become the majority opinion of the Supreme Court for another sixty years, and the "separate, but equal" doctrine having been sanctioned, was promulgated through legislative actions throughout the South.[15]

Almost as soon as the *Plessy* decision was handed down, the issue arose as to who would determine when public facilities, such as public schools, were equal. In the case of *Cumming v. Richmond County Board of Education* (1899), blacks in Augusta, Georgia sued the local School Board to close the white high schools, after the high school for black children was closed. According to the opinion in *Plessy,* the county was supposed to provide "equal" facilities for blacks and whites. The Supreme Court ruled, however, that the School Board did not have to maintain a high school for blacks.

> While all admit that the benefits and burdens of public taxation must be shared by the citizens without discrimination against any class on account of their race, the education of people in schools maintained by state taxation is a matter belonging to the respective states, and any interference on the part of Federal authority with the management of such schools cannot be justified except in the case of a clear and unmistakable disregard of rights secured by the supreme law of the land.

This unanimous decision was written by Justice John Harlan, and had the effect of sanctioning the unequal distribution of public school funds between blacks and whites in many states.[16]

During the latter part of the nineteenth century, the values and beliefs of the white majority not only determined how much schooling black children were to receive, but also influenced the type of schooling which was made available. While the social and political position of blacks was being defined by the courts and state legislatures, many educators and southern leaders were determining the most appropriate form of education for blacks, given their inferior social position. At the end of the Civil War, many newly-emancipated blacks actively sought to try and improve their status in southern society. General Samuel Armstrong, who became Principal of Hampton Institute in 1868, believed that blacks should learn "respect of labor ... for the sake of character"; and supported industrial education as the most appropriate form of schooling for the "uplifting" of an "inferior race."[17] The idea that the white race was superior in cultural and biological development to the "darker races" became a generally accepted belief among whites in the last quarter of the nineteenth century. Therefore, when General Armstrong suggested that blacks could not benefit from or appreciate "higher" or "classical" education, but needed "to replace stupid drudgery with skilled hands..."; he received support from many "friends of the Negro" throughout the nation. Ex-president Rutherford B. Hayes, J.L.M. Curry of the Slater Fund, Railroad magnate Collis P. Huntington, Philanthropists William H. Baldwin and George Foster Peabody, and the indominable Andrew Carnegie were only a few of the northern industrialists and financiers who supported the introduction of basic industrial training for the masses of blacks throughout the South.[18]

It should be noted, however, that Armstrong did not provide training in the "skilled trades" for blacks attending Hampton in order to insure that they did *not* compete with skilled white tradesmen and craftsmen in the South. Manual labor and basic reading and writing skills were about all students could count on after three or four years at Hampton. But these were considered by Armstrong to be the only skills needed by black teachers and leaders. Some supporters of industrial education, such as Rutherford B. Hayes, believed that blacks should have advanced industrial skills to become "good mechanics and good businessmen ... architects, civil engineers and the like." But during the 1870s and 1880s the curriculum and instruction at Hampton, and later Tuskegee Institute and the various other industrial schools supported by the northern foundations, merely prepared black students to teach others the "joys of manual labor."[19]

By the 1890s throughout the South, industrial education had become almost synonymous with "Negro education." Booker T. Washington, the leading Negro disciple of Armstrong, rose to fame as a result of his accommodating political stances and support for industrial education. Washington received a great deal of financial support from northern philanthropists to travel throughout the United States spreading the "gospel of uplift through industry."[20] White southerners, who already had a bias in favor of "classical" education, came to think of industrial education as being only for the Negroes. Although the Progressive reformers were able to convince many lower class and foreign-born whites in the North that industrial and vocation education would prepare them for many "higher industrial pursuits," southern whites were very slow in jumping on the "industrial education bandwagon."[21]

The beliefs and values of the dominant white majority determined the social goals of American society, and the role of the public schools in achieving these goals. Since most whites believed that blacks were inferior mentally and culturally, and white leaders controlled the public expenditures for schooling; it is not surprising that public schools for blacks primarily consisted of the elementary grades and emphasized manual labor and industrial training. Though the official policies and laws in the southern states called for "separate, but equal"; the reality between 1896 and 1954 was "separate and unequal." Studies sponsored by Atlanta University in 1901 and 1911, Horace Mann Bond's famous examination of the *Education of the Negro in the American Social Order,* published in 1934, and the numerous investigations conducted by the black and white lawyers of the National Association for the Advancement of Colored People (NAACP) in the 1930s and 1940s documented the fact that the public educational facilities provided for black children in most southern states were far from equal to those provided for white children in the same states.[22]

In its campaign for school desegregation, the NAACP first attacked those states which provided graduate and professional education at public expense for whites, and nothing for blacks. After winning several favorable Supreme Court decisions in the 1930s and 1940s which opened Law and other professional schools to blacks in Maryland, Virginia, and several other states, the NAACP lawyers believed there were enough legal precedents for the Court to overturn the "separate, but equal" doctrine. In May 1954, in the case of *Brown v. Topeka Board of Public Education,* the United States Supreme Court declared that segregation in public education was unconstitutional.[23]

In that opinion, Chief Justice Earl Warren acknowledged the fact that in some states attempts had recently been made to "equalize" the public educational facilities between blacks and whites, but these were only the more "tangible factors." "Our decision, therefore, cannot turn on merely a comparison of these tangible factors in the Negro and white schools involved.... We must look to the effect of segregation itself on public education." Then Warren described the social purposes of the public schools "in our democratic society."

> It is required in the performance of our basic public responsibilities, even service in the armed forces. It is the very foundation of good citizenship. Today it is a principal instrument in awakening the child to cultural values, in preparing him for later professional training, and in helping him to adjust normally to his environment. In these days, it is doubtful that any child may reasonably be expected to succeed in life if he is denied the opportunity of an education. Such an opportunity, where the State has undertaken to provide it, is a right which must be made available to all on equal terms.[24]

Equality of Opportunity, Pluralism, and the Desegregated School

In the *Brown* decision the Supreme Court sanctioned the basic social goal of "equality of educational opportunity" and called for the desegregation of American public education "with all deliberate speed." Problems arose, however, in the implementation of school desegregation because although this important social goal was restated, it did not rest on values held by a majority of Americans. Whereas opposition to the establishment of the free, universal, common schools was unsustained; most school boards continually exercised their prerogative to open separate public schools for black children. Whereas few whites opposed the introduction of a special industrial curriculum into predominantly black schools, the mandate for school desegregation in order to achieve equality of educational opportunity met with a great deal of white resistance. Legal suits often were brought to stall the desegregation of the local public schools. State legislatures enacted laws which attempted to "nullify" the enforcement of the Court's decision. In Georgia, Alabama, and Virginia, for example, legislation was passed which forbade the desegregation of the public schools, while the Texas legislature tried to withhold funds from school districts which attempted to desegregate. Eventually mobs of white citizens in cities and towns in the North and the South tried to thwart school desegregation by protest and violence.[25]

In addition, several attempts were made to undercut the goal of equality of educational opportunity by questioning whether or not desegregation will bring "equality" between blacks and whites given the "innate mental inferiority of the Negro" as measured by "intelligence tests." Arthur Jensen, for example, in a series of books and articles suggested that the fifteen point difference in "intelligence quotient" (IQ) scores between blacks and whites was due to the superior intellectual ability of whites. Jensen believes that environmental and cultural factors would not account for the difference, and that improvements in the environment of blacks would not be reflected in the intelligence test scores.[26] Although a few other social scientists, and one famous non-social scientist, William Shockley, supported Jensen's thesis; many others questioned Jensen's manipulation of the evidence and grandiose statements about the heritability of intellectual abilities. In any case, those who opposed the social goal of equality of educational opportunity found comfort in the "findings" of Arthur Jensen.[27]

It has also been suggested that some of the attempts to bring about the goal of equality of opportunity for blacks and other minorities in the United States led to the creation of "special benefits" for these groups. Legislation calling for equal opportunities for minorities led to attempts to bring about "statistical parity" in employment and other areas. According to several writers, Affirmative Action guidelines have resulted in the establishment of a virtual "quota system" in many areas of employment. Thus in the attempts to end discrimination against blacks and other minorities, white males became the victims of discrimination. In his recent book, *Affirmative Discrimination,* Nathan Glazer summarized many of the arguments opposing the further extension of the goal of equality of opportunity to blacks and other minority groups. He believes that the efforts to redress the inequalities between blacks and whites provided a special benefit to blacks as a group, which in turn led to demands for special benefits by "all deprived groups." This new emphasis on racial and cultural groups, however, was contrary to what Glazer believes is the "American orientation to ethnic difference and diversity..." With regard to ethnic groups Glazer claims that the United States government historically has followed a policy of "salutary neglect." While the "entire world" was allowed to enter this country, no separate ethnic group was to be allowed to establish an "independent polity." At the same time, Glazer argued that these racial and cultural groups were not forced to give up their own "character and distinctiveness" and become fully assimilated into American culture and society.[28]

During the 1960s as a result of the attempts to correct the inequalities between blacks and whites, there was an overemphasis on racial and ethnic groups and a general drift away from the traditional American concern for the rights of the individual. Glazer believed that Americans have "abandon[ed] the first principle of the liberal society, that the individual and the individual's interests and good and welfare are the test of a good society, for we now attach benefits and penalties to individuals simply on the basis of their race, color, and national origin." He argued that Americans should "work with the intellectual, judicial, and political institutions of the country to reestablish the simple and clear understanding that rights attach to the individual, not the group, and that public policy must be exercised without distinction of race, color, or national origin."[29]

Nathan Glazer's statements coincide very closely with what has been termed "liberal pluralism" by sociologist Milton Gordon. According to Gordon, liberal pluralism "is characterized by the absence, even prohibition, of any legal or governmental recognition of racial, religious, language, or national origins groups as corporate entities with a standing in the legal or governmental process, and a prohibition of the use of ethnic criteria of any type for discriminatory purposes, or conversely for special or favored treatment."

> Many members of such groups would, of course, receive benefits provided by legislation aimed at the general population in connection with problems produced by lack of effective economic participation in the society: for example, anti-poverty measures, housing, education and welfare measures, and so on. Members of disadvantaged ethnic groups would thus benefit as individuals under social programs in relation to their individual eligibility, but not in a corporate sense as a function of their ethnic background.

In contrast to liberal pluralism, Gordon posited the ideal of "corporate pluralism," in which "racial and ethnic groups are formerly recognized as legally constituted entities with official standing in the society. Economic and political rewards, whether in the public or private sector, are allocated on the basis of numerical strength in the population or on some other formula emanating from the political process. Egalitarian emphasis is on equality of condition rather than equality of opportunity, and universalistic criteria of reward operate only in restricted spheres...."[30] Nathan Glazer argued against "corporate pluralism," but his defense of "liberal pluralism" is severely flawed due to his selective use of historical and empirical data, and his suggestions that certain issues were settled when, in reality, they are still being hotly debated by social scientists and political theorists. Acceptance of "liberal pluralism" and the social goal of equality of opportunity in education, employment, and other areas, and thus the rejection of the goals of "corporate pluralism" and "equality of condition" among groups must rest on solid historical evidence and reasonably reliable economic and sociological data.

Glazer stated that the "American ethnic pattern" was "to allow all to enter." But he also points out that crucial distinctions among potential immigrants on the basis of race and national origin did not end until the passage of the Immigration Act of 1965. Thus between 1924 and 1965 the "pattern" of American immigration had been to recognize racial and ethnic backgrounds, and individuals were discriminated against on the basis of their group membership or national origin. Moreover, in states with large numbers of Chinese and Japanese, there were laws specifically addressed at limiting the rights and privileges of these groups. Native and Mexican Americans were the victims of discriminatory legislation in many of the southwestern states. These laws defined the social position of these racial and ethnic groups in those areas, just as the Supreme Court's *Plessy* decision defined the social position of blacks with respect to whites throughout the country.[31]

The "pattern" of defining the status of racial and cultural minorities extended into the area of public schooling. Thus we find numerous laws for segregated public schools for Mexican-Americans, Native Americans as well as blacks in various states.[32] To accept Glazer's view that the United States did not define groups on the basis of race or ethnicity would, in effect, deny the historical reality which underpins the pattern of analysis developed by historians and sociologists over the last three decades. Although Glazer presents a rather novel interpretation of the history and sociology of racial and ethnic groups in the United States, most American social historians would find it difficult to accept without further documentation.[33]

The notion that "no separate ethnic group was allowed to establish an independent polity in the United States," has validity in that it accounts for the lack of political parties based entirely on racial or ethnic origin in various cities or states. But there is evidence that from the late nineteenth century and throughout the twentieth, many trades, trades unions, municipal departments, and political machines were dominated in many cities by one or another white ethnic group. Italians would control the municipal sanitation department, while the Irish commanded the police force. The local Democratic or Republican political machine may have been in the hands of either the Italians or the Irish, while the Jews might control teaching positions in the public school system. Although these groups may not be considered "independent polities," they were active in the political arena, and supported or opposed issues and candidates on the basis of their own ethnic interests.[34] Glazer appears concerned about the possibility that blacks will begin to function as a political and cultural interest group as do the Jews, Irish, and Italians in many areas. This would lead, according to Glazer, to a situation of "heightened ethnic conflict" in many cities and various sectors of the economy. But according to tradition the American political system is supposed to thrive on competition. Many white ethnic groups have used politics and political maneuvers to gain social and economic concessions from those in power. When several new "corporate entities" begin to make demands on the political process, it is suggested that there is a need to place more emphasis on the "individual" rather than racial or cultural "groups." In this instance, Glazer's liberal argument supports the more conservative objective of maintaining the status quo.

With regard to assimilation, though Glazer would have us believe that there was little or no pressure brought to bear on European immigrants to become "Americanized," there is too much historical evidence which suggests the contrary. The Americanization campaigns have been well documented by educational and social historians. Some American industries penalized immigrant workers who did not learn to read and write English.[35] Voluntary associations and social centers were active in sponsoring special "Americanization classes." And public school systems with large immigrant and ethnic populations provided special Americanization textbooks and curricula for immigrant children in the elementary grades.[36] Even the foreign-language newspapers which circulated in immigrant neighborhoods often supported the learning of English for advancement in American society.[37]

At the same time, the influx of large numbers of southern and eastern European immigrants into this country during the "new immigration", 1880 to 1924, did not seriously challenge the prevailing Anglo-Saxon cultural hegemony in this country. The dominant cultural motif was sustained by both the political and economic power of the Anglo-Americans, and the lack of sustained opposition to the existing cultural values and traditions by the southern and eastern European immigrant groups. Although it would be unfair to say that all members of the white immigrant groups accepted Anglo-American culture and "Americanization," especially in light of the large numbers of immigrants who returned to their native lands after only a few years of working in the United States; many white immigrants did submit to the "ordeal of assimilation."[38] It was only very recently that many second and third generation white ethnics began to "rediscover their ethnicity" and to demand greater recognition of their cultural backgrounds and traditions in the United States.[39]

The issue of cultural assimilation brings us back to our earlier discussion of the desegregated school in American society. The numerous researchers who have analyzed various aspects of the school desegregation process not only ignored the more important social and political reasons why it should be supported, but they also were extremely ethnocentric in their suggestions of how the new desegregated public school should look and function. One of the reasons why many minority parents and educators have had difficulty supporting the new desegregated school was because it resembles too closely the old white segregated school in many important areas. With respect to curricular content, teaching, administrative, and counseling staff, and cultural orientation, most desegregated public schools reflect the values, traditions, and political power of the dominant white majority in this society. However, the minority group students who have been "integrated" into previously segregated public schools also possess cultures, but the new "desegregated" school either denies or merely pays lip-service to the cultural background of the new minority student population.[40]

The contemporary bias of the desegregated school toward the Anglo-American culture and heritage has its origins in the earlier campaigns to "Americanize" and assimilate the southern and eastern European immigrant groups during the first three decades of this century. These groups were not just "assimilated," they were assimilated into the dominant Anglo-American cultural milieu. The goal was the obliteration of the "foreign-ness" of the new immigrants, and the elimination of competing cultural values and traditions on the American social scene. Thus in many areas there was opposition to the recognition of racial and cultural "corporate entities" but most scholars in the area would probably agree that ethnicity was significant in the evolution of social, economic, and political ideas and practices in many parts of the United States. One important result of the *non*-recognition of minority cultures in this country, especially in the area of artistic expression, has been the lack of public support for the maintenance and expansion of minority cultural forms and traditions. Whereas the federal, state, and local governments through support of cultural centers and institutions of higher learning guaranteed the development of Anglo-American cultural traditions, the various minority cultural groups have had to support both Anglo-American culture through taxes, and their own cultural traditions through contributions to social organizations involved in the maintenance of their cultural heritage in this country.[41]

The social goal put forth by the Supreme Court in the Brown decision was equality of opportunity in public education. Spokespersons for liberal pluralism continue to support the goal of equality of opportunity for individuals in social, political, and economic areas, and Nathan Glazer and other liberals oppose any further recognition of racial or cultural groups in American society believing that prohibiting discrimination against "individuals" in education, employment, housing, and other areas is a satisfactory societal objective. However, continued acceptance of the goal of equality of opportunity must hinge upon evidence that sufficient numbers of individuals from the various racial and cultural minority groups are able to take advantage of opportunities and compete for the limited social and economic resources of the society. Although there is some historical evidence that individuals from various European backgrounds were able to take advantage of opportunities for advancement in various areas, social and economic data on blacks and other historically oppressed racial and cultural minorities suggest that laws and court decisions guaranteeing equality of opportunity have not succeeded in greatly improving their social and economic conditions.[42] In fact, in the case of black Americans, there is evidence that they were "loosing ground" in several occupational pursuits and educational attainment in the 1970s. A recent thorough study of the educational, employment, health care, income, and housing conditions among blacks in this country from 1960 to 1975 conducted by the Center for Manpower Policy concluded that the possibility of blacks attaining parity with whites in these areas in the near future was "Still A Dream."[43]

The goal of equality of opportunity does not insure the proportionate representation of racial and cultural minority groups in the more important sectors of the national economy. Thus when oppressed minorities begin to lose ground in areas where gains had previously been made, the advocates of liberal pluralism are not overly concerned because nothing was promised to these groups. The fluctuations in the national economy and political power to a very large extent determines economic conditions among the various racial and cultural groups, and the federal government has generally been reluctant to intervene unless the economic downturn has begun to affect the middle classes among the dominant ethnic groups.

During the late 1960s, rioting broke out in many large cities among blacks who perceived that they were not participating in the social and economic rewards of the wartime economy. During the 1970s, black Americans and others see the minor advances made in the 1960s in education and employment being eroded away by the postwar economic recession. At the same time that blacks, Chicanos, Puerto-Ricans, and other traditionally oppressed minorities are finding that the decrease in economic and educational opportunities is greatly limiting the possibility of individual or group advancement, liberals are calling for less emphasis on racial and cultural background in the allocation of the social, economic, and political resources of the society. The oppressed condition of these minority groups historically was determined for the most part by the values and beliefs of the dominant white society. Institutional practices and contractions in the national economy often prohibits the improvement of the conditions of these groups. The rejection of the ideals and goals of corporate pluralism very likely will mean that these oppressed racial and cultural minorities will have to resort to alternative strategies, especially political mobilization, in order to focus attention on their deteriorating social and economic condition in American society.

Some researchers have projected the desegregated school as an important vehicle for the attainment of a desegregated society.[44] But when one examines the curriculum, staffing, and cultural orientation of the desegregated school, one finds that there is really no reason to believe that it is preparing children for participation in a "desegregated American society." At the same time, with regard to the participation of minorities in higher education and various sectors of the national economy, there seems to be very little likelihood that the country as a whole is moving toward greater desegregation. Historically the values and beliefs of the dominant white majority have determined the social and economic position of minority groups in the United States, and the amount and type of public schooling to be received by minority children. Until that majority believes it is in their best interest to truly desegregate the public schools and the entire society, we can expect little progress in these areas. It is fairly clear that blacks and other historically oppressed minority groups must mobilize their social and political resources and demand greater participation in the desegregated public school and increased access to the economic and social rewards of the entire society. To do otherwise would probably mean the continued deterioration of the social position of these oppressed minorities in American society.

NOTES

1. *See,* for example, Robert Crain, *et al., Political Strategies in Northern Desegregation* (Lexington, Ky., 1973); Elizabeth Cohen, "The Effects of Desegregation on Race Relations: Facts or Hypothesis," Meyer Weinberg, "The Relationship between School Desegregation and Academic Achievement: A Review of the Research," and Edgar G. Epps, "Impact of School Desegregation on Aspirations, Self Concepts, and Other Aspects of Personality," *Law and Contemporary Society,* 39 (Spring 1975), pp. 248–313; Harold B. Gerard and Norman Miller, *School Desegregation: A Long Term Study* (New York, 1975); for information on black teachers in the school desegregation process, *see* Frederick A. Rodgers, *The Black High School and Its Community* (Lexington, Mass., 1975).

2. "Special Issue: Is School Desegregation Still A Good Idea?" *School Review,* 84 (May 1976). This special issue was recently reprinted as a book entitled, *School Desegregation: Shadow and Substance,* F. Levinsohn and B. Wright, editors (Chicago, 1976). *See also,* Lloyd R. Henderson, "Is It Worth It?" *Journal of Law and Education,* 4 (January 1975): 43–62.

3. *See,* for example, Nathan Glazer, "Is Busing Necessary"; David Armor, "The Evidence on Busing"; reprinted in *The Great School Bus Controversy,* Nicolaus Mills, editor (New York, 1973). This book contains a number of articles on busing, pro and con.

4. This famous excerpt from Jefferson's *Notes on Virginia* has been reprinted numerous times. *See,* for example, John H. Best and Robert T. Sidwell, *The American Legacy of Learning: Readings in the History of Education* (Philadelphia, 1967), pp. 90–93.

5. Webster quoted from *The American Magazine,* May, 1788, in *ibid.,* pp. 117–120.

6. Excerpts from Jedidiah Morse's *American Geography* may be found in Best and Sidwell, *American Legacy of Learning,* pp. 126–127; 167–168.

7. Sections of the Vermont, New Hampshire, and Pennsylvania state constitutions for the years 1784, 1792, and 1838 are reprinted in *ibid.,* pp. 127–129.

8. Quoted from the *Twelfth Annual Report of the Board of Education Together with the Twelfth Annual Report of the Secretary of the Board* (1848), reprinted in *ibid.,* pp. 183–199.

9. Sumner's arguments were reprinted in *The Black American and Education,* Earle H. West, editor (Columbus, Ohio, 1972), pp. 43–45.

10. *Roberts v. The City of Boston,* 5 Cushing 204–210, reprinted in *ibid.,* pp. 40–43. It should be noted that Massachusetts passed legislation in 1855 prohibiting discrimination in the public schools on the basis of race.

11. For information on patterns of school segregation in northern cities, *see* Vincent P. Franklin, "The Persistence of School Segregation in the Urban North: An Historical Perspective," *The Journal of Ethnic Studies,* 2 (February 1974): 51–68. The most recent history of southern black education is Henry Bullock's *A History of Negro Education in the South from 1619 to the Present* (Cambridge, Mass., 1969).

12. The background to the *Plessy* case is detailed in Richard Kluger's *Simple Justice: The History of Brown v. Board of Education and Black America's Struggle for Equality* (New York, 1976), pp. 73–74.

13. *Plessy v. Ferguson,* 163 U.S. 537 (1896).

14. *Ibid. See also,* Kluger, *Simple Justice,* pp. 73–83; and George Frederickson, *The Black Image in the White Mind: The Debate Over Afro-American Character and Destiny, 1817–1914* (New York, 1971), pp. 218–319.

15. *Plessy v. Ferguson;* Kluger, *Simple Justice,* pp. 81–82; Barton J. Bernstein, *Plessy v. Ferguson:* Conservative Sociological Jurisprudence," *Journal of Negro History,* 48 (July 1963): 196–205, and "Case Law in *Plessy v. Ferguson,*" *Journal of Negro History,* 47 (July 1962): 192–198.

16. *Cumming v. Richmond County Board of Education,* 175 U.S. 528; *see also* June O. Patton, "The Black Community of Augusta and the Struggle for Ware High School," in this volume.

17. General Samuel C. Armstrong, "The Founding of Hampton Institute," *Old South Leaflets,* 4 (1890): 6–7.

18. For a discussion of the financial and philanthropic support for the industrial education of blacks at Hampton, see James D. Anderson, "Education As A Vehicle for the Manipulation of Black Workers," in *Work, Technology and Education,* Walter Feinberg and Henry Rosemont, editors (Urbana, Ill., 1975), pp. 15–40; and "The Hampton Model of Normal School Industrial Education, 1878–1900" in this volume.

19. *Ibid.; see also,* Louis D. Rubin, editor, *Teach the Freeman: The Correspondence of Rutherford B. Hayes and the Slater Fund for Negro Education,* I (Baton Rouge, La., 1959), pp. 41–50.

20. *See,* Louis B. Harlan, *Booker T. Washington: The Making of a Black Leader, 1856–1901* (New York, 1972).

21. For a discussion of the attitudes of southern whites toward industrial education, during the late nineteenth century, *see* Berenice Fisher, *Industrial Education: American Ideals and Institutions* (Madison, Wisconsin, 1967), pp. 155–158; and Charles B. Dabney, *Universal Education in the South,* II (Chapel Hill, North Carolina, 1936), pp. 205–206; and Linda M. Perkins, "Quaker Beneficence and Black Control: The Institute for Colored Youth, 1852–1903," in this volume.

22. W.E.B. DuBois, editor, *The Negro Common School* (Atlanta, 1901); and *The Common School and the Negro American* (Atlanta, 1911); Horace Mann Bond, *The Education of the Negro in the American Social Order* (1932, reprinted New York, 1956). For a discussion and excerpts from the investigations of the NAACP lawyers, *see* Kluger, *Simple Justice,* pp. 163–165.

23. For the complete background of the various cases leading up to the *Brown* decision in 1954, *see,* Kluger, *Simple Justice.*

24. *Brown v. Board of Education of Topeka,* 347 U.S. 483 (1954). The opinion is reprinted in Kluger, *Simple Justice,* pp. 779–785; and Mills, *The Great School Bus Controversy.*

25. Several articles have dealt with the attempts to thwart school desegregation, *see* H. Rodgers and C. Bullock, "School Desegregation: Nine Parts Deliberation and One Part Speed," in *Law and Social Change: Civil Rights Laws and Their Consequences* (New York, 1972), pp. 69–111; and Betty Showell, "The Courts, The Legislature, The Presidency, and School Desegregation Policy," *School Review,* 84 (May 1976); 401–416.

26. Arthur Jensen, "How Much Can We Boost IQ and Scholastic Achievement," *Harvard Educational Review,* 39 (Winter 1969): 1–123; and *Genetics and Education* (New York, 1972).

27. There have been numerous critical analyses of Jensen's findings and suggestions, *see,* for example, Jerry Hirsch, "Behavior-Genetic Analysis and Its Biosocial Consequences," and Leon Kamin, "Heredity, Intelligence, Politics, and Psychology," in *Shaping of the American Educational State 1900-to the Present,* Clarence Karier, editor (New York, 1975), pp. 348–392; Philip Green, "Race and IQ: Fallacy of Heritability," *Dissent,* 23 (Spring 1976): 181–196 and "The Pseudo Science of Arthur Jensen," *Dissent,* 23 (Summer 1976): 284–297; Daniel Kohl, "The IQ Game: Bait and Switch — A Review Essay," *School Review,* 94 (August 1976): 572–604.

28. Nathan Glazer, *Affirmative Discrimination: Ethnic Inequality and Public Policy* (New York, 1975), pp. 5–25, passim.

29. *Ibid.*, p. 221.

30. Milton Gordon, "Toward A General Theory of Racial and Ethnic Group Relations," in *Ethnicity: Theory and Experience,* Nathan Glazer and Daniel P. Moynihan, editors (Cambridge, Mass., 1975), pp. 105–106.

31. Excerpts from state laws which discriminated against Asian, Mexican, and Native Americans are reprinted in *In Their Place: White America Defines Her Minorities, 1850–1950* (New York,1972), pp. 8–11, 157–162, 236–239. *See also,* Manuel Ruiz, *Mexican American Legal Heritage in the Southwest* (Los Angeles, Calif., 1972).

32. For a discussion of legislation which segregated Mexican American children, *see* U.S. Commission on Civil Rights, *Education of the Spanish-Speaking: Report I — Ethnic Isolation of Mexican Americans in the Public Schools of the Southwest; Report II — The Unfinished Education; Report III — The Excluded Student* (Washington, D.C.: 1972); Rudolph De La Garza, *Chicanos and Native Americans: The Territorial Minorities* (Englewood Cliffs, N.J., 1973).

33. Glazer does cite several histories of immigrants and immigration in the United States, but these works do not support Glazer's idea that America did not define the position of racial and ethnic minorities in laws and customs. Carlson and Colburn, however, reprint a number of documents which defined the social position of blacks, Native Americans, Mexican Americans, and other minorities, *see In Their Place,* sections I–V.

34. There have been numerous studies of the role of ethnicity in the political process, *see* Harry Bailey and Ellis Katz, editors, *Ethnic Group Politics* (Columbus, Ohio, 1969); Lawrence Fuchs, editor, *American Ethnic Politics* (New York, 1968); Brett Hawkins and Robert A. Lorinskas, editors, *The Ethnic Factor in American Politics* (Columbus, Ohio, 1970); and Mark R. Levy and Michael S. Kramer, *The Ethnic Factor: How America's Minorities Decide Elections* (New York, 1972).

35. Robert A. Carlson, "Americanization As An Early Twentieth Century Adult Education Movement," *History of Education Quarterly,* 10 (Winter 1970): 440–464; *see also,* George E. Hartman, *The Movement to Americanize the Immigrants* (New York, 1948).

36. *Ibid., see also,* Edward Stevens, "Social Centers, Politics, and Social Efficiency in the Progressive Era," *History of Education Quarterly,* 12 (Spring 1972): 17–33.

37. This point is elaborated upon in Timothy Smith's "Immigrant Social Aspirations and American Education, 1889–1930," *American Quarterly,* 21 (Fall 1969): 523–543.

38. For a documentary history of this topic, *see* Stanley Feldstein and Lawrence Costello, editors, *The Ordeal of Assimilation: A Documentary History of the White Working Class* (Garden City, N.Y., 1974).

39. The literature on the rediscovery of white ethnicity has become voluminous. The ones most helpful to this author were, Michael Novak, *The Rise of the Unmeltable Ethnics* (New York, 1971); L. Dinnerstein and D. Reimers, *Ethnic Americans: A History of Immigration and Assimilation* (New York, 1975); Sallie Te Selle, editor, *The Rediscovery of Ethnicity; Its Implications for Culture and Politics in America* (New York, 1973); and Andrew Greeley, *Ethnicity in the United States: A Preliminary Reconnaissance* (New York, 1974).

40. In reviewing the numerous studies of school desegregation, it became very clear that few researchers have even discussed the cultural orientation of the desegregated school. *See,* for example, the book-length report on the desegregation of the Riverside School System, Gerard and Miller, *School Desegregation.* There are chapters on "Adjustment and Personality," "Social Contact in the Desegregated Classroom,"

"Teacher Influences," "Attitudes," "Family Values," but nothing on cultural values and traditions in the desegregated school.

41. The lack of public support for the maintenance of minority cultures is discussed by James D. Anderson in "Black Cultural Equality and American Education," in *Equality and Social Change,* Walter Feinberg, editor (Urbana, Ill.), forthcoming.

42. For discussions of the social conditions among the historically oppressed minorities, *see* Gilberto Lopez y Rivas, *The Chicanos: Life and Struggles of the Mexican Minority in the United States* (New York, 1974); Raymond J. Flores, *The Socioeconomic Status Trends of the Mexican People Residing in Arizona* (San Francisco, 1973); Julian Samora, editor, *La Raza: Forgotten Americans* (South Bend, Ind., 1966); Francesco Cordasco and Eugene Bucchioni, *The Puerto Rican Experience: A Sociological Source Book* (Totowa, N.J., 1973); Cesar Parales, "Puerto Rican Problems in Integration," *Integrated Education,* 13 (May–June 1975); 8–10. This issue of *Integrated Education* deals with "Inequality in Metropolitan America: Schools, Housing, Employment," and provides some very useful information on the contemporary status of racial and cultural minorities in urban America. For reports on the declining status of blacks, *see* "Blacks on A New Plateau," *Newsweek,* October 4, 1976, p. 73; and "Black College Gains Called Major, But Inadequate," *The New York Times,* August 11, 1976.

43. Sar A. Levitan, William B. Johnson, and Robert Taggert, *Still A Dream: The Changing Status of Blacks Since 1960* (Cambridge, Mass., 1975).

44. Many researchers have suggested that school desegregation is related to the attainment of the desegregated society, *see,* for example, "Is School Desegregation Still a Good Idea," in *School Review;* and Elizabeth Cohen, "The Effect of School Desegregation Upon Race Relations."

Contributors

JAMES D. ANDERSON is an Assistant Professor of History of Education at the University of Illinois, Urbana-Champaign. Mr. Anderson received his Ph.D. from Illinois in 1973 and is presently completing a study of philanthropy and black education.

VINCENT P. FRANKLIN is an Assistant Professor of History and Afro-American Studies at Yale University. He received his Ph.D. from the University of Chicago in 1975 and is completing a book on the education of the Philadelphia black community. 1900–1950.

DARLENE CLARK HINE is an Assistant Professor in the Department of History at Purdue University. Ms. Hine received her Ph.D. from Kent State University in 1975 and is author of a forthcoming monograph on the Texas White Primary to be published by Kraus-Thompson.

GENNA RAE McNEIL is Assistant Professor of History in Law at Howard University School of Law, where she is completing a history of the Law School. A graduate of the University of Chicago, Ms. McNeil is on leave (1976–1978) from the Department of History of the University of North Carolina at Chapel Hill. She recently completed a monograph on Charles Hamilton Houston and the Struggle for Black Civil Rights.

JUNE O. PATTON teaches Afro-American History at Governors State University. A doctoral candidate at the University of Chicago, Ms. Patton is completing a study of Major R.R. Wright and Black Higher Education in Georgia, 1870–1920.

LINDA MARIE PERKINS is a doctoral candidate in Administration and Higher Education at the University of Illinois, Urbana-Champaign. She is completing a study of Fannie Jackson Coppin and the Institute for Colored Youth, 1852–1903.

LILLIAN S. WILLIAMS is an Instructor in the Department of History at Howard University and a doctoral candidate in History at the State University of New York at Buffalo. Ms. Williams is completing a study of the history and development of the Buffalo black community, 1900–1930.